Building Migrant Cities in the Gulf

Building Migrant Cities in the Gulf

Urban Transformation in the Middle East

Florian Wiedmann and Ashraf M. Salama

I.B. TAURIS
LONDON • NEW YORK • OXFORD • NEW DELHI • SYDNEY

I.B. TAURIS
Bloomsbury Publishing Plc
50 Bedford Square, London, WC1B 3DP, UK
1385 Broadway, New York, NY 10018, USA

BLOOMSBURY, I.B. TAURIS and the Diana logo are trademarks of
Bloomsbury Publishing Plc

First published in Great Britain 2019

Cover design by Charlotte Daniels
Cover image: Dubai skyline during sunset
(© FilippoBacci / Getty Images)

A catalogue record for this book is available from the British Library.

A catalog record for this book is available from the Library of Congress.

ISBN: HB: 978-1-7883-1068-0
ePDF: 978-1-7883-1625-5
ebook: 978-1-7883-1626-2

Typeset by Deanta Global Publishing Services, Chennai, India
Printed and bound in Great Britain

To find out more about our authors and books visit www.bloomsbury.com
and sign up for our newsletters.

Contents

Illustrations

Figures

All images belong to the author.

Tables

Acknowledgements

This book would have not been developed and written without working in teaching and conducting research in the Gulf and at Qatar University, in particular. Many people have contributed directly or indirectly to this book. We are indebted to our colleagues and students alike who have encouraged and participated in many research activities and discourses in Qatar, Bahrain and the United Arab Emirates.

Much of our research productivity, which led to the development of this book, would not have been possible without the major support of the Qatar National Research Fund (QNRF), who awarded our project of the National Priorities Research Program (NPRP 09-1083-6-023) during the period between 2011 and 2014. Special thanks are due to the leadership of Qatar University, which has always supported our international and regional research collaborations.

Our thanks are extended to students and colleagues, who have made special contributions to some of the key materials of this book. Our former students Ahood Al-Maimani and Fatma Khalfani, who were intelligently engaged in various field studies; Velina Mirincheva, who skilfully supported our GIS studies; and Simona Azzali, who coordinated research on everyday urbanism in Qatar. Many thanks are also due to Dr Khaled Alawadi (Khalifa University, Abu Dhabi) and Wafa Al-Ghatam (University of Bahrain), whose insights helped us understand urban developments in the United Arab Emirates and the Kingdom of Bahrain. Finally, we are thankful to the University of Strathclyde's Department of Architecture, which offered a supportive academic environment to develop this book.

Preface

During the last twenty years, cities in three small Gulf States, namely Bahrain, Qatar and the United Arab Emirates have witnessed rapid urban growth due to new development visions and strategies to establish emerging hubs in global networks. The subsequent extensive migration has produced and transformed urban landscapes. This is particularly expressed in new housing dynamics, which reflect the extensive need for shelter on one hand and the opposing phase of speculative tendencies on the other. Today, more than 80% of the combined population of the capital cities is of foreign descent where an absolute majority has migrated over the last two decades. The various cultural backgrounds coupled with the segregation of income groups engaging in certain economic sectors have led to unique migrant societies. Urban transformation driven by housing development and its underlying dynamics seem to be a nexus of many urban concerns from environmental, socio-economic to sociocultural aspects and have thus been chosen as main premise for this book.

Building Migrant Cities in the Gulf offers a comprehensive analysis carried out to reveal the various complex layers of contemporary urbanism in the world's biggest urban growth scenario rooted in foreign migration. Within real-estate markets housing has become the top commodity and thus a main factor of economic growth in all Gulf cities. The direct interdependency of economic growth and housing has led to the paradox of increasing land prices and the resulting lack of affordable housing and growing challenges for future growth built on continuously exchanging migrant societies. Today, Gulf cities are expressions of controversies: Vacant mega projects and crowded high-density agglomerations; themed spectacles and monotonous built environments; continuous urban sprawl and intense high-rise conglomerates; and rapid internationalization and traditional conservatism. All these internal factors and external influences represent tensions that have led to highly fragile entities. The authors identify housing development as the most crucial element keeping Gulf cities alive or eventually leading to exacerbating these tensions if not comprehensively considered from an integrated perspective of sustainable urbanism.

This book is an endeavour to develop a holistic overview of interdependent factors within the urban development process. It provides in-depth insights of housing and migration dynamics in major Gulf cities and explores the lessons learned from one of the prevalent urban experiments in human history. The scale and diversity of foreign migration has never been witnessed in the context of engineered hub cities. The top-down approach of controlling development dynamics is a crucial element in understanding both migration and housing dynamics in Gulf cities. The book's aim is to contribute to an overall understanding of the role of contemporary governance from initiating development visions, reorganizing decision-making to implementing distinctive strategies. The book includes a thorough exploration of how investor-driven mechanisms, new economic sectors and demographic transformations have impacted the demand and supply of housing as well as the specific spatial characteristics of the resulting urban transformation. Conclusively, the direct interrelationship between inhabitants and their home environments is explored by demonstrating the divergent living standards and the new lifestyle tendencies resulting in various representations.

The authors follow a strategic approach that integrates scientific analyses, discourses and impressions. Such approach describes past development patterns and establish and validate new concepts and terminologies to define a phenomenon, as well as introduce and debate emerging issues and how they can be seen as opportunities or threats for future development. Primarily, this is to establish a comprehensive interpretation and not a documentation of historic facts. Thus, the mission of this book is to raise the important questions and to point out to possible solution scenarios. How are migrant Gulf cities produced? And what role does housing play in future scenarios of urban consolidation? Are two key questions the books places emphasis upon. These specific questions are methodologically explored, first by investigating the overall development vision and strategies examined through exploring the impact of mega projects and general housing patterns on the reconfiguration of urban structures. Following this assessment, analyses of the newly evolving urban landscapes, the multicultural migrant communities and their lifestyles and perceptions are studied before the question of everyday urbanism and its future.

Any urban transformation can only be discussed holistically by linking empirical analyses and explorations to a well-founded theoretical framework. In this respect, the book concludes by postulating a new framework, rooted in space production theories, how housing is a main driver of urbanism and thus the most crucial factor in establishing more efficient and diverse urban environments reflecting shared identities rather than fragmented and segregated parallel societies. The framework is the result of a theoretical exploration on how housing can contribute to more sustainable cities in the Gulf or how housing can become a crucial factor leading to the economic decline of these newly established hubs. In this context, migration entered the main premises of this discourse, since all urban environments are currently built for a hypothetical future society. Building migrant cities of this scale without any officially implemented strategy to attract foreigners to settle long-term and to build communities has led to the main subtext of any major debate about the future of urbanism in the Gulf.

Human history has seen many settlements being transformed or completely erected by arriving foreigners from various places, such as all cities in the United States or Australia. The main difference to the Gulf region is the fact that most of these foreigners have been immigrants aiming to build their new lives in a new world they have perceived as an opportunity to settle rather than as a place to transit. Migration patterns in the Gulf however follow the path of the latter and the emerging airport societies have reached the scale of millions of guest workers, hardly engaged in their new society or attached to their new environment. This refers to both low-income labourers, mainly hired to work in construction industries as well as to higher income groups, who often perceive the Gulf as an opportunity for retirement or for developing their special expertise by managing large-scale projects or new business branches. '*Building migrant cities in the Gulf*' is a timely effort to draw an abstract outline of this unique urban phenomenon substantiated by concrete examples and empirical research.

The authors have lived and worked in the Gulf including Qatar, Bahrain and the United Arab Emirates, and other countries during various periods between 2004 and 2014. Being able to witness the boom before and the downturn after the international financial crisis and being migrants themselves led to major impulses to explore Gulf cities from macro and interconnected perspectives rather than to focus on singular parameters within the built environment. As academic architects and urban designers specialised in urbanism and the complex dynamics between people and places the authors have attempted to build new bridges of understanding continuous demographic and social changes, economic developments and new forms of governance impacting urban transformations. This aspiration is rooted in the role of architecture and urbanism as a scientific field touching the various crossroads of humanities, social sciences and engineering, which can be summarized in one main motive: To decode the key qualities needed for sustainable urbanism and the distinctive roles of planning and design to establish more resilient cities.

1

Introduction: Migration and
urban transformation

This opening chapter introduces a contextual background on migration and urban transformation including a historic overview of how Gulf cities have evolved from desert vernacular settlements to modern conurbations since the middle of the twentieth century and to the most recent phenomenon of emerging hub cities within global networks. The introduction sets the stage for the main objective of this book and develops an overarching argument of why migration has always been a main catalyst of urban transformation and why contemporary Gulf cities have been witnessing a special case of migration-driven urbanism. Thus, it is crucially urgent to understand the various layers and interdependencies of migration and urban dynamics, which are expressed by new housing developments and the resulting neighbourhood patterns as well as diverse spatial practices and consumption patterns. Migration is seen as one of the most important factors transforming urban identities of cities worldwide and, in particular, Gulf cities. Therefore, it is essential to depict how migration has been affecting urban developments and to highlight the various dimensions and variables, which must be explored to understand contemporary urbanism in the Gulf.

Migration is either rooted in incentives to leave challenging living conditions behind or to gain opportunities needed to achieve higher living standards. According to the United Nations Statistics Division and the annual World Migration Report, the Gulf States have become the countries with the biggest share of migrants worldwide.[1] Apart from international migration, as it can be studied in the Gulf, internal migration has also become a crucial factor in many developing countries, where populations living in rural areas have been moving to cities leading to densely urban areas. Most international migration to developed countries has thus its starting point in rapidly growing cities in the Global South. According to the World Bank's Migration and Remittances

Factbook 2016, migrants have been sending a big share of their salaries back to their families, worth more than US$441 billion, which is three times of official aid.[2] A large share of this amount originates from all six Gulf Cooperation Council countries, where US$98 billion in outward remittance flows were calculated in 2014.[3] Today more than 247 million people, which is equivalent to 3.4 per cent of the world's population, live outside their countries of birth. The volume of South-South migration has increased to 38 per cent and is thus dramatically exceeding the South-North migration with around 34 per cent, which is the result of recently emerging cities in the Global South and the growing economies they are experiencing.[4]

Based on the 'Recommendations on Statistics of International Migration' by the United Nations Statistics Division, there is a clear distinction between short-term and long-term migrants.[5] While short-term migrants stay between three and a maximum of twelve months in a foreign country, long-term migrants stay more than a year. This definition is rooted in the assumption that most migrants establish a source of income and a legal permission to stay during this period. Regarding short-term working contracts of two to three years in emerging cities, this definition is rather problematic, since most guest workers would never gain any long-term perspective to settle. Another important aspect of international migration is the size of the diaspora including first, second and third generations.[6] According to the World Bank Group, there is no basic data on the descendants of migrants available for countries other than those in Europe, Australia and the United States.[7] These native-born generations with migrant parents often have a special role in being rooted in their countries of residence but with still remaining cultural ties and affiliations to the home countries of their parents.

Due to significant differences in development, demography and the quality of governance, the United Nations are expecting the scale and scope of migration to grow.[8] The main argument is the dependence of the global economy on enhanced urban migration. Scientific evidence demonstrates that various sectors of the economy in both developing and industrialized countries would collapse without a continuous migration of foreign labour.[9] The rapid exchange of information has led to a new global awareness and especially young generations have a rising incentive to become an increasingly mobile workforce to achieve better living conditions than in their home countries. To improve the working and living conditions of this growing and rather vulnerable group of migrants, various commitments were signed, such as the Monterray Consensus.[10] Furthermore, the welfare benefits of the Doha round of trade negotiations underlined the importance of enabling the populations in developing countries to have access to livelihoods and a growing prosperity in their countries.[11] Another important aspect is the implementation of new incentives with respect to increasing the impact of remittances sent back by migrants to their families left behind as well as how new skills learnt abroad could be reinvested more efficiently after the return to home countries.

According to the United Nations, the full integration of long-term migrants is important to establish social cohesion and to enhance the contributions made by migrants towards instituting sustainable urbanism. One important aspect is the transparent communication of rights, obligations and perspectives to enhance association and attachment and thus the integration of migrants into the host society. In this context, active citizenship and opportunities to own and manage businesses should be promoted. The dynamic integration of migrants must be supported by local and national authorities as well as employers and members of civil society. To improve the coordination of migration and to prevent exploitation one of the rising challenges has been the governance of international migration via coherence, sufficient capacities and cooperation. Consequently, transparent migration policies need to be implemented according to agreed objectives, which respect and integrate international law. At the United Nations, the Global Commission on International Migrations (GCIM) has been installed to ensure a more effective institutional response to the opportunities and challenges of international migration.[12]

In 2017, the World Bank Group identified nine main themes of migration, which were included in a vision for the global compact on migration.[13] The theme with the greatest priority is the creation of jobs in developing countries to prevent migration forced by local economic conditions. Another important theme is the integration of migrants in host communities followed by a high awareness regarding the emerging job competition for native workers in host countries. Policies and control need to be in place to prevent trafficking and abusive working conditions of migrants. In this context, a key theme is the improvement of migrant rights. Additional themes include the particular circumstances of many migrants, as they often have to leave their families behind, who usually depend on their income abroad, and the loss of workforce in origin or home countries. Last but not least, the rising congestion and fiscal costs of social services have to be taken into account.[14] The recent globalization dynamics have created an extensive international division of labour and a complex situation in most developing countries facing migration consequences.

A study by the OECD (Organisation for Economic Co-operation and Development) in 2010 revealed that 43.6 per cent of all migrants must be considered low skilled due to limited educational backgrounds followed by migrants with intermediate skill level (35 per cent) and highly skilled migrants (21.5 per cent). Thus, low-skilled workforce dominates migration in absolute terms in both the OECD and non-OECD countries. One important fact is the magnitude of the global migration rate of highly skilled persons from developing countries, particularly from Africa since it is the highest at 10.6 per cent in comparison to the world average of 5.4 per cent.[15] The socio-demographic characteristics can widely differ by country of origin. While migrants from Africa are mainly low skilled, Asian migrants are rather diverse. The loss of highly skilled workforce has had a negative impact on local economic development in the Global South. The migration of low-skilled workforce however has become an important economic factor for developing countries due to remittances and the training of new skills abroad.[16] Thus, international migration has developed into a distinct phenomenon where many economic and political forces have been redefining demographic and social structures worldwide.

Migration and housing

Since most economic growth is located in cities, the most significant share of migration can be observed in the urbanized areas worldwide. The ongoing regional and global movement of people to find work or better living conditions has led to a substantial population change, in which the net migration is usually significantly larger than the natural population growth of cities. The overall resulting population growth feeds into projections of household growth and housing needs. In England, for instance, the household numbers are projected to increase by 27 per cent in 2033, which can be translated into the development of 232,000 new housing units every year.[17] Net migration is expected to account just under two-fifth of the rising demand. In most countries, a smaller percentage of the foreign-born population own their homes, and new migrants are more than twice as likely to be renters. In recent years there has been a tendency that recent migrants in the UK are more likely to be living in social housing, while long-term migrants live in housing developments similar to that of the settled population.[18]

In many parts of the world housing has become highly affected by migration due to continuously changing demands and the tenure effects of short- and long-term stays. The negative impact of insufficient housing is problematic since both general well-being and health can be highly affected. Migrants are particularly vulnerable since housing is a rather crucial factor for how they are integrating within their new host societies. In many places worldwide migrants have been witnessing severe social segregation and a limited access to established living standards. Most frequently, migrants reside in overcrowded areas, built with poor standards, and even homelessness is widespread. A common phenomenon is the clustering of migrants in rather problematic urban environments, such as deteriorating neighbourhoods in proximity to industrial areas. According to many international studies, migrants face significantly less housing opportunities and choices than native populations.[19] The typical pattern of migrants residing in deprived areas can lead to problematic urban and social conditions.

Housing is a crucial factor in how life is generally experienced including the various individual opportunities.[20] Accordingly, housing conditions can be studied from a three-dimensional perspective including the functional realities, such as demographic, economic and spatial transformations, coupled with an assessment of how the newly developed housing environments are used by migrants and finally how they are perceived and experienced. The emerging diversity in most urban environments inhabited by migrants often leads to complex housing markets, in which the needs and interests of many different groups must be addressed.[21] Historically migration has always been a key feature in demographic and economic dynamics worldwide defining urban development patterns. Trading networks have been an essential driver in shaping new markets and thus the beginning of major settlements. Trade led to an extensive exchange of goods and services and the successful migration of influential merchants has often been accommodated through the provision of suitable and attractive housing.[22]

The basic spatial and social challenges imposed by migration have already occurred in the very first settlements. The main difference today is the extent and speed of rural-urban and international migration due to a fierce competition between major global and emerging cities aiming to attract the investment of an increasingly mobile capital.[23] The resulting need for growth has fuelled a new form of migrant urbanism, in which both advanced skilled and manual labour are the preconditions of growing service and consumption centres within global economic networks. In many ways the relocation of industrial production to regions, such as the Pearl River Delta in China, and the rise of cities as hubs for new advanced producer services and high technology sectors have instigated new social and spatial structures and place typologies worldwide.[24] The frequently

cited term 'knowledge economies' has become highly dependent on both the
continuous migration of skilled workforce and a functioning housing market
supplying high-quality living standards.[25] Therefore visionaries and scholars,
such as Saskia Sassen, highlight the importance of the emerging knowledge
capital including its complexity and fragility due to the ongoing pressure to
enhance and sustain investment returns in real estate resulting in an increasingly
challenged quality of urban life.[26]

The preceding analysis reveals that migration can be seen as a complex
factor impacting housing markets worldwide. On the one hand labourers are
needed as construction workers, and on the other hand expanding financial
and other advanced producer services related to real estate demand broad and
diverse expertise.[27] Thus, a substantial part of any emerging housing market is
created by migrants themselves. In many cases migration has been a crucial
factor in sustaining land values and thus to prevent a major drop of real estate
prices. This, however, has had a negative impact on the availability of affordable
housing. While there is, for example, certain empirical evidence in the UK
that house prices can drop in certain areas, where low-income migrants led to
a move of native inhabitants, this move has resulted in housing shortages and
concomitantly higher land prices in other places.[28] The affordable housing crises
in most cities worldwide are essentially linked with continuous urban growth
leading to rising land prices as well as construction and infrastructure costs due
to the growing demand and shrinking availability of already developed land.
By introducing incentives to lower growth rates, many cities would witness a
dramatic impact on local economic development.[29]

By and large, a significant share of migration should be perceived as a direct
consequence of newly initiated urban development. Cities worldwide have
turned into the most efficient concentrations of consumption spaces and thus
into important protagonists of contemporary globalization. Expanding housing
markets are clear expressions of connected hubs generating new capital via
rising land prices and thus an important determinant for economic growth.
Building migrant cities has become increasingly defined by property-led
development dynamics, in which new urban expansions have turned into major
catalysts for enhanced economic activities.[30] The accumulation of capital in
comparatively few cities worldwide has enabled both an enhanced connectivity
between places and a new role of urban development as a major accelerator of
economic growth. While in the past capital was mainly created by producing
goods, the anticipated future consumption has turned into the key factor of
capital growth today. Consequently, contemporary urbanization is regarded as

an expression of how investment patterns are evolving. Nonetheless, this capital-driven form of urbanism is detached from environmental and social concerns. Migration has thus become a necessity, which is mainly expressed in growth rates and segregation instead of integration and diversity that represent desired multicultural realities.

Today, the development of migrant cities towards sustainable and liveable environments is anticipated to highly depend on the rise of intermediate economies serving the advanced sectors in an efficient and innovative manner. The resulting global interdependence and increasing competitiveness rely on a stable and consolidated knowledge capital. In this sense, the spatial environment, including buildings and infrastructures, must be seen as an important tool in establishing and nurturing the relationship between people and places. The access to an attractive environment can compensate various daily challenges, such as commuting times and rising living costs.[31] Housing as everyday environment is thus the core driver of urbanism due to its economic role as well as environmental impact in addition to its importance to attract long-term investments by individuals. Architects worldwide are increasingly challenged by the automated production of housing, the fragmented gated communities and the mass housing schemes, which have become detached from the contextual particularities of places including historic, sociocultural and environmental characteristics. Consequently, repetitive, replaceable and scattered environments have been produced by recent housing dynamics, hardly defined by a proactive and participatory integration of an enhanced social diversity.

Migration as historic heritage in the Gulf

The geopolitical location of the Gulf coast along one of the most important trading routes to Asia and East Africa led to various engagements of European, Ottoman and Arab as well as Persian powers throughout history to secure this important passage.[32] The contemporary debate about the Gulf as being either referred to as 'Arab' or 'Persian' is an indicator of its crucial role as border region along the lines of different cultural and ethnic backgrounds rooted in a rich history of regional and global trade. While Bedouin tribes have occasionally left major inland oases or settlements and moved to coastal regions, mainly due to conflicts or the harsh desert environment, fishermen and merchants have often moved throughout the Gulf coasts. Thus, larger settlements, where regional markets emerged, became expressions of diverse compositions of settled and semi-nomadic inhabitants. During the nineteenth century the intensified trading activities between Europe and Asia and the associated rise of the British East India Company led to new economic potentials along the Gulf coast.[33] After piracy was defeated via contractual agreements, the emerging pearl trade enabled a new economic basis turning fishing villages and coastal settlements into ports. The move of Indian and Persian merchants as well as East African slaves to the region created distinctive social groups residing in newly built environments.[34]

Despite the fact that the leadership of dominant tribes usually decided which land could be used and how, there has been an established process of decision-making within so-called *majlis*, which can be best described as a council formed of representatives of influential clans to reach consensual agreements. Major decisions regarding the development of new settlements included the important access to fresh water and the preservation of fertile land. Besides, corridors were established towards the sea to enable a natural ventilation of rather densely built neighbourhoods. Bedouin tribes settled in tents and *barasti* huts, which were made of palm leaves, at the periphery during certain seasons to trade their animals and animal products.[35] Each social group lived segregated in their own areas and the main centres of social interaction were the harbour, market and mosque. While the residences of leading tribes were often located within small separate settlements, Persian, Arab and Indian immigrants often lived in the precincts of the market, known as *souq*, due to their daily trading activities. Natives and migrants residing in proximity to the coast and harbour were often fishermen or craftsmen who were engaged building and maintaining boats. Another social group were East African slaves, who were involved in pearl diving activities.[36]

Based on the socio-economic importance of the market each neighbourhood was directly linked to it via hierarchical roads. The organic road network was not a result of conscious planning but rather the consequence of the collective building efforts of each family and clan. The role of the ruler concerning the administration of the settlement development was limited to incentives regarding where to build a palace and mosque in addition to the macro-distribution of land and key functions including markets, cemeteries and new residential districts. Furthermore, within the tribal structure the local ruler was also seen as the leading sheikh and thus as executor of Islamic law, which covered building violations.[37] However, most construction concerns were dealt with at lower levels within tribal clans and thus it can be argued that this early development of larger settlements in the Gulf region was mainly governed by dynamic bottom-up processes rather than centralized top-down decision-making. This flexibility was a necessary requirement to avoid conflicts and to lower the risk of losing control, while establishing attractive regional hubs for merchants.

Houses were built following the inherited knowledge of the indigenous and migrant populations using local building materials such as palm fronds and trunks as well as coral, stones and mud. Houses varied in scale and size from simple buildings with one space and entrance to courtyard houses with two floors and multi-functions.[38] The design followed the cultural tradition of dividing male and female spaces and the high degree of family privacy, which was further mirrored in the complex system of winding streets within neighbourhoods that served as access to individual houses.[39] In these neighbourhoods, known as *fareej*, each family clan built their houses in close proximity to each other, usually wall on wall, due to their strong affiliation and social interaction.[40] The high density of the built area was also influenced by the hot climate and the necessity to shade walkways and exterior walls. The market itself was often partly roofed and located in proximity to the port. In many cases, markets stretched in linear fashion along main roads and side roads from the harbour area towards inland. The settlement centre was identified by the Friday Mosque, which acted as a landmark and a point of reference. In some cases, colonial buildings, such as forts, or cemeteries interrupted central areas, which were generally densely covered by low-rise residential buildings.

Despite colonial interests and military presence, no Gulf settlement witnessed any major colonial urbanization, as in other parts of the wider Middle East due to harsh climatic conditions and a lack of fresh water. Thus, the traditional urban form remained intact until the middle of the twentieth century when the oil production commenced. Its vernacular structure and architecture were the result of direct human interaction and participation within the building process. Climate and cultural traditions had shaped a built environment reflecting not only how its spaces were used from a functional point of view but also how these spaces expressed the inner world of a society that was highly dependent on its natural environment and the origins of its social groups including tribal affiliations.[41] This was reflected in structural aspects of the local architecture that were adapted to desert climate and in decorative elements such as plant images or geometric patterns on walls and doors indicative of the people's origins in central Arabia, Persia or India. The use of Persian building techniques such as wind towers and *barasti* huts built by Bedouin tribes are key elements of the traditional built environment.

Although most settlements along the Gulf coast evolved as former fishing villages at the beginning of the nineteenth century and thus represent a relatively short history, their urban and architectural forms are thousands of years old and quite diverse.[42] Inherited knowledge and traditions created a vernacular space by following no planning or centralized regulations. Despite the allocation of land by tribal rulers, it was generally free to use and build on. Spontaneous settlement patterns evolved based on the principle of a cell, in this case the courtyard house, multiplying into clusters to form neighbourhoods that connected to the central backbone of the settlement – the market, port and mosque. These settlements were the product of the collective efforts of its inhabitants, their intuition, value system, customs, traditions and behaviours. Capitalist incentives resulting from the pearl trade or the interaction with colonial powers had not yet led to centralized planning and state regulations impacting local structures. Migrants imported both their know-how and lifestyles and thus formed key spaces expressing the diversity of Gulf societies.

One of the most important stakeholders in shaping the historic settlement forms were merchant families from Iran and India, who were highly respected. Their move to Gulf settlements, such as Dubai, was a crucial factor in increasing the revenues of trading activities. Persian and Indian merchants were therefore given land to build their own neighbourhoods, one of which was rediscovered during the early 1990s and restored in 2005 in Dubai. The neighbourhood is known as Al Bastakiya which dates back to the year 1901, when Dubai was declared a duty-free port (Figure 1.1). Raised taxes led to the decline of the Iranian port city Bandar Lengeh, which was the main centre of the regional pearl trade at the turn of the nineteenth century. As a result, many Persian merchants resettled and moved to Dubai, where free land was offered in Shindagha.[43] The move of craftsmen to build the new neighbourhoods according to the design techniques established in Southern Iran led to a distinct architectural style which was different from the surrounding neighbourhoods. The same import of architecture can be found in the historic market Souq Waqif in Qatar's capital Doha, which was reopened in 2008 after an implementation of a comprehensive conservation plan that commenced in 2006.[44]

The preceding discussion suggests that contemporary Gulf cities are all rooted in a very dynamic history of flourishing trading networks during the nineteenth century. Therefore, they should be perceived as rather young migrant cities and that migration itself has always been part of their legacy. The will and risk-taking of merchants from inland and offshore enabled extending settlements of few 10,000s of inhabitants and thus the basis for subsequent development patterns during modern urbanization, which started in the late 1940s. Notably, this first period of major migration was the result of economic ties and that each migrant

Figure 1.1 The restored Al Bastakiya neighbourhood in Dubai.

group, except for slaves, had its own unique spatial development. Despite all economic dependencies, migrant communities lived a rather segregated life behind the walls of a private realm preserving their own customs. This spatial segregation and introversion is an evidence of the preference to avoid conflicts. In this respect, many contemporary debates about identity conflicts in Gulf cities must be therefore questioned by integrating a historic understanding of migration and urbanism along the Gulf coast. There has never been one identity but multiple identities.

Welfare states, migration and urban transformation

The commencing oil production during the middle of the twentieth century introduced new political and economic realities that led to a transformation of Gulf societies in a few decades. To enable a coordinated and an increasingly efficient oil trade, oil companies needed regional alliances securing political stability. Thus, nation building was an important priority to consolidate political leadership and to enable a reliable environment for major infrastructure investments required for production and export. After regional attempts to unite all small Gulf States failed, the borders of each country and emirate had to be defined via major diplomatic efforts.[45] Based on their status as official protectorates, which involved British and American presence through political and military engagements, the rulers of these new nations were identified according to the way in which they are perceived as capable and able to secure regional stability. This was dependent on their tribal affiliations and thus the size of their immediate fellowship enabling a direct communication as well as a general acceptance of the rulers' privileges.

A few decades after the small Gulf States were formed, rulers were granted independence after major negotiations during the 1960s. The first strategy of all rulers was the quick introduction of higher living standards to stabilize and justify their increasingly dominant political role as leaders of oil-rich nations. The first oil revenues made from oil were mainly invested in the development of infrastructure such as the construction of major roads linking oil fields, settlements and first ports and airports.[46] The new capital cities were developed in the same location as the residences of the ruling families. From the 1950s to 1970s settlements, such as Doha, grew from around just 14,000 inhabitants to over 83,000, with foreign immigrants constituting about 67 per cent.[47] Almost 90 per cent of the working population was non-Qatari in 1970 due to a lack of educated workforce among the indigenous population and the introduction of subsidies, which turned the young nation into a classic welfare state reliant on its fossil resources. In Qatar only about 25 per cent of around 30,000 Qataris were counted as workforce by a census in 1970 and most were engaged in the newly established public administration in Doha.[48] The private sector was mainly run by immigrants, primarily from South Asia and other Middle Eastern countries, who worked in the expanding trade businesses or as employees in the growing civil and lower service sectors.

During the 1950s and 1960s, settlement patterns in Gulf cities were determined by the development of modern infrastructure such as roads and the supply of fresh water and electricity. The modern administration was just in its infancy and despite the introduction of first public housing laws and affordable housing schemes, planning and regulations had still limited impact on the general development process.[49] Yet, a major impact was made on the urban form by imported goods, particularly cars and air conditioning, and the vast migration. Subsequently, roads were widened in central areas to provide vehicular access and the old courtyard buildings were replaced by modern building blocks made of cement and imported construction materials (Figure 1.2). Likewise, new housing areas were developed in an uncoordinated manner around the former

Figure 1.2 Replaced traditional typologies in Manama during the first modernization.

city peripheries to accommodate expatriate labour as well as natives moving from other parts of the country to the emerging capitals. Subsequently, cities grew in all directions with development mainly concentrated along growth corridors towards oil fields, ports or airports. Due to the rapidly growing trade of imported goods, many informal shopping areas grew along the peripheries of city centres and in proximity to the old market areas.[50] Gradually, vernacular and traditional urban spaces faced their rapid end as a result of growing investments in developing modern infrastructure and the increasing purchasing power of urban populations. After the common practice to build affordable low-rise housing in proximity to historic centres to accommodate the growing population, including former Bedouin tribes, the rising expectations for modern living standards led to the move to suburban areas and the replacement of traditional settlements with mixed-use developments or the occupancy of these dwellings by low-income migrants. The modern suburban lifestyle required cars and air conditioning and established urban structures with low built densities, extensive road grids and cement block architecture.

While initial public administrations were already established in the middle of the twentieth century and first municipalities were founded during the 1960s to coordinate infrastructure developments and basic land uses, it was only after the declaration of national independence that an efficient central administration came into being in most Gulf States.[51] The first major public administration included several ministries that dealt with future urbanization, of which the most important were the ministries of works, the ministries of housing as well as the ministries of municipalities, which were often in charge of physical planning. The centralization of governance enabled oil revenues to be efficiently invested in the urbanization process, leading to rapid urban growth during the 1970s and 1980s when oil prices reached their peak. During this period, many Western consultants were involved in the first phase of central urban planning to establish modern capital cities. For instance, in 1974 the British consultant Llewelyn Davis was appointed by the new town planning authority in Qatar to design the first master plan of Doha for 1990.[52]

The first master plans followed the Western vision of car-based urbanism and were rooted in a well-defined functional distribution of land uses within a grid road structure. This basic structure was the foundation for the development of hierarchical road systems during the 1970s as well as for subsequent land allocations and suburban sprawl on the city outskirts (Figure 1.3). Based on the initial zoning plans and the newly introduced land policies, new city centres were created consisting of commercial developments, services and multi-storey housing. During the 1970s, most traditional neighbourhoods were replaced, and the local population moved to new suburban developments. This was made possible by land policies that included the free replacement of properties with allocated plots of land with defined measurements, such as 30 × 30 metres in Qatar, and the provision of interest-free loans for the construction of housing or financial compensation, which usually exceeded the market price of real estate at that time.[53]

Subsequently, the 1970s witnessed increasing land speculation within the city centres and adjacent areas. In most Gulf cities planning departments were in charge of subdividing land into parcels, while public housing programmes were the domain of the ministries of social affairs and housing as well as public works. These responsibilities led to various coordination challenges, which were further exacerbated by the fact that high-profile projects were usually under the supervision of special task forces or committees and thus not part of the general legalization process within ministries. Despite these challenging factors, the main elements of first master plans were implemented, such as road grids and proposed land reclamation projects. Another important objective of these first plans was to establish modern city centres. For this purpose, informal

Figure 1.3 Suburban sprawl in Dubai.

commercial buildings were no longer possible and traditional buildings were replaced to make room for access roads and multi-storey developments.

While in the transition period during the 1950s and 1960s old traditional structures were gradually replaced by a still rather uncoordinated process of modernization, the implementation of first master plans and the first major land reclamations were determining steps, carried out by newly established public authorities during the 1970s. Subsequently, the population of metropolitan areas grew rapidly. In Doha, for instance, the population increased from 89,000 inhabitants in 1970 to over 434,000 in 1997.[54] In addition to this rapid growth, land policies and real estate speculation caused the total urban area to increase exponentially. Thus, Qatar's capital grew from around just 130 hectares in the middle of the twentieth century to over 7,100 hectares in 1995.[55] The urban sprawl during the oil boom led to scattered urban landscapes with low densities resulting from the prevalence of suburban typologies and a large percentage of un-built land due to missing regulations and speculation. While the two-storey housing areas, one of the peripheries of the capital, became the residence of Qataris as well as high-income guest workers, the central areas became the residence of foreign labour. This led to a reduction in investments and subsequently to decreasing urban qualities in city centres.

In parallel, many areas within city centres continued to deteriorate, some areas became the new focal points of investment, with government buildings being erected as modern landmarks, and first major public spaces were created in the form of parks and promenades. In Qatar, the Government House was built on reclaimed land in the east of the market area, followed by the Qatar National Bank and the Ministry of Foreign Affairs. The most significant landmark at the time was the new palace, known as Diwan Al Amiri, completed in 1972, which replaced Government House as the official seat of the Emir and his government (Figure 1.4). The Diwan was constructed in a prominent location at the point where the Corniche begins and the old centre in the west ends.[56] To its west the Grand Mosque and the Clock Tower were built to complete a modern architectural ensemble intended to represent Qatar's independence. In Dubai, the World Trade Centre was built in 1979. With thirty-nine floors it became the tallest high-rise in the entire MENA region and thus an early manifestation of emerging economic ambitions in the small emirate.[57]

The transformation of the local built environment from compact and vernacular settlements to increasingly car-centric and sprawling urban areas was sudden and as precipitous as the oil boom that instigated it. The introduction of modern Gulf cities was rapidly and simply executed by importing the expertise and labour necessary. This transition to modernity was reflected in the architecture and urban design of the period, which broke away abruptly from traditional and participatory forms of urbanism to principles imposed by the state. This can be seen best in the replacement of the former neighbourhoods

Figure 1.4 Diwan Al Amiri in Qatar's capital Doha.

of the native populations, consisting of courtyard houses and winding streets, with modern suburban dwellings that stood on equally sized rectangular plots accessed by an orthogonal grid of roads. The Western consultants, who endorsed this process since the 1950s, applied their Western understanding of modern space in the newly established capitals in the Gulf. Thus, all cities developed into functional entities rooted in rigid grids defined by road hierarchies and an increasing consumption of spaces by areas dedicated to roads and parking sites, which meant the end of compact settlements.

Since the introduction of centralized governance, state planning has obliterated the earlier practice of self-governed neighbourhoods and thus the local inhabitants' direct access to shape urban environments. This meant the end of the traditional *fareej*, in which most locals lived in proximity to their extended family. Today, the heritage of these traditional neighbourhoods surrounding shared public buildings and spaces can still be found and studied in villages in the Kingdom of Bahrain. In most places, modern environments were quickly accepted due to welfare state mechanisms and the subsequent tremendous rise in living standards. Within only three decades native families found themselves in an urban Western lifestyle that enabled and promoted consumption on a scale never experienced before. While Western consumption industries entered and redefined urbanism, cultural traditions were however preserved, for example, by erecting large walls around dwellings to protect the privacy of families (Figure 1.5). The most significant impact of local populations on local urban developments has been the increasing interest to invest in land rather than accumulating wealth in bank accounts or stock markets, which led to a high percentage of over 50 per cent vacant land within most Gulf cities in the mid-1990s.[58]

This growing interest in owning land was rooted in the early practice of rulers distributing land to politically influential families to share wealth and secure their own leadership. While in the past land could only be owned, when it was directly used, the newly established modern banking system was followed by new land ownership rights and land purchase programmes, which have become important factors defining urban structures in the Gulf.[59] Over a period of two decades or so, merchants, fishermen and Bedouins found themselves as speculators, landlords and sponsors of foreign businesses benefiting from enhanced migration and the associated economic activities. However, the most significant share of the national population became dependent on public sector jobs, free services, such as health care and education, as well as housing programmes in the form of social housing, free plots and loans, while securing high living standards due to continuous oil revenues.

Figure 1.5 Villas with surrounding walls in the Kingdom of Bahrain.

On a different level, the private sector was fostered by migrants whose entrepreneurial incentives and general rights have been limited due to sponsorship requirements. The short-term perspectives of most migrants to stay in Gulf cities led to growing amounts of remittances sent back to home countries and thus a significant economic loss. Accordingly, the economic model of welfare states founded on oil revenues and service sectors dependent on foreign workforce was increasingly questioned during the 1990s. Instead of changing migration policies, rulers decided to open and deregulate local real estate markets for enhanced foreign investment interests stimulating growth and thus avoiding economic downturns caused by stagnant or even declining oil revenues. This new strategy to stimulate urban growth was rooted in the general vision to benefit from the geopolitical location of Gulf cities as main service hubs and thus to reconnect to the past as emerging trading ports between Eastern and Western global markets. While successful city states, such as Singapore, became a new role model for economic development visions, the importance of migrants and housing dynamics has hardly been addressed.

The structure of the book

The current vision of future cities in the Gulf is directly linked with the aim to initiate economic diversification, which has, however, only been possible by extensive migration. Chapter 2 introduces the various visions of how governments conceive cities and what role continuous migration is considered to play. The overview of most recent development visions is accompanied by a review of global development tendencies and contemporary social and economic realities in the Gulf region, which form the main context of establishing any new vision for future urbanism. In particular, the chapter places emphasis on one key aspect: the official political communication of migration-driven growth and economic diversification. In this respect, four major development visions are explored to introduce the main characteristics of top-down visions guiding major-decision-making in four cities. The chapter offers a juxtaposition of the realities of an increasing dependence on migration against publicized strategies mainly focusing on shrinking minorities of the local population but ignoring the needs of migrants. The resulting conflict of the two is viewed as one of the important determinants of housing production and urban dynamics as a whole along the Gulf coast.

The new visions of establishing global service hubs have been followed by extensive reforms of how urban development has been organized and guided in all small Gulf States. Thus, Chapter 3 focuses on new forms of entrepreneurial governance and the subsequent decentralization of urban development, which has led to new alliances between public and private sectors as well as the emergence of semi-public holdings. In this context, the authors introduce this reorganization of urban governance and the important role of holdings in initiating urban growth and hence restructuring contemporary housing markets by focusing on the pioneering role of the Emirate of Dubai. The chapter also provides insights into a new episode of how urban planning is viewed and practised in public institutions and the concomitant roles and structures via a small excursion to the Kingdom of Bahrain. The particular focus in this respect is on the analysis of how urban developments are managed and what kind of planning structure is followed in order to enable both profitable investment in real estate and local housing supply for migrants and national citizens.

Chapter 4 discusses the economic transformation ignited by property-led development incentives as the most important factors for extensive migration in Gulf cities. The chapter highlights key characteristics of mega projects and their impact on urbanism. Since the end of the 1990s large-scale mega projects have been initiated to enable an unprecedented urban growth and the expansion of new economic sectors. Mega projects have played an important role in shaping emerging economies and transforming housing dynamics in Gulf cities. The chapter also introduces the first pioneering developments in Dubai and Bahrain and their distinctive roles in redefining urban typologies. Examples, which have been built during the construction boom between 1999 and 2008, are outlined. During this phase many themed projects were accompanied by the rapid development of mass housing in downtown areas and the emerging suburbs to accommodate millions of newly arriving migrants.

Since the vision of establishing international service centres was introduced in the Gulf region, various new housing typologies have been built. Following the role of recent development dynamics, Chapter 5 identifies and analyses key trends in the context of rapid urban growth. The main objective of this chapter is to deliver an overview of typical trends of urban transformation in rapidly growing migrant cities in the Gulf, which are still relying on cars as main mode of transport resulting in contemporary urban conditions. The authors debrief new development patterns with respect to investment interests and migration dynamics leading to particular neighbourhoods and urban fragmentation tendencies in Gulf cities. The spatial distribution of the identified housing typologies has been investigated via various studies to explore the new structure of six urban districts in Bahrain's capital Manama and Qatar's capital Doha. The outcomes of this investigation offer new insights regarding spatial fragmentation in the Gulf and the role of housing development.

Chapter 6 investigates the relationship between main lifestyle groups, emerging neighbourhoods and multicultural perceptions in Gulf cities. In general, four major lifestyle trends can be observed, which are rooted in the earlier initiated development and the current urban transformation ignited by extensive migration. Therefore, new lifestyle patterns are particularly visible in the various neighbourhoods and their distinctive social and spatial contexts. The chapter argues that recent international migration patterns have redefined Gulf cities. Key lifestyle trends and the multicultural perceptions of migrants are investigated, who have been engaged in emerging economies and who are therefore important factors for future developments. The chapter places emphasis on the diverse urban experiences with respect to cultural backgrounds and the social segregation in various neighbourhoods that have different particularities. While general lifestyle trends were investigated by analysing demographic structures and consumption patterns as well as spatial practices, cultural perceptions were studied through direct engagement with inhabitants.

Chapter 7 focuses on the move of long-term residents from traditional neighbourhoods due to new developments and the arrival of thousands of migrants with short-term contracts and incentives to stay. Today, both deterioration and redevelopment threaten remaining traditional forms of everyday urbanism which, over the years, reflected integrated and engaged migrant communities in the surroundings of historic centres. The chapter interrogates the way in which this everyday urbanism in Gulf cities has changed from a common and unquestioned reality into an increasingly marginalized phenomenon. Differences between the historic urban spaces defined by traditional housing in dense mixed-used districts and the modern replaceable urban landscapes are explored. Districts such as Al Asmakh and Al Jadeeda in Doha or Al Satwa in Dubai are important sites to study the recent spatial transformation and the associated human behaviour of their communities. Through fieldwork in the form of systematic observations, the study reveals key questions on how future innovation and urban manufacturing can take place in spaces produced by continuous growth and replacement instead of long-term social and spatial consolidation.

The concluding chapter offers an outlook on future trends and how housing can become a crucial factor in establishing more sustainable migrant cities in the Gulf. Most urban developments will face a major challenge in responding to the paradox of contemporary Gulf urbanism created by the high dependency on migration while simultaneously neglecting a long-term integration of migrant communities and their needs. The perception of cities as growth machines and thus corporate entities, rather than organic incremental development within planning frameworks, has never been more manifest than in contemporary Gulf cities. Integrated development will however play an important role in enabling Gulf cities to evolve as true expressions of their inhabitants rather than as shells of replaceable societies only migrating to work and consume for limited periods. Despite the undeniable reality that a large factor in recent urban growth patterns in the Gulf region has been a result of specific globalization patterns, the role of housing in establishing more sustainable built environment must be underscored. Thus, the book concludes with a holistic framework introducing the various interdependencies of the production of urban qualities for more sustainable migrant cities.

Notes

1   United Nations, *International Migration Report 2017*. Available at: www.un.org/en/ development/desa/population/migration/publications/migrationreport/docs/Migr ationReport2017_Highlights.pdf (accessed 7 March 2018).

2   World Bank Group, *Migration and Remittance Factbook 2016. Third Edition*. Available at: www.siteresources.worldbank.org/INTPROSPECTS/Resources/334934-1199807908806/4549025-1450455807487/Factbookpart1.pdf (accessed 7 March 2018), p. 4.

3   Ibid., p. 6.
4   Dilip Ratha and William Shaw, 'South–South Migration and Remittances', Working Paper 102, World Bank (Washington, 2007).
5   United Nations, *Recommendations on Statistics of International Migration*. Revision 1, 1998. Available at: www.unstats.un.org/unsd/publication/SeriesM/SeriesM_58r ev1e.pdf (accessed 7 March 2018).
6   Dilip Ratha and Sonia Plaza, 'Diaspora and Development: Critical Issues', in S. I. Rajan (ed.), *India Migration Report* (London, 2014).
7   World Bank Group, *Migration and Remittance Factbook 2016*, p. 11.
8   United Nations, *Fourth Coordination Meeting on International Migration. Department of Economic and Social Affairs*, 2005. Available at: www.un.org/esa/popul ation/meetings/fourthcoord2005/P09_GCIM.pdf (accessed 7 March 2018), p. 3.
9   Ibid.
10 United Nations, *Monterrey Consensus on Financing for Development*. 2002. Available at: www.un.org/esa/ffd/monterrey/MonterreyConsensus.pdf (accessed 7 March 2018).
11 United Nations, *Fourth Coordination Meeting on International Migration*, p. 3.
12 Ibid., p. 10.
13 World Bank Group, *Migration and Remittances. Recent Developments and Outlook. Special Topic: Global Compact on Migration*, 2017. Available at: www.pubdoc s.worldbank.org/en/992371492706371662/MigrationandDevelopmentBrief27.pdf (accessed 7 March 2018), p. 14.
14 Dilip Ratha, 'Migration and Development: A Roadmap to a Global Compact', *Presentation to Meeting of the Regional Conference on Migration on the Global Compact on Migration*, 29 March (Washington, 2017).
15 Jean-Christophe Dumont, Gilles Spielvogel and Sarah Widmaier, 'International Migrants in Developed, Emerging and Developing Countries: An Extended Profile', in *OECD Social, Employment and Migration Working Papers*, No. 114, 2010. Available at: www.oecd.org/migration/46535003.pdf (accessed 7 March 2018).
16 International Monetary Fund, *International Transactions in Remittances: Guide for Compilers and Users* (Washington, 2009).
17 John Perry, 2012, *Housing and Migration. A UK Guide to Issues and Solutions*. Available at: www.cih.org/resources/PDF/Policy%20free%20download%20pdfs/ho usingandMigration2012.pdf (accessed 7 March 2018), p. 10.
18 Ibid.
19 Ya P. Wang, Yanglin Wang and Jiansheng Wu, 'Housing Migrant Workers in Rapidly Urbanizing Regions: A Study of the Chinese Model in Shenzhen', *Housing Studies*, 25 (2010), pp. 83–100; Sarah Wayland, 'The Housing Needs of Immigrants and Refugees in Canada', Canada Housing and Renewal Association (Ottawa, 2007).
20 Valentina Antoniucci and Giuliano Marella, 'Immigrants and the City: The Relevance of Immigration on Housing Price Gradient', *Buildings*, 7/91 (2017),

pp. 1–14; Hubert Jayet, Glenn Rayp, Ilse Ruyssen and Nadiya Ukrayinchuk, 'Immigrants' Location Choice in Belgium', in *Institut de Recherches Economiques et Sociales de l'Universite catholique de Louvain*, 2014. Available at: www.sites. uclouvain.be/econ/DP/IRES/2014004.pdf (accessed 7 March 2018); Weiping Wu, 'Temporary Migrants in Shanghai, China: Housing Choices and Patterns', *Human Settlement Development*, Volume 3, 2009.

21 Marcello Balbo and Giovanna Marconi, 'International Migration, Diversity and Urban Governance in Cities of the South', *Habitat International*, 30/3 (2006), pp. 706–15.

22 Adrian Jarvis and Robert Lee, *Trade, Migration and Urban Networks in Port Cities, 1640-1940* (Liverpool, 2008).

23 Blair Badcock, *Making Sense of Cities* (London, 2002).

24 Victor F. Sit and Chun Yang, 'Foreign-investment-induced Exo-urbanisation in the Pearl River Delta, China', *Urban Studies*, 34/4 (1997), pp. 647–77.

25 Walter W. Powell and Kaisa Snellman, 'The Knowledge Economy', *Annual Review Sociology*, 30 (2004), pp. 199–220.

26 Saskia Sassen, 'Cities Today: A New Frontier for Major Developments', *The Annals of the American Academy of Political and Social Science*, 626/1 (2009), pp. 53–71.

27 Libertad Gonzalez and Francesc Ortega, 'Immigration and Housing Boom: Evidence from Spain', in *Institute for the Study of Labor*, 2009. Available at: www.ftp. iza.org/dp4333.pdf (accessed 7 March 2018).

28 Dawn Foster, *Is Immigration Causing the UK Housing Crisis?* Available at: www. theguardian.com/housing-network/2016/jan/25/is-immigration-causing-the-uk-housing-crisis (accessed 7 March 2018).

29 World Bank Group, *World Development Report, 1999/2000: Entering the 21st Century* (New York, 1999).

30 Susanne Heeg, *Von Stadtplanung und Immobilienwirtschaft* (Bielefeld, 2008).

31 Robert W. Marans, 'Quality of Urban Life Studies: An Overview and Implications for Environment-Behaviour Research', *Social and Behavioural Sciences*, 35 (2012), pp. 9–22.

32 Lawrence G. Potter, *The Persian Gulf in History* (New York, 2009).

33 J.E. Peterson, 'Britain and the Gulf: At the Periphery of the Empire', in L. G. Potter (ed.), *The Persian Gulf in History* (New York, 2009), p. 278.

34 Matthew S. Hopper, 'The African Presence in Eastern Arabia', in L. G. Potter (ed.), *The Persian Gulf in Modern Times* (New York, 2014).

35 Ronald Hawker, *Traditional Architecture of the Arabian Gulf: Building on Desert Tides* (Southampton, 2008).

36 Hala Fattah, 'Social Structures and Transformation in the Gulf and Arabia until 1971', in J.E. Peterson (ed.), *The Emergence of the Gulf States* (London, 2016), p. 250.

37 Besim S. Hakim, 'Revitalizing Traditional Towns and Heritage Districts', *Archnet-IJAR: International Journal of Architectural Research*, 1/3 (2007), pp. 153–66, p. 154.

38 Ibrahim Jaidah and Malika Bourenane, *The History of Qatari Architecture 1800-1950* (Milan, 2009), p. 30.

39 Ibid., p. 22.

40 Mustapha Ben-Hamouche, 'Complexity of Urban Fabric in Traditional Muslim Cities: Importing Old Wisdom to Present Cities', *Urban Design International*, 14/1 (2009), pp. 22–35.

41 Saleh A. Al-Hathloul, *The Arab-Muslim City* (Riyadh, 1996).

42 Fadl A. Al-Buainain, *Urbanisation in Qatar: A Study of the Residential and Commercial Land Development in Doha City, 1970 – 1997* (Salford, 1999) p. 186.

43 Shahnaz R. Nadjmabadi, 'The Arab Presence on the Iranian Coast of the Persian Gulf', in L. G. Potter (ed.), *The Persian Gulf in History* (New York, 2009), p. 135.

44 Hassan Radoine, Souk Waqif, Doha, Qatar, 2010. Available at: www.archnet.org/syst em/publications/contents/8722/original/DTP101221.pdf?1396271815 (accessed 7 March 2018).

45 David D. Commins, *The Gulf States: A Modern History* (London, 2012) p. 120.

46 Fred Scholz, *Die Kleinen Golfstaaten* (Gotha, 1999), p. 77.

47 Al-Buainain, *Urbanisation in Qatar*, p. 217.

48 Ibid., p. 168.

49 Florian Wiedmann, *Post-oil Urbanism in the Gulf: New Evolutions in Governance and the Impact on Urban Morphologies* (Stuttgart, 2012).

50 Scholz, *Die Kleinen Golfstaaten*, p. 201.

51 Rosemarie S. Zahlan, *The Creation of Qatar* (London, 1979).

52 Florian Wiedmann, Ashraf M. Salama and Alain Thierstein, 'Urban Evolution of the City of Doha: An Investigation into the Impact of Economic Transformations on Urban Structures', *METU Journal of the Faculty of Architecture*, 29/2 (2012), pp. 35–61, p. 41.

53 Sharon Nagy, *Social and Spatial Process: An Ethnographic Study of Housing in Qatar* (Pennsylvania, 1997).

54 Wiedmann et al., 'Urban Evolution of the City of Doha', pp. 35–61, p. 42.

55 Al-Buainain, *Urbanisation in Qatar*, p. 407.

56 Salma S. Damluji, *The Diwan Al Amiri, Doha, Qatar* (London, 2012).

57 Colin Simpson, *Dubai World Trade Centre Building: An Example for the Future*, 2012. Available at: www.thenational.ae/uae/dubai-world-trade-centre-building-an-example-for-the-future-1.362159 (accessed 7 March 2018).

58 Al-Buainain, *Urbanisation in Qatar*, p. 407.

59 Laura El-Katiri, Bassam Fattouh and Paul Segal, *Anatomy of an Oil-based Welfare State: Rent Distribution in Kuwait*, 2011. Available at: http://eprints.soas.ac.uk/1426 5/1/Kuwait_2011.pdf (accessed 7 March 2018), p. 9.

2

Visions of migration-based urbanism

The formulation and introduction of holistic economic development visions for cities is a rather recent phenomenon. Historically, the industrial city has been shaped by manufacturing industries and their needs for labour and infrastructure. Since the 1980s, the new form of globalization built on the international division of labour led to emerging service hubs in more and more complex networks.[1] Cities in the Global North witnessed a rapid process of transformation due to dominant knowledge economies, such as advanced producer services or high-tech research and development. In parallel, many cities in the Global South experienced a rather rapid urbanization and modernization overnight, in which cities became the main employers due to manufacturing industries and rural areas lost their population. One main factor of the extensive migration to cities worldwide was urban development itself. The construction of cities, from complex infrastructure to diverse real estate markets, led to their new role as engineered places of an increasingly debt-driven consumption industry. Consequently, the definition of a vision regarding future development dynamics became an important tool to attract investment interests.

The rising advanced industrial production and the highly efficient connection of cities via modern infrastructure and new communication technologies enabled a complex hierarchy of hubs, determined and driven by their access to growing markets. The result was an inevitable competition between cities worldwide to attract the headquarters of various key international corporations and thus to position themselves as major hubs in extending networks of capital flows.[2] The main preconditions of any emerging hub include advanced connectivity, enabled by modern infrastructure, the overall political stability and the local growth potentials to establish an increasingly important marketplace. Since these preconditions are viewed as factors that can be initially established by rigorous top-down decision-making in places with strategic geopolitical location and existing resources, many new hub cities were initiated in recent decades. According to the Boston Consulting Group, there are more than 100 emerging hubs worldwide, which can mainly be characterized by their proximity to the development of local natural resources or industrial production.[3] These cities are experiencing the highest growth rates worldwide and share common characteristics regarding their migration-driven type of urbanism.

The main factors of postmodern urbanization are closely linked to the basics of generating fast growth relying on rising land values and therefore the prospects of accumulating consumption. Accordingly, the new consumption-driven economies have become dependent on an increasing number of individuals investing in private homes, resulting in a complex system of rising debt and a new dependency on continuous growth to reassure the prices of properties.[4] One important consequence of an increasing tendency towards private land ownership coupled with the introduction of the car as preferred mode of transportation was the phenomenon of urban sprawl. This was always associated with a high level of spatial fragmentation between core urban areas and the surrounding countryside.[5] The very pragmatic approach of modern urban development schemes, which were mainly established during the 1960s and 1970s, led to an efficient formula of new city building worldwide. This formula is directly based on selling undeveloped land to private investors and reinvesting in infrastructural networks. Thus, one key factor of any successful city project has been the established trust of investors in continuously rising land prices by generating the confidence in future growth and economic consolidation.

Contemporary urbanism has thus led to scattered and segregated urban landscapes, which are often described as contradictive yet dependent worlds of leisure and labour, wherein the role of inhabitants is largely reduced to either consume or produce. This structure has gradually become efficient due to a newly emerging sociotechnical organization, also referred to as the informational mode of development,[6] which enabled new opportunities for an extending global capitalism. Furthermore, the fast globalization of capitalism has challenged and weakened the national state as a geographically defined form of governance and led to an ongoing conflict between local concerns and global forces.[7] The enhanced consumption and the resulting waste led to complex environmental challenges, whereby cities became the main threat for natural habitats worldwide.[8] The dominant role of top-down envisioned and planned urbanization has resulted in the general conflict between quantity and quality due to the very limited access of majorities to impact spatial structures.

Contemporary urban developments in the Global South are often analysed as highly contrasted due to extreme poverty and small wealthy elites. The rapid industrialization process is currently evolving in developing countries within less than half a century and as a direct consequence of recent globalization patterns instead of a regional emancipation of local markets built on innovation and knowledge. Due to this dependency on the developed world and its rising or decreasing need for certain products or resources, emerging cities in the Global South have been facing similar challenges based on a rather fragile and often-speculative existence. Gated communities for higher-income minorities are surrounded by walls to be protected from squatter settlements, mass housing or decaying ghettos. The pressure of rural migration extended urban slums and disabled an efficient integration of urban structures built on state-of-the-art infrastructure and a high level of liveability.[9]

While growth has become a main threat for the quality of urban life due to enhanced waste and unsustainable structures, made of fragmentation and isolation, it has also become an inevitable precondition for remaining part of the global network. Modern infrastructure and thus access to global networks can only be developed and maintained in few places of the developing world, which have the prospect of serving an increasingly hierarchical and centralized global economy. The capital-driven globalization has thus led to problematic structures, in which cities must enter a fierce competition to attract investment.[10] Consequently, the emerging gates to global markets and the dependency on rising investments have caused a clear divide between the economic opportunities in urban and rural areas. The inevitable liberalization of local markets has resulted in an increasingly limited agricultural production due to monocultures in the developing world and the rising dependency on global imports.

While emerging hub cities can be initially launched by investing in state-of-the-art infrastructure and the liberalized markets, the sustenance of the overall growth momentum has become a rising challenge worldwide. Real-estate-driven developments can lead to rapid urban growth and thus new-born cities for millions. But economies independent from construction industries and associated services must grow in parallel and as fast as possible to sustain settlements. This economic diversification is however often victim of the rapid development itself, since neither investments nor communities themselves are establishing the capacities needed for highly advanced economies. Instead, emerging cities have become fragile entities depending on accelerated urban growth and have consequently entered a rather short-sighted competition to attract global investment flows. The direct result has been a rather speculation-driven form of urbanism, in which urbanized land has become an exchangeable commodity within international markets.[11] Growing land prices however are the first and main factor in preventing diversified urban economies. The exclusion of bottom-up economies led to a severe lack of opportunities for the masses of people and their dependency on being employed as labourers rather than becoming initiators of local businesses.

In summary, it is argued that the contemporary form of globalization, which is mainly built on capital flows towards an increasing and highly efficient accumulation, has prevented the integration of the needs of many communities worldwide. Extensive migration is leading to an accelerated urbanization process and to the pressing question of what role cities will play in the future. The increasingly transparent hierarchical system of cities and the resulting threat for any local development has challenged every city to either enter the competition or face a rather quick isolation and the associated economic struggles. While mega cities are complex entities with enormous scales integrating almost all aspects of modern urbanization in the Global South, from forgotten slums to emerging high-tech centres, the newly born hub cities are rather dynamic but recently engineered places, which share rigorous top-down strategies to enter global networks. The following sections offer an exploration of the repercussions of the global condition in the Gulf region, articulate the background and key characteristics of hub visions in the Gulf region and demonstrate how various preconditions such as the wealth of fossil fuels as well as the fortunate geopolitical location have enabled a new dimension of engineered hub cities built on global migration.

The social and economic realities along the Gulf coast

Prior to discussing the contemporary visions of urbanism in the Gulf region, the overall demographic results of the urbanization during recent years should be introduced in more detail. Since the turn of the centuries, the Gulf region has witnessed rapid growth, which led to an overall population increase in all four small Gulf States, including the UAE, Qatar, Kuwait and Bahrain, from only around eight million inhabitants in 2005 to more than seventeen million in 2017.[12] Almost 70 per cent of all inhabitants live in only six cities, including all four capital cities in addition to Dubai and Sharjah. The overall share of the national population along the Gulf coast has decreased from 27 per cent in 2005 to around 18 per cent in 2017. The lowest share with less than 10 per cent can be found in Dubai, while the Kingdom of Bahrain enjoys the highest share with approximately 45 per cent.[13] In addition to the overall urban population increase due to migration, the overall urban sprawl has led to major metro urban regions integrating previously rural settlements. The largest urban agglomeration can be

found in the merging urban landscapes of the Emirate of Dubai, Sharjah, Ajman
and Umm Al Quwain covering more than 960 square kilometres (Table 2.1).

The rapid migration led to a new demographic structure and with an average
of 82 per cent of an overwhelming majority of migrant groups in all major Gulf
cities. For instance, during 2005 and 2015 more than three million migrants
moved to Doha, Dubai and Abu Dhabi and Manama. A large share of these
migrants has been staying in these cities for a limited number of years due to
short-term contracts, which has led to rather high turnover rates. The most
significant share of all migrants, around 80 per cent, is South Asians, particularly
from the Indian subcontinent (Figure 2.1). Since most of these migrants are

Table 2.1 Overall demographic and growth profile in four Gulf States[14]

Country	Qatar	United Arab Emirates	Bahrain	Kuwait
Population (2005)	836,924	4,106,427	867,014	2,263,604
Population (2017)	2,324,346	9,505,870	1,412,416	4,235,549
Maximum Growth Rate (2007)	17.74%	15.3%	8.08%	5.31%
National population	14%	11%	45%	30%
Migrant population	86%	89%	55%	70%
Male population	75%	69%	62%	60%
Female population	25%	31%	38%	40%
Median age	30,8	33,5	30,5	31,1

Figure 2.1 South Asian inhabitants in Dubai Creek.

low-income male labourers being engaged in construction sectors, logistics and manufacturing industries, an average of almost 70 per cent of the total urban population along the Gulf coast are men and the median age is thirty years.[15] These labourers are housed in specific accommodations, which are provided by employers in either deteriorating downtown districts or in industrial areas. In all Gulf cities labourers are typically provided with accommodation by their employers and they are not permitted to move into the countries with their families.[16] Based on the evaluated statistics of all four cities, these labourers make up at least 40 per cent of the urban population.[17]

The next lowest income group can be described as low to medium income, mainly from the Indian subcontinent, the Philippines and the MENA region (Middle East and North Africa). This group is engaged in service sectors, such as construction, trade and tourism, and includes many migrants and their families, who have settled in the four Gulf cities over several decades. Therefore, a large share of this group is from countries like India, Pakistan, Egypt, Iran and Sudan. Although medium-income groups with a minimum monthly wage, for instance around $2,700 in Qatar and the UAE, are usually permitted to move with their families, a large share has moved as singles due to short-term contracts and a big majority of young professionals.[18] This migrant group counts to another 30 per cent to 40 per cent of the urban population in each city.

The remaining share of the urban population can be divided into two groups: the national population, who in all four major Gulf cities constitutes only around 10 per cent to 20 per cent of the urban population, and the medium- to high-income expats, who make up around 10 per cent. The medium- to high-income migrants are the most diverse group including a large share of migrants from Western, Asian and Middle Eastern countries. Based on similar historic and regional contexts, a very distinctive overall demographic structure can be detected in the case of Doha, Manama, Abu Dhabi and Dubai, despite their different sizes and differing political leadership (Table 2.2).

Apart from this new demographic structure of Gulf cities, rapid migration has led to new challenging questions regarding the socio-economic development. The local populations have found themselves over night in a transforming environment moving away from the previous welfare state mechanisms towards accelerating hub dynamics. Today, all statistics show a very low active participation of most locals in the private sector. Only in Bahrain, many locals are engaged in the private sector. In all other GCC countries, the majority is involved in public sector occupations in addition to their roles as landlords, sponsors and investors.[19] According to recent statistics, an average of approximately 20 per cent of nationals

Table 2.2 The basic demographic structure of urban populations in four Gulf cities

City (metro)	Doha	Manama	Abu Dhabi	Dubai
Population (2016)	1,351,000	411,000	1,720,000	2,663,000
Origin	Western 3%, Local 12%, Indian Subcontinent 56%, South-east Asia 10%, Middle Eastern 17%	Western 3%, Local 22%, Indian Subcontinent 55%, South-east Asia 7%, Middle Eastern 12%	Western 2%, Local 16%, Indian Subcontinent 52%, South-east Asia 8%, Middle Eastern 21%	Western 3%, Local 9%, Indian Subcontinent 57%, South-east Asia 9%, Middle Eastern 20%
Age structure	0-24: 25%, 25-54: 70%, 55<: 5%	0-24: 36%, 25-54: 56%, 55<: 8%	0-24: 33%, 25-54: 62%, 55<: 5%	0-24: 28%, 25-54: 66%, 55<: 6%
Gender	Female 25%, Male 75%	Female 38%, Male 62%	Female 34%, Male 66%	Female 31%, Male 69%

have a public sector job, a clear indication of a rather low employment rate.[20] The general lack of qualifications combined with the fact that foreign employees are cheaper and thus more attractive has led to an extensive exclusion of nationals within new economies. Furthermore, due to the rapid internationalization, most locals left cities and currently reside in the periphery or in satellite settlements. Their homogeneous suburban neighbourhoods are rooted in a separate housing market, guided by the land distribution of governments and rigid development policies. This economic and spatial division of national populations has been the result of the former urbanization in welfare states.

In order to establish emerging hubs, particular development strategies were implemented, which can be traced back to the first incentives during the 1970s in Bahrain and Dubai. At first, major ports and airports enabled a new level of regional and international connectivity and thus the establishment of main trading centres. These trading centres were associated with the attraction of service sectors and industries related to the production of oil and gas and the concomitant attraction of financial institutions. While trade was accelerated by newly launched free trade zones, offshore banking led to rising international attention. During the 1990s the rulers of both Bahrain and Dubai recognized the vacuum of leisure opportunities in the region and embarked on an effort for their cities to become major touristic centres.

The turn of the twentieth century was marked by the liberalization of local real estate markets, which led to an unprecedented urban growth rate and a new dimension of international migration.[21] The 9/11 terrorist attacks and the subsequent move of Saudi capital from the United States contributed to an extensive interest in local freehold properties along the Gulf coast. The local construction boom and the extending tourism sectors were furthermore enabled by the increasingly important role of airports and national airlines connecting the new hub cities. The general linking of infrastructure investments and a particular form of market liberalization dominated by holdings, which are directly governed by decision-makers, became the model for all Gulf cities. However, the overall realization of these city projects would have not been possible during a period of less than three decades without accelerated migration and thus globalization and its resulting realities in the developing world.

Governments have however applied various limitations for migrants to move freely on the private labour market to reduce the danger of entirely excluding nationals from the newly emerging economies. The dependence of each migrant to obtain an official sponsorship by a locally registered company or a national citizen has led to a fairly controlled migration. This restriction has always been seen as a necessary step to prevent an irreversible internationalization and the associated loss of identity as well as to establish an important channel for nationals to become sponsors and thus to benefit from the overall growth. The latter has however benefited a relatively low percentage of well-established nationals, who have been able to achieve key roles as sponsors of emerging economies or as landlords. In general, it can be argued that the sponsorship concept has led to the widespread preference of employers to only hire migrants due to their limitations of changing employers and their comparatively low wages as well as their, in average, higher qualifications and work ethics.[22] In recent years, various nationalization strategies and policies were applied in most Gulf countries to enforce an increasing percentage of nationals being employed in the private sector.

The highly differing living standards, which are rooted in state subsidies and which can still be found in high wages for public sector jobs, led to the situation of nationals often earning 600 per cent of the equivalent foreigner's salary.[23] This extreme gap between nationals with relatively low qualifications but high salary expectations on the one side and the competitive migrant community with differing salary perceptions led to a socio-economic structure made of a relatively controllable but frequently exchanging international workforce and a national population either benefiting from new developments as sponsors, investors or landlords. A significant majority of nationals has however been remaining dependent on state subsidies and nationalization policies. Most newly established economies from logistics, trade and tourism to financial sectors and higher education rely on qualified migrants, who have been witnessing no progress regarding their labour rights or long-term career perspectives, while in parallel facing increasing living costs due to the general loss of momentum of urban growth since the international financial crisis in 2008.

Overall, the decreasing benefits of short-term migration and the resulting frequent exchange in the Gulf region are viewed as major threats for consolidating new economies in the long-term but enable national populations to develop the needed qualifications as well as openness to acquire key roles within expanding service sectors. Made of an extreme dependency on continuous migration and the lack of time to integrate national populations as drivers of new economies, this fragile situation has become the core driving force for initiating development visions in most Gulf countries. While further investment and growth must be stimulated, the widespread perception of Gulf cities as shells for temporary migration rather than as sustainable hubs has to be encountered by sound holistic visions drawing realistic scenarios for future development. The evident question of a desired future Gulf society requires a governmental response to avoid the increasing loss of confidence in the entire idea of establishing hub cities in this desert region.

Despite the evidence of this urgent matter since the conscious and strategic attempt to establish hub cities during the end of the twentieth century, most formulated and published development visions were introduced in 2007 and 2008. Most governments hesitated to formulate and implement an officially declared vision for building cities for millions of international migrants to avoid fears and conflicts within national communities, who might begin to object major growth strategies initiated by large-scale investments and market deregulations. In the beginning, the necessity of economic diversification was announced as main driver to initiate growth and thus to sustain wealth during a future era without oil and gas production. The new dimension of middle- and higher-income migrants moving to the Gulf region to build cities and to establish the desired service economies however led to an increasing need for an official clarification of how migrant urbanism should be directed towards social and economic consolidation and how a future Gulf city will function with shrinking growth rates.

Key characteristics of recent development visions

Recent visions for future urban development in the Gulf region must be understood as a product of a top-down mediation between the new challenges to be part of global networks and the rising question of how Gulf societies will transform towards consolidated and sustainable structures. In the following, the most recently published visions in Qatar, Abu Dhabi, Dubai and Bahrain are introduced and discussed to identify the main characteristics of contemporary tendencies to guide migrant-driven urbanization in Gulf cities. Each vision is rooted in the distinctive history of each place, local economic conditions and the incentives of current ruling elites. Thus, despite all parallels, differences can be detected between places facing shrinking oil revenues since the 1970s, such as Dubai and Bahrain, and places with still abundant resources and the opportunities of an accelerated production of fossil fuels.

The Qatar National Vision 2030

Qatar's new political leadership in 1995, when Sheikh Hamad Bin Khalifa Al Thani came to the throne, enabled a completely new path of postmodern development dynamics for what was once known as a relatively conservative country avoiding rather than seeking regional or international attention.[24] Despite the immediate implementation of new development strategies accompanied with extensive investments during the 1990s, a new holistic vision was only introduced in 2008 stating the overall aim to develop the capital city Doha into an emerging service hub in the region and beyond. In general, three major factors can be identified as catalysts for this new development vision in Qatar including the rising investment pressure because of rapidly increasing gas revenues, the accelerating regional competition to attract oil- and gas-independent service sectors, such as transit and logistics, and thirdly and perhaps most decisively the individual ambitions of Qatar's new leadership to transform the small emirate into a progressive hub linking both a political and economic role in the entire region.

Qatar's prosperity is mainly based on the world's second largest gas field, known as North Field, which is considered to be the major economic driver for the following several decades. The investment of gas production revenues in state-of-the-art infrastructure has led to an increasing connectivity and thus the main basis of enabling fast urban growth. Apart from the fortunate geopolitical location as potential transit hub and the vast investment potential due to the wealth on fossil fuels, the overall vision to develop a hub within global networks is also rooted in the particular individual interests of the ruling elites. Sheikh Hamad Bin Khalifa Al Thani and his wife, Sheikha Mohza Bint Nasser Al Missned, aimed to shape Qatar into a think-tank highly engaged Middle Eastern affairs accompanied by the ambition to be perceived as a modern and progressive nation.[25]

While global sports events were understood as an important catalyst to generate international attention, as exhibited in the form of the Qatar Open (since 1993), the Asian Games in 2006 and most recently the successful bid for the FIFA World Cup 2022, the Qatar Foundation was initiated to establish state-of-the-art education and research facilities as well as to sustain Qatar's identity by launching conservation strategies and by integrating the young national population in various development efforts (Figure 2.2). The proclaimed role of the Qatar Foundation can be understood as an indirect sign that the initiated internationalization and liberalization process was conceived by Qatar's ruling elite as a significant departure from former social structures during the following years.[26] The formulation of a clear hub vision itself could only be established as an outcome of a gradual process reshaping the overall perception of Qataris regarding their country and their future role within globalization.

At the end of the twentieth century, the remaining adherence to old tribal structures was one of the main reasons that a paradigm shift within governance, from conservative welfare state mechanisms towards liberalized markets and internationalization, was established gradually over a period of more than ten years. Although the initial vision to transform the capital city Doha into an international hub cannot be found in the form of any major political documents

Figure 2.2 The Convention Centre of Education City in Doha.

or published reports, an accumulation of various strategies and projects was a clear sign for the new development direction. Qatar's new chapter of urbanization was therefore initially not guided by any comprehensive framework defining clear development goals. This has led to a fairly fragmented and scattered urban development built on the case-by-case decision-making of new mega projects. Due to increasing development conflicts and unclear regulations, the leadership decided to introduce a new framework of policies built on a holistic vision for society, economy and environment.

The General Secretariat of Development Planning (GSDP) was founded as a governmental agency in 2006 and its main remit was the introduction of this comprehensive vision for Qatar, which later became known as the Qatar National Vision 2030 (QNV). After having been under preparation for two years, the QNV was introduced in 2008 and became the foundation for several subsequent strategies and frameworks reshaping Qatar's development directions by promoting an enhanced integration and a definition of future milestones. The new vision identifies five key challenges including the preservation of local traditions, the needs of future generations and the overall growth management as well as the size and the quality of the expatriate labour force and the general sustainability concerns. The main focus of each challenge is conceived from the angle of the shrinking share of the national population and not from any perspective acknowledging Qatar's emerging and growing multicultural society. This is particularly evident given the overemphasis on preserving local cultural identities while perceiving the Qatari traditional family as the main basis for any future development.[27]

In order to address the five key challenges, the QNV defines four main pillars, namely, Human Development, Social Development, Economic Development and Environmental Development. The Human Development Vision focuses on promoting the development of sufficient facilities for education and health as well as programmes for engaging nationals. One key aspect in this regard is the further establishment of higher education and research funds to enhance the international and intellectual activities. The Qatar Foundation and its subsidiaries, such as Education City and QNRF, have been set up within the overall vision to be perceived as main drivers of these human development goals. The main aim is to develop an increased and diversified participation of Qataris within the newly emerging economies on the basis of an improved access to education.[28]

In addition to the focus on the needs of Qatari nationals to become more competitive, the Social Development Vision has been introduced in order to emphasize the importance of establishing sound social structures on certain key principles, such as the preservation of local heritage rooted in Islamic values and identity. Furthermore, civic organizations should be improved by more accessible services with high qualities including legal, business and safety concerns. While this vision is mainly based on internal affairs, it also includes the future international cooperation in the region and Qatar's role as centre for cultural and political dialogues. No migrant concerns are specifically named as part of the overall social vision, which is underlining the impression of perceiving migration as an inevitable but temporary phenomenon rather than recognizing the existing and the increasing dependency on migrant and expatriate communities and thus the need for social integration.[29]

The Economic Development Vision is based on the establishment of sustainable growth rates by balancing between regional and local conditions as well as the interests of the public and private sectors. In addition to management concerns regarding economic developments, the vision integrates the future role of oil and gas industries, which is expected to remain a major economic driver. Furthermore, the economic diversification process is envisioned on the basis of a gradually decreasing dependency on hydrocarbon industries and the important role of emerging knowledge economies. In this respect, the vision emphasizes the design and development of economic activities in which Qatar can gain a special role by including the human development requirements. This can be translated as the overall vision that new economies will be essentially driven and guided by a national highly skilled and productive labour force.[30]

With respect to the Environmental Development Vision, the GSDP decided to emphasize the necessary balance between development needs for urban growth and environmental protection. Thus, it introduced the vision of efficient governance with specialized institutions as well as a holistic legal framework to regulate developments and enhance consolidation of organizations and decision-making.[31] This fourth pillar is introduced in a relatively brief manner within the overall QNV and without explicitly linking rapid growth caused by extensive migration and major environmental concerns. Instead, the QNV refers to a comprehensive urban development plan, known as the Qatar National Master Plan, whose major development framework was introduced three years later, in 2011.

In 2009 the GSDP published the *Second Human Development Report*, also known under the title *Advancing Sustainable Development*, which identifies water supply, maritime environment and climate change as the main challenges of sustainable development in Qatar. This study was intended to reflect the urgent environmental challenges and thus to be used as the basis for future policies and plans.[32] The particular role of the existing economic model relying on increasing migration is again hardly addressed. Therefore, this official report is mainly an overview study of existing environmental risks rather than an actual reflection of the key factors instigating these risks. Neither the brief summary of social equity concerns nor other sections specifically focus on the rapidly exchanging migrant communities, who are only mentioned regarding increased emissions.[33]

After the introduction of the Qatar National Vision, its actual implementation began with the introduction of the Qatar National Development Strategy (QNDS) in 2011. The QNDS has been prepared for a period of five years to achieve the first development goals. The main emphasis of this first national development strategy is the promotion of human and social development. Based on assessments regarding current challenges, the QNDS prioritizes the establishment of an evolutionary and integrated health care system, sufficient supply of high-quality educational facilities as well as incentives to integrate Qataris in the private sector.[34] With respect to social development, the QNDS integrates measures for fostering family cohesion, the social responsibilities of the private sector, safe and healthy living environments and cultural identity.[35]

The QNDS follows the basic structure of the previous national vision and in spite of recognizing migrant-driven urbanism within certain sections, there has been no explicitly named strategy targeting the overall conception of how to integrate migrant communities and how a future multicultural society should function. Both rights and needs of migrants are largely excluded in this strategic framework. The most striking aspect is the introduction of a desired population figure for the year 2030, in which the population should be stabilized in the range of 2.2 to 2.8 million inhabitants. This figure is mainly rooted on the assumption that low-income labourers will be less needed and that only the segment of migrants with higher educational background will grow in future. Qatar's current population of more than 2.3 million is expected to witness major transformation in future. More recently, the annual growth rates already dropped from the peak of almost 20 per cent in 2007 to 2 per cent in 2017.[36] Thus, it is even more surprising that future demographic changes caused by new migration patterns are not further emphasized within a clear strategy. Instead, new restrictions and regulations for immigration are proposed as necessity for a more strategic demand for expatriate workforce. Furthermore, increasing crime rates are referred to migration without addressing the current living situation of low-income labourers. The actual needs of immigrants are only mentioned in the context of listing civil society organizations dealing with urgent matters.[37]

In general, it can be stated that the topic of continuous immigration has been treated as an unspoken reality and less desired as an integral component in the future vision of Qatar's society. Thus, every major vision, strategy or planning effort emphasizes enhanced Qatarization and thus the associated aim to become gradually independent of foreign expertise. One major step has been made earlier in 2005, when a new law was introduced permitting expats to apply for citizenship. This citizenship is however granted on a rather individual basis and any applicant has to have a record of residing in Qatar for twenty-five years, and it is dependent on their income level and cultural background.[38] Labourers in low service sectors are still perceived as inevitable and exchangeable necessity to sustain the overall social equity within national communities but less needed in future, once the consolidation phase has been entered and economic growth has become less dependent on actual urban growth itself. Although the overemphasis on nationalization and thus the integration of nationals in future development dynamics must be understood as important domestic political necessity, the introduced demographic vision itself contradicts this desired future. Based on current growth rates of the national population, a clear majority of Qatar's population will remain foreign in the year 2030, which is leading to the inevitable question of how a society should evolve towards more stable and integrated structures, if the needs and desires of majorities are not part of any overall strategic framework and subsequent policies.

The Abu Dhabi Economic Vision 2030

Similar to Qatar's leadership, the rulers of Abu Dhabi initiated a relatively comparable approach to introduce a macro vision to explain and link decision-making rooted in basic but key objectives. The Abu Dhabi Economic Vision 2030 was published in 2007 and distinguishes between four key priority areas, namely economic development, social and human resources development, environmental sustainability and the optimization of government operations. The overall vision is summarized in defining the vision for Abu Dhabi in achieving a secure society and a dynamic open economy. Like Qatar's development context, Abu Dhabi's economy has mainly been relying on the production of fossil fuels, which led to the establishment of a rather conservative place built on welfare state mechanisms following the guidance of the UAE founder Sheikh Zayed bin Sultan Al Nahyan and his approach in prioritizing and satisfying the needs of the population, rather than seeking fast growth. Since 2004, the immense development of Dubai as emerging global hub and the new leadership of

Abu Dhabi marked a new beginning of reconfiguring the general vision and role of the largest emirate of the United Arab Emirates.

As other Gulf States, Abu Dhabi's new leadership identified knowledge economies as essential factor in sustaining economic wealth and regional importance. Instead of remaining in the previous structure of top-down wealth distribution, the initiation of liberalized markets and new investments in infrastructure were perceived as an ideal basis for opening a large variety of opportunities for the national population, from becoming sponsors of new businesses to establishing themselves as major landlords of large developments. Thus, the economic vision explicitly declares the aim to develop a large and empowered private sector as well as a knowledge-based economy by 2030. This should be achieved through a transparent regulatory environment, while continuing the strong and diverse international partnerships. In comparison to Qatar's National Vision, the Abu Dhabi Vision clearly identifies the needs of international migrants, particularly in the case of security, as an important aim. But similar to Qatar's visionary approach, the new vision emphasizes the priority of promoting the national population via improved education and new policies to enter the private sector and to become important drivers of the economic diversification in the immediate future.

The vision itself was developed by a concerted effort of the public sector as well as joint public–private sector entities, including the Department of Planning and Economy, the Abu Dhabi Council for Economic Development (ADCED) and the General Secretariat of the Executive Council. The ADCED was established as a joint public–private advisory body, which includes representatives of all the major stakeholders in the economy to directly integrate major concerns regarding economic as well as general sustainability matters.[39] The Economic Vision 2030 was designed to identify all key priority areas for economic development and a realistic set of socio-economic development goals. Similarity with Qatar's National Vision is also witnessed in other areas. Five-year strategic plans were recognized as important drivers to provide a more focused framework for immediate economic policies. The general framework recognizes stable human capital and physical as well as financial capital as important preconditions for economic development and stability built on productivity and competitiveness.[40]

An interesting aspect can be unveiled in the case of conceiving the stimulation of faster economic growth as part of the same list of aims focusing on integrating young people and women as well as attracting skilled international workforce. These are aimed at establishing a more balanced social and regional development that brings benefits to all segments of society.[41] Thus, instead of perceiving growth as a general consequence of global and regional dynamics and as a challenge for integrating national communities, it is listed as a precondition for balancing the local economic development. The vision is clearly influenced by the confidence that further liberalization, particularly in financial markets, will enable economic consolidation rather than the evident threats of a speculation-driven development. This confident vision is mainly explained by excluding the current migrant majority within the overall development approach to develop an economy, which will benefit all inhabitants. Abu Dhabi's decision-makers introduce the national population as main asset for future economies and the expected attraction of highly skilled migrant workforce replacing a large number of current labourers. According to recent statistics the share of male labourers has significantly decreased between 2005 and 2015, which is a clear sign for an increasing shift within low service sectors.[42]

The major difference to the QNV can be found in one clear statement: 'The economy will be reliant on foreign labour for the foreseeable future, and so efforts will be made to attract and retain foreign talent and skilled labour, including an assessment of immigration procedures.'[43] In spite of this open realism, the entire Abu Dhabi Economic Vision as well as its subordinated strategies, such as the Plan Abu Dhabi 2030, does not include any clear vision on how current demographic tendencies and the shrinking share of nationals will lead to a cohesive and balanced future society. The terminology of multiculturalism is avoided as well as future perspectives of how to attract highly skilled migrant workforce long-term.

The Dubai Strategic Plan 2015 and the Dubai Plan 2021

While in Qatar and Abu Dhabi the incentives of initiating local urban growth needed to þe framed under macro visions in 2007 and 2008, the rulers in the Emirate of Dubai, where the model of initiating growth in the Gulf region was originally tested, have always proclaimed a clear business ratio for the overall plans to establish a hub city. The biggest factor can be found in the shrinking oil wealth and thus a relatively easy-to-communicate necessity to diversify the local economy. But beyond this fact, Dubai's historic roots and its diverse migrant community made of merchants play a key role in the exhibited confidence in entering global economic competitions without internal conflicts between the ruling decision-makers and local communities. When the Emirate of Dubai under the leadership of Sheikh Mohammed Al Maktoum pursued the new development path as early as in the 1980s, when the first free trade zone was launched in Jebel Ali, a new dynamic was introduced to the entire region exhibiting the various potentials of becoming a highly connected trading hub.[44]

Due to limited oil revenues the leadership of Dubai was forced to initiate a new development model for turning into an emerging service centre on a regional and global scale by particularly focusing on trade and financial sectors. When Dubai's rulers followed their vision of developing the first global city in the Gulf by liberalizing local markets, an unprecedented construction boom turned the small settlement into a rising hub with more than one million inhabitants at the beginning of the new millennium (Figure 2.3).[45] This model of initiating rapid growth began to affect urban development visions in the entire region since it constituted a potential solution as to how to sustain prosperity in a future post-oil era. Thus, despite their tremendous wealth of still remaining fossil fuels, the new leaders in Qatar and Abu Dhabi began to enter the ignited competition for new economic sectors, convinced that only an immediate participation in this economic diversification process could guarantee the development of the complex socio-economic structures needed for establishing service centres in the Gulf.[46]

The general aims of the economic development are summarized in the Dubai Strategic Plan 2015, which was introduced in the year 2005 with emphasis placed on eight main goals including the focus on key economic

Figure 2.3 Construction sites in Dubai.

sectors, enhanced productivity and human capital excellence. Thus, one major element of a successful economic transformation was recognized in the form of attracting and retaining highly skilled employees in addition to improving the qualifications of the national population. Another goal of the strategic plan was ensuring and maintaining Dubai's competitiveness by managing rising living costs for both migrant and national communities. Furthermore, the goal of quality of life improvement integrates the needs of migrants as well as an improved institutional frameworks and regulations. Consequently, it was assumed that an estimated 882,000 additional workers would be required by the year 2015, bringing total employment to 1.7 million with a significant shift towards higher skilled employment.[47] This goal was already surpassed in 2012. The most important foundation is the concept of a liberal market with only few restrictions to attract both regional and global investors and to strengthen public–private partnerships, which have become essential for the economic diversification process.

In spite of recognizing the importance of migration in the Strategic Plan, Dubai's main social development challenge was identified as the future integration of the national population within all sectors of the economy to preserve national identity and culture and to become more independent from foreign labour. Today, however, less than 10 per cent of the population enjoy a national citizenship.[48] Most of the over one hundred-thousand jobs that are created in Dubai each year are in the private sector and according to statistics only 1 per cent of this workforce comprises nationals. The majority of the population is formed by South Asian migrants and most of this foreign labour works only temporarily in Dubai in order to send remittances or to save their salaries for their return to their homelands. The result has been an ever-changing and multicultural society. As in Qatar or Abu Dhabi the fear of long-term internationalization and the associated dependence on migrants was addressed by the encouragement and support of the national population as a main goal of the Dubai Strategic Plan 2015.

In 2015 the government of Dubai announced the 2021 Dubai Plan, which currently forms the new basis for guiding economic and social growth and includes various strategies, such as the Dubai Industrial Strategy 2030.[49] In the case of the envisioned society the new Dubai Plan moved away from the previous plan and emphasizes a 'vibrant and sustainable multicultural society', which it translates into a 'population that is economically and demographically sustainable and for which multiculturalism is a source of strength and pride'.[50] It furthermore announces that it aims for an enhanced proportion of individuals who are satisfied with the cultural diversity of Dubai and the proportion of individuals who consider Dubai a suitable place to live for expatriates of different nationalities.[51] Despite the general openness towards migrants' needs in the past, this new emphasis on progressive multiculturalism and the desired identification of expatriate communities with Dubai can be seen as an enhanced willingness to recognize migrants not only as temporary necessity but also as the actual and essential asset for Dubai's future development.

Dubai's current overall ambition is to develop into a high-ranking global city with the best international standards by becoming completely independent from fossil resources. To achieve this, the structure of urban governance has more and more adopted a business-like attitude to efficiently guide Dubai towards becoming the main gate of any global business in the region. While the semi-public and private holdings have occupied the key role in shaping Dubai, the central decision-making has always remained in the hands of the ruler, who has understood his role as a corporate manager integrating the needs of all service sectors in addition to his genuine function as political representative. The establishment of the Dubai Executive Council, which has always included major stakeholders within key economies, as the actual government has particularly affected the ability of enforcing top-down strategies and rather quick reactions on emerging challenges.

Due to the historic context and the perception of Dubai as historic trading port, migration has never been perceived as a major threat, like in places with a more conservative development background or places with conflicts between the various national communities. But as in all other Gulf States, Dubai's government has remained restrictive regarding the long-term integration of migrant communities by offering political rights and by removing the system of local sponsorship. Thus, the new shift towards integrating migrants as Dubai's main identity must be merely interpreted from a business perspective and the recognized importance of migrants as drivers of new economies, rather than as actual sign for a paradigm shift redefining migrant urbanism in the Gulf.

Bahrain's Economic Vision 2030

In the year 2008 King Hamad bin Isa Al Khalifa launched the Economic Vision 2030 to guide the overall development of Bahrain. The proclaimed aims of the new vision include the restructuring of government, society and the economy to realize a better life for every Bahraini. The main driver of the new vision has been the Economic Development Board, which collaborated with various ministries to compile the first national economic strategy as a roadmap to achieve the overall vision. Several new committees were founded upon the instigation of the Economic Development Board (EDB), which was established under the leadership of Crown Prince Sheikh Salman in 2002. To implement the new vision, the EDB took over much of the previous responsibility of ministries, particularly regarding the creation of a new strategic plan for Bahrain.

The main urgency of redirecting development patterns in Bahrain can be found in three core areas. The first factor is Bahrain's high economic dependence on Saudi Arabia due to its location in direct proximity to the main oil producing region in the Eastern Province and its own very limited oil resources, which have defined the small island kingdom as major touristic centre for Saudis and as hub for businesses and their international employees preferring to commute to the Eastern Province via a causeway, which was established in 1986. The second factor is the challenging social and political structure rooted in the historic divide between the ruling Sunni leadership and a Shia majority within the national population, which has led to long-term tensions and the outbreak of frequent riots, as most recently in the form of the uprising during the Arab Spring in 2011. And finally, the fast growth of Dubai and other new regional service centres have challenged certain economic sectors, such as offshore banking, which have been established in Bahrain since the 1970s.

The small group of islands only cover 765 square kilometres limiting the expansion of urban centres and until recently there was always a clear majority of a national population in Bahrain. Unlike the other Gulf States, Bahraini citizens are mainly engaged in the private sector including low service sectors, such as employees in supermarkets or taxi drivers. Thus, the resulting socio-economic structure highly differs from the previous welfare states, such as Qatar and Abu Dhabi, and offers both an easier integration of national workforce in emerging economies and a challenging income gap between national communities. Subsequently, the vision underlines that Bahrainis need to become the employees of choice for high-value-adding companies as a major development goal. The main economic sector envisioned to become the key driver has been identified in the form of the financial sector, which should be expanded, in order to work as major benchmark for all other sectors, such as tourism, manufacturing and logistics (Figure 2.4).[52] As in all other Gulf States, the first introduced strategy is the extensive liberalization and privatization of governance to achieve an accelerated interest of investors and thus the rapid growth of needed advanced services to cater these investments, either in the form of offshore banking, investment banking or investment in local real estate.

Figure 2.4 The Bahrain Financial Harbour in Manama.

Within its economic vision the government ensures that the desired fast economic growth will benefit all Bahrainis by ensuring that the new service sectors will generate a lot of medium- to high-wage jobs. Furthermore, the government seeks to reform immigration and to revise labour laws to promote a bigger nationalization of all workforce in the private sector. Third, the government announces to support programmes and lifelong training to integrate Bahrainis.[53] In comparison to other visions in the Gulf region, the loss of national identity is not mentioned as a major challenge in Bahrain. Similar to regulations in Qatar, migrants are permitted to apply for citizenship after legally residing twenty-five consecutive years, but with the condition of owning a registered real estate in Bahrain.[54] However, there is no general vision how migrants will be integrated as main asset for economic sustainability. Thus, despite quite contradictory social and economic conditions and continuous crises, Bahrain's rulers have followed the same agenda of liberalizing markets and igniting a construction boom to build new urban landscapes housing a more and more internationalized society, while they officially proclaim that these newly built environments will found the basis for national communities and their future economic prosperity. The vision of most Bahrainis being engaged in emerging service sectors in future clashes with current realities of a large number of unqualified nationals experiencing increasing economic challenges to support their families.

Conclusion

The accelerated globalization at the end of the twentieth century and the resulting competition between emerging service centres have set the backdrop of the most recent transformation of urbanism in the Gulf region. The general fear of uncertainty regarding the future economic role and the expected depletion of oil and gas has led to a rather instant reaction of all rulers along the Gulf coast to initiate fast growth to proclaim their proactive governance towards economic diversification. While Dubai and Bahrain have instigated their role as regional service centres as early as in the 1970s, the new opportunities at the turn of the centuries to open local markets for international investments have led to the immediate recognition of tremendous development potentials. The geopolitical location of the small Gulf States is not only fortunate because of its centrality between emerging Asian and established Western markets, but it has also become an important factor for rapid growth due to the ongoing conflicts in the wider Middle East and the resulting need for secure logistic centres, investment havens as well as leisure oases in close proximity.

These particular settings have pressured decision-makers to enable growth and to function as global border towns, built on masses of Asian labourers and imported Western expertise, and as rising beacons of economic success exhibiting modern consumption worlds in an increasingly troubled Middle East. Underneath the instant rise of Gulf cities as new pioneers of economic reforms in the region, the main social question has become more and more urgent: How to balance rapid growth built on migration and the needed integration of national communities and their identity? Only in the case of the Emirate of Dubai, this question has gradually lost its significance, due to the rather low share of nationals, the corporate-driven management style of urban governance and the overall premise of economic success as well as the long history of economic diversification built on trade. In all other countries, visions have been introduced to draw new perspectives of how national communities will become the driving force in future development scenarios while avoiding any major emphasis on the importance of ongoing migration.

In general, two major purposes of introducing development visions can be distinguished: On the one side, visions clearly aim to portrait progressive nations with ambitious economic goals to attract and stabilize regional and global investment. On the other side, these visions address national communities to communicate a convincing political outline of how their prosperity and cultural identity will be preserved and, in many cases, re-established. These two approaches contradict in one major aspect: continuous international migration needed for fast economic growth and the inevitable consequence of migrant majorities transforming local identities. Investment flows can only be secured if growth can be guaranteed. Fast urban growth along the Gulf coast however will always depend on migration due to missing hinterlands and rural population. Low-income labourers are needed to develop the newly emerging cities, while middle- and higher-income migrant groups are the key drivers of new service sectors in a highly competitive environment. The previous welfare state environments and the missing promotion of higher education led to a national population, who is neither prepared nor willing to compete with an international workforce, attracted by relatively high salaries, compared to the ones in their home countries, and career opportunities.

The highly ambitious vision that the national workforce can transform during a period of twenty years into a major factor within advanced economies can only be understood as needed political act to address rising domestic concerns regarding the increasing dependency on migrants, particularly in Qatar and Abu Dhabi. Dubai's rather brief summary of a new vision focusing on short-term goals rather than blurry ideal scenarios is a clear indication, how a completely internationalized migrant city adjusts to its actual realities and focuses on maintaining the momentum in a more and more challenging world. Dubai's decision-makers have achieved a clear separation between the overall business concerns of their hub project and general domestic concerns, which are just one aspect among many others. Therefore, they directly proclaim and promote multiculturalism as core of Dubai's identity, a still unthinkable act in all other Gulf countries and emirates, where the emphasis on local culture and the key role of nationals within the future development path has become the driver of most visions. Consequently, it can be stated that Dubai has managed a new development phase, in which migrant urbanism is not denied as necessity and even promoted as essential part of the emirate's future. But despite this changed tone of visions and strategies, one core question has even remained in Dubai: How are migrant communities provided with a more stable perspective to settle and invest long-term?

Today, Gulf cities are clear cases of migrant cities, if only general demographic statistics are taken into account. But a closer look reveals that in most countries migration is conceived and communicated as undesired short-term necessity to build rather than sustain new hub cities. The sponsorship concept has led to a clear division between national communities and frequently exchanging expats. No current vision aims for reforming this basic social structure, which has been successful in accelerating urban growth, but which needs to be questioned in developing more complex knowledge economies relying on a well-established permanent workforce. The contemporary airport societies are therefore the result of a new development phase, in which the actual construction of cities itself has become the main catalyst of economic growth. The resulting urban shells are however a product of the new form of migrant urbanism in the Gulf. Thus, the rapidly built urban landscapes are clear reflections of this phenomenon, built on the unprecedented scale of recent migration rates. Finally, one question needs to be asked in the case of any current development vision: How do cities become consolidated and competitive hubs if migrant communities are not going to be integrated with new perspectives, choices and rights?

Notes

1 Robert B. Cohen, 'The New International Division of Labor, Multinational Corporations and Urban Hierarchy', in M. Dear and A. Scott (eds), *Urbanization and Urban Planning in Capitalist Society* (London, 1981), pp. 287–317.

2 John Friedmann, 'The World City Hypothesis', *Development and Change*, 17/1 (1986), pp. 69–83.

3 Boston Consulting Group, *Winning in Emerging Markets* (2016). Available at: www.bcgperspectives.com/content/articles/globalization_growth_winning_in_emerging_market_cities/?chapter=2 (accessed 27 November 2016).

4 Peter Hall, 'The Urbanization of Capital and Consciousness and the Urban Experience: Studies in the History and Theory of Capitalist Urbanization', *Economic Geography*, 63/4 (1987), p. 354.

5 Peter Hall, *Cities of Tomorrow* (Oxford, 1988), p. 48.

6 Manuel Castells, *The Informational City* (Oxford, 1989).

7 Saskia Sassen, 'Locating Cities on Global Circuits', *Environment and Urbanization*, 14/1 (2002), pp. 13–30, p. 29.

8 Peter Newman and Jeffrey Kenworthy, *Sustainability and Cities: Overcoming Automobile Dependence* (Washington, 1999), p. 5.

9 Philipp Aerni, 'Coping with Migration-induced Urban Growth: Addressing the Blind Spot of UN Habitat', *Sustainability*, 8/8 (2016), p. 800.

10 Saskia Sassen, *The Global City: New York, London, Tokyo* (Princeton, 1991), p. 169.

11 Hank V. Savitch and Paul Kantor, *Cities in the International Marketplace* (Princeton, 2002).

12 Worldometers, *Bahrain Population*. Available at: www.worldometers.info/world-population/bahrain-population/ (accessed 22 March 2017); Worldometers, *Kuwait Population*. Available at: www.worldometers.info/world-population/kuwait-popu lation/ (accessed 22 March 2017); Worldometers, *Qatar Population*. Available at: www.worldometers.info/world-population/qatar-population/ (accessed 22 March 2017); Worldometers, *United Arab Emirates Population*. Available at: www.worldo meters.info/world-population/united-arab-emirates-population/ (accessed 22 March 2017).

13 Bahrain Information & eGovernment Authority, *Bahrain Open Data Portal, 2014*. Available at: www.data.gov.bh/en/DataAnalysis (accessed 22 March 2017).

14 Worldometers, 2017.

15 Françoise De Bel-Air, *Demography, Migration and the Labour Market in Qatar, 2014*. Available at: www.cadmus.eui.eu/bitstream/handle/1814/32431/GLMM_ ExpNote_08-2014.pdf?sequence=1&isAllowed=y (accessed 22 March 2017); Françoise De Bel-Air, *Demography, Migration and the Labour Market in the UAE, 2015*. Available at: www.cadmus.eui.eu/bitstream/handle/1814/36375/GLMM_ ExpNote_07_2015.pdf?sequence=1&isAllowed=y (accessed 22 March 2017); Françoise De Bel-Air, *Demography, Migration and the Labour Market in Bahrain, 2015*. Available at: www.cadmus.eui.eu/bitstream/handle/1814/35882/GLMM_ ExpNote_06_2015.pdf?sequence=1&isAllowed=y (accessed 22 March 2017).

16 Andrew Gardner, 'Gulf Migration and the Family', *Journal of Arabian Studies*, 1/1, pp. 3–25.

17 Abu Dhabi Statistics Centre, *Statistical Yearbook of Abu Dhabi 2016*. Available at: www.scad.ae/en/Pages/ThemesReleases.aspx?ThemeID=4 (accessed 22 March 2017); Bahrain Information & eGovernment Authority, 2014; Dubai Statistics Center, *Population Bulletin*, 2017. Available at: www.dsc.gov.ae/Publication/Pop ulation%20Bulletin%20Emirate%20of%20Dubai%202015.pdf (accessed 22 March 2017); Ministry of Development Planning and Statistics, *Population and Social Statistics*, 2016. Available at: http://www.mdps.gov.qa/en/statistics/Statistical%2 0Releases/Population/Population/2015/1_Population_2015.pdf (accessed 22 March 2017).

18 Françoise De Bel-Air, *Demography, Migration and the Labour Market in Qatar*; Françoise De Bel-Air, *Demography, Migration and the Labour Market in the UAE*.

19 Steffen Hertog, 'Arab Gulf States: An Assessment of Nationalisation Policies', in: *Gulf Labour Markets and Migration*, 2014. Available at: www.cadmus.eui.eu/ bitstream/handle/1814/32156/GLMM%20ResearchPaper_01-2014.pdf?sequence=1 (accessed 22 March 2017), p. 4.

20 Ibid.

21 John Fox, Nada Mourtada-Sabbah and Mohammed Al-Mutawa, *Globalization and the Gulf* (New York, 2006), p. 3.

22 Maysa Zahra, 'Bahrain's Legal Framework of Migration', in: *Gulf Labour Markets and Migration*, 2015. Available at: www.cadmus.eui.eu/bitstream/handle/1814/34579/GLMM_ExpNote_01_2015.pdf?sequence=1 (accessed 22 March 2017).

23 Hertog, 'Arab Gulf States: An Assessment of Nationalisation Policies', p. 7.

24 Scholz, *Die Kleinen Golfstaaten*, p. 185.

25 Allen J. Fromherz, *Qatar: A Modern History* (London, 2012), p. 77.

26 Ibid, p. 111.

27 General Secretariat of Development Planning, *Qatar National Vision 2030* (Doha, 2008), p. 5.

28 Ibid., p. 10.

29 Ibid., p. 12.

30 Ibid., p. 15.

31 Ibid., p. 17.

32 General Secretariat of Development Planning, *Advancing Sustainable Development, Qatar's Second Human Development Report* (Doha, 2009), p. 5.

33 Ibid., p. 105.

34 General Secretariat of Development Planning, *National Development Strategy 2011 – 2016* (Doha, 2011), p. 151.

35 Ibid., p. 161.

36 Ministry of Development Planning and Statistics, *Population and Social Statistics*, 2016. Available at: www.mdps.gov.qa/en/statistics/Statistical%20Releases/Populat ion/Population/2015/1_Population_2015.pdf (accessed 22 March 2017).

37 General Secretariat of Development Planning, , *National Development Strategy 2011 – 2016*, p. 181.

38 Maysa Zahra, 'Qatar's Legal Framework of Migration', in: *Gulf Labour Markets and Migration*, 2016. Available at: www.cadmus.eui.eu/bitstream/handle/1814/32154/GLMM%20ExpNote_02-2013.pdf?sequence=1 (accessed 22 March 2017).

39 Abu Dhabi Council for Economic Development, 'Sustainability – Playing a Central Role in Abu Dhabi's Economic Growth', *The Economic Review*. Issue 19, (Abu Dhabi, 2014).

40 Abu Dhabi Council for Economic Development, *The Abu Dhabi Economic Vision 2030*, 2007. Available at: www.adced.ae/sites/En/ev/Documents/Measures%20of%2 0Sucess.pdf (accessed 22 March 2017), p. 12.

41 Ibid., p. 17.

42 Abu Dhabi Statistics Centre, *Statistical Yearbook of Abu Dhabi 2016*, p. 143.

43 Abu Dhabi Council for Economic Development, *The Abu Dhabi Economic Vision 2030*, p. 75.

44 Heiko Schmid, 'Dubai: Der schnelle Aufstieg zur Wirtschaftsmetropole', in E. Blum and P. Neitzke (eds), *Dubai – Stadt aus dem Nichts* (Berlin, 2009), pp. 56–73, p. 58.

45 Christopher Davidson, *Dubai: The Vulnerability of Success* (New York, 2009), p. 128.

46 Florian Wiedmann, *Post-oil Urbanism: New Evolution in Governance and the Impact on Urban Morphologies* (Stuttgart, 2012), p. 53.

47 Government of Dubai, *Dubai Strategic Plan 2015*, 2005. Available at: www.dubaiplan2021.ae/dsp-2015-2/ (accessed 22 March 2017).

48 Dubai Statistics Center, *Population Bulletin*.

49 Government of Dubai, *Dubai Industrial Strategy 2030*, 2016. Available at: www.dubaiplan2021.ae/wp-content/uploads/2016/06/Dubai-Industrial-Strategy-2030.pdf (accessed 22 March 2017).

50 Government of Dubai, *Dubai Plan 2021*, 2016. Available at: www.dubaiplan2021.ae/dubai-plan-2021/ (accessed 22 March 2017).

51 Ibid.

52 Bahrain Economic Development Board, *Bahrain Vision 2030*, 2008. Available at: www.bahrainedb.com/en/about/Pages/economic%20vision%202030.aspx#.WNJCtvnysuV (accessed 22 March 2017), p. 14.

53 Ibid., p. 15.

54 Zahra, 'Bahrain's Legal Framework of Migration', p. 7.

3

Enabling housing supply through new forms of governance

Rapid urbanization processes worldwide have to be understood as both the result of the rise of global finance resulting in hierarchical city networks and the local restructuring of urban governance permitting enhanced growth rates of cities, particularly in emerging countries.[1] New models of governance, such as urban entrepreneurialism, state-led development initiatives and various forms of public–private partnerships, are only a few examples of new approaches to face the increasing challenge to balance the necessity to stimulate growth and the increasing evidence of the need for urban consolidation to limit urban sprawl and fragmentation. Contemporary urban governance is confronted by global financial events and their direct impact on capital movements and by the growing social inequalities.[2] The overall result has been a highly conflicted period of urbanization, in which growth has become a necessity to balance municipal debts accumulated by infrastructural investments. Accelerated growth has however led to hazardous effects on social equity, economic diversity and consequently on the natural environment in many places worldwide.[3]

The resulting urban crises are particularly visible in housing development, which is a direct mirror of how an urban society has access to play an active role within the housing development process. During the early periods of modern urbanization, governments mainly had to provide sufficient infrastructure for a flourishing housing market supplied by the private sector, while they also supported various forms of affordable and social housing to integrate deprived social groups. The globalization and the increasing competition to attract major service sectors led to new growth strategies including liberalization and privatization.[4]

These development patterns in emerging cities worldwide have led to increasing challenges to establish a dynamic housing market catering all communities.[5] The rising land prices in particular have led to the almost impossible integration of sufficient affordable housing in many areas, which has reinforced both social segregation and spatial fragmentation. Subsequently, new forms of urban governance have begun to launch housing strategies and new models of engaging the private sector in supplying housing for lower-income groups. After a period of deregulation, governance has thus become more and more challenged to reinforce a balance between stimulating and regulating urban growth to guide overall housing dynamics and to ensure a certain level of affordability.[6]

Emerging cities in the Global South are witnessing rapid transformation processes, mainly as a result of initiatives to access global networks to either export natural resources or to attract various international industries. In addition to traditional urbanization strategies, the emerging real estate markets have been deregulated to establish property-led developments and thus attract advanced producer services, such as finance. This new development path is usually accompanied by city-branding strategies including the promotion of international tourism.[7] The first precondition for initiating this urban transformation however is the development of new and extensive infrastructure to establish the required level of regional and global connectivity.[8]

Consequently, international and regional migration has been transforming these emerging hubs by adding new markets, particularly in the form of real estate and services. The increasing complexity of social structures, rooted in various income and the diversity in cultural backgrounds, has led to the demand on a wide spectrum of new housing typologies. While upper real estate markets have witnessed a rapid diversification leading to a wider range of new housing dynamics, lower-income groups have however found themselves in an increasingly challenging environment between informal settlements, over-occupied dwellings and mass housing in urban peripheries.[9] The main challenge of any new form of governance has therefore been a proactive mediation between investment interests and the needs of majorities of urban populations.[10]

According to UN Habitat, urban governance is the software that enables the urban hardware to function. Thus, urban governance can be defined as the many ways that institutions and individuals organize the day-to-day management of a city, and the processes used for effectively realizing the short-term and long-term agenda of a city's development.[11] In this sense, urban governance must be viewed as the holistic framework integrating all key decision-makers in both public and semi-public sectors interwoven with the rapidly growing private sector. The key stakeholders of urban governance are first of all the elected or non-elected governments, who are in charge of major urban development directions due to investments, political reforms or the promotion of new economic development visions. These decisions usually lead to the restructuring of administrative processes including their overall regulatory frameworks. The major decision-making procedures are thus followed by the various administrative bodies of the public sector on national, regional and local levels. Consequently, these authorities are in charge of translating visions into physical plans and introducing new investment or regulatory strategies, whose successful implementation highly depends on integrating the interests of the private sector.

In this chapter, the role of new forms of urban governance in defining urbanization in the Gulf region is introduced by highlighting and summarizing the major historic roots of the first phase of modern urbanization, which particularly evolved after the national independence of the small states during the 1960s and 1970s. Since the end of the twentieth century, globalization led to major transformation processes in the Gulf region.[12] The new development path of urban entrepreneurialism, which was first introduced in the Emirate of Dubai, is analysed in the context of how this new form of governance has been impacting general urbanism and housing dynamics in particular. The chapter concludes with an argument on how contemporary tendencies within local urban governance could respond to the increasingly challenging supply of housing in emerging migrant cities along the Gulf coast.

Historic governance and housing supply in the Gulf

Before the oil production commenced in the middle of the twentieth century, the management of the very few settlements were in the hands of dominant tribes and their respected leaders. The harsh climatic circumstances have formed hierarchical communities to guarantee an efficient process of macro decision-making as basis for collective survival.[13] Land for settlement was therefore centrally controlled and distributed to avoid any hazardous impact on scare water sources and agricultural soil. This basic hierarchical structure of tribes and clans led to defined territories and alliances, which predefined the later introduction of national and regional boundaries along the Gulf coast during the British protectorate in the nineteenth century.[14] The main realm of social interaction was the main market, where trading became an essential part of building a settled society with nomadic roots.[15] Since the middle of the twentieth century the sudden oil wealth and the associated social structure under one leading tribe led to hierarchical welfare states, in which rulers found themselves as both traditional patriarchs distributing the newly gained wealth and visionary political leaders exploring new development paths towards modern urbanization.[16]

The foundation of national states since the end of the 1960s led to the rapid development of modern governmental institutions, which had to regulate and administer the newly initiated urbanization process. Because of the existing political order, government and administration have been developed from top following a clear and centralized structure. Therefore, the king or Emir and his ministers held the greater responsibility for all decisions made regarding the country's development. It has often been the ruler's initiative to develop new strategies such as physical planning, budget plans or even single projects and new regulatory frameworks in cooperation with committees and councils of ministers, which have always been directly appointed.

The ministries themselves have developed plans and programmes within their own planning departments. Ministries for municipal affairs and works have usually been put in charge of physical planning units, while housing has often been governed by a separate authority due to the urgent need to provide modern housing units for the local population.[17] While the physical planning units have been responsible for spatial planning at the national, regional and local levels including the definition and distribution of residential land uses, the ministries of housing have been in charge of launching general housing programmes, the monitoring of housing as well as housing research. The ministries have been responsible for the actual procurement of housing and the general management of major social housing projects.[18]

In conjunction with the economic and social transformation, a new way of living was introduced due to the import of a new form of mobility. British and American oil companies introduced car as the main mode of transportation and, in doing so, also introduced a new type of housing when they built the first settlements for their employees, which had a large impact on building regulations in most Gulf States. The rather simplistic physical plans, built on a suburban car-based settlement structure, were introduced by an administration, mainly concerned about supplying a higher living standard to local populations.[19] Particularly in the 1960s, many major infrastructure projects were carried out by most Gulf countries, which included road networks, harbours and first airports. During this time, the planning instruments used were limited to so-called guide plans, which were in effect reduced land-use plans concerning, for example, use, building heights or housing density. These guide plans were difficult to implement because of the lack of an effective legal framework for their enforcement.[20]

Under the general ministerial structure on a national level or regional level, municipalities were installed to manage developments within their respective districts or territories. During the 1970s, new building laws were established together with new master planning and zoning regulations via Western consultancies. Traditional building laws were not included in this new legal framework due to their divergent concept of the spatial organization of dense settlements rooted in walkability. The import of modern infrastructure permitted new forms of urban typologies. Development policies were introduced to solve predominantly technical problems such as the supply of sufficient infrastructure as well as the support of private land ownership.

For example, in the case of land trade, rules emphasized the importance of specifying the precise area of such lots of land in accordance with official plans. Furthermore, there were regulations as to what percentage of one lot could be built upon and what distance a house had to be from the street of the width of the street.[21] This top-down spatial planning based on regulating uniform developments was a large paradigm shift in an environment, which was previously relying on self-management and rare interventions of building violations, only in cases interfering with others and their rights. These initial building laws were generally limited to strict but simple rules to cope with the development of infrastructure and the creation of lots for private or public use in the context of rapid urban growth and the import of new building types and construction techniques.

During the first period of modern urbanization in the Gulf region, the whole concept of spatial development and the associated management process were imported from established Western planning systems without any major local adjustments or adaptation. An example of one of the first master plans in the region is the 1973 Doxiadis master plan for Riyadh. The Greek consulting company Doxiadis Associates International developed a plan with a linear growth imperative as the basic development concept. This master plan had to be extended over time to accommodate an ever-growing urban sprawl. A city-wide gridiron network of highways circumscribed 'super blocks' of 2 by 2 kilometres in size. Land use was strictly divided according to function leading to repetitive and replaceable suburban landscapes with one of the lowest urban densities worldwide.[22] In almost all major cities new comprehensive master plans were developed and implemented during the 1970s.

The key common feature which all share is that governments were mainly concerned about securing sufficient land for new neighbourhoods for a rapidly increasing local population due to rural migration and the move of communities from historic centres towards the outskirts. The various housing strategies of distributing land, buying old central properties above the usual market price and supporting a newly built financial system granting mortgages were accompanied by major government efforts to develop new towns as dormitory settlements in urban peripheries. Examples can be found in the case of any major settlement, particularly in the surroundings of newly established capital cities.[23] In spite of the size of these new residential settlements, the impact of these projects as property-led form of development can be regarded as rather minor, since all these initiatives aimed at meeting the supply of affordable housing for permanent residents rather than stimulating the growth of local real estate markets.

In order to understand the general patterns to supply sufficient housing, the Kingdom of Bahrain can be introduced as a case example. The local government was involved in various housing programmes, which have included extensive new town projects, to support local citizens and their families. While 'Isa Town' was already established at the end of the 1960s and gradually expanded during the 1970s, 'Hamad Town' was designed and developed by the Ministry of Housing after a proposal of the Physical Planning Department in 1979.[24] The Ministry of Housing was established in 1975 to solve the increasing problem of a lack of housing units for citizens. The main goal was to provide adequate housing for every Bahraini family that was unable to finance its own house.

In this respect, as well as constructing dwelling units in the form of houses and apartments, the ministry began to establish policies related to housing loans and the allocation of plots. In 1975, the Physical Planning Directorate moved from the Ministry of Agriculture and Municipalities to the Ministry of Housing, thus restructuring the entire planning process and making the Ministry of Housing in charge of all planning directorates concerning urban development. Between 1975 and 1996, the ministry accomplished the development of 15,690 housing units, mainly in the form of detached villas. While 'Isa Town' was developed for about 35,000 inhabitants, 'Hamad Town' was designed for 60,000 people. Thus, in 1991, more than 12.5 per cent of the overall population of Bahrain lived in these two towns.[25]

Before a new paradigm shift within urban development governance in Gulf cities commenced during the end of the twentieth century, housing supply already underwent a major transformation from a relatively self-managed process of developing homes to a top-down supply of either allocated defined lots with strict regulations, financial support and entirely built dormitory towns. The widespread tendency of local citizens buying residential plots as investments led to rather low urban densities in many areas coupled with the need for expanded infrastructure to access new development areas (Figure 3.1). While in the past undeveloped land could not be possessed by any individual, the newly introduced form of property rights permitted any citizen to invest in land and to become a major landlord benefiting from the fast-growing demand on housing, particularly during times of extensive migration.

In addition to the implementation of land use regulations, the urbanization phase after national independence was marked by the first industrialization and economic diversification. Some countries and emirates, such as Bahrain and Dubai, faced serious economic challenges due to limited oil wealth. The favoured development strategy in these cases was the initiation of large ports and airports to become regional trading centres together with the promotion of tourism and the introduction of a progressive finance sector introducing Islamic Banking.[26] Thus, the Emirate of Dubai and the Kingdom of Bahrain were pioneers of establishing emerging regional service hubs. The initiation of economic free trade zones, such as Jebel Ali in 1985 and Mina Salman in 1979, expanded trade and certain industrial sectors. The geographic location between emerging markets in Asia, Africa as well as the Middle East led to the initiation of well-connected hubs based on the publicly funded extension of

Figure 3.1 The large percentage of un-built land in urban peripheries (Emirate of Dubai).

infrastructure as well as national airlines. The new role of cities as emerging hubs led to increased opportunities in local real estate markets. During the 1990s, first measures have explored possibilities to organize and benefit from property-led development mechanisms in the Gulf region.[27] This has led to a major and highly significant transformation from managing cities as centres of rather introverted welfare states towards positioning cities as branded hubs within an increasingly globalized world. The resulting form of urbanism has highly impacted housing dynamics.

Urban entrepreneurialism as a new form of governance

In order to introduce the transition from centralized urban management to rather particular forms of entrepreneurial urban governance in the Gulf region, the development of the Emirate of Dubai can be taken as an important case example. At the beginning of 2006, Sheikh Mohammed bin Rashid Al Maktoum became the ruler of Dubai after the death of his older brother Sheikh Maktoum bin Rashid Al Maktoum, who had been in charge since 1990. While their father Sheikh Rashid bin Saeed Al Maktoum led Dubai through the decisive time of the oil boom and the foundation of the UAE from the 1950s to the late 1980s, it was his third son, Sheikh Mohammed, who took over the initiative to develop Dubai into a regional and global hub. This was made possible during the reign of Sheikh Maktoum, who left Dubai's economic development to his younger brother and mainly focused on the political day-to-day business of the UAE. Thus, since the early 1990s, Sheikh Mohammed was already able to start creating his vision of a modern Dubai by introducing new economic strategies rooted in a reformed concept of governance.[28]

Sheikh Mohammed, who was educated at Cambridge in the UK, was introduced into the political leadership at a very young age of twenty-three, when he became Minister of Defence, and thus the youngest minister of the UAE, at the beginning of the 1970s. His entrepreneurial skills were first proven in 1985, when he decided to develop the first airline of the UAE, Emirates, involving an investment of US$10 million. In the mid-1990s, he initiated the expansion of the tourism sector by founding the Shopping Festival, which soon became one of the biggest regional attractions. It was this entrepreneurial ambition and its positive economic impact that led to his appointment as Crown Prince by Sheikh Maktoum instead of his older brother Sheikh Hamdan in 1995.[29]

In the 1990s, Sheikh Mohammed created the cornerstone of the rapid urban growth of the following decade by instigating the establishment of large real estate companies to develop freehold properties for sale to non-UAE nationals. In cooperation with other investors, the joint stock company Emaar was founded in 1997 with an equity capital of 2.65 billion dirhams. Because of the allocation of land for the development of real estate, the Maktoum family became the key shareholder with 33 per cent of the stock. Mohammed Al Abbar was appointed as chairman of Emaar, who has proven his skills as a financial expert in earlier projects in Dubai. Emaar's first project in 1999, 'Emirates Hills', was also the first freehold property project in Dubai. In 2007, the company had an annual net profit of more than 6.5 billion dirhams that continued to grow over the following years due to the company's expansion within the region and globally.

In parallel with Emaar, Sheikh Mohammed initiated the establishment of a second large real estate company, Nakheel, named after its signature project of reclaimed islands along Dubai's coast in the form of a palm tree. The intention of Sheikh Mohammed was to create a real estate company wholly owned by the Al Maktoum family unlike Emaar. Nakheel was directly linked to the government and the fact that Emaar was already running at full capacity; Nakheel soon became the major real estate developer of Dubai. The first appointed chief executive of Nakheel was Sultan Ahmad Bin Sulayem, who already had previous senior management experience in relation to his leadership role at Jebel Ali Harbour and the free trade zone. The net profit of Nakheel in 2007 was 4,688 billion dirhams.[30]

Although since the 1970s all ministries have been established in Abu Dhabi to govern the major internal and external affairs of the United Arab Emirates, each emirate has remained in charge of their own local governmental institutions that have been playing a major role in the local economic development process. The Dubai Municipality, which had already been established in the 1950s, was followed by the Dubai Commerce and Tourism Promotion Board in 1989, which was later replaced by the Department of Tourism and Commerce Marketing (DTCM) in 1997, the Dubai Ports Authority (DPA) in 1991, the Department of Economic Development (DED) in 1992 and furthermore the Dubai Development and Investment Authority (DDIA) in 2002.

The DED was mainly developed to analyse the economy unlike the DDIA, which was put in charge of executing the outcome of these analyses within the sectors of infrastructure development, project management and investment expansion. Thus, the DDIA was one of the most important institutions and consequently put under the direct supervision of Sheikh Mohammed himself, who appointed Mohammed Abdallah Al Gergawi as its chairman.[31] In the following years these public institutions were often reformed and restructured, particularly the DDIA. After four years of its existence it was completely privatized and subordinated to the private Dubai Holding, which was developed in parallel at the beginning of the millennium as a semi-public version of the DDIA, and due to its economic success and future perspectives as a private cooperation, Dubai Holding was able to establish a strong position for itself.

Dubai Holding was established as a holding of seven company conglomerates of the Al Maktoum family, covering thirteen different economic sectors including finance, real estate, tourism, communication, technology, industrial manufacturing, education and research. The Jumeirah Group was one of the first conglomerates of Dubai Holding, which included companies working in hospitality, education, leisure and entertainment (Figure 3.2). In addition, the conglomerate Tatweer was established as the parent company of various companies in the entertainment industry, including, for example, 'Dubailand', as well as additional companies involved in real estate, health care, industrial manufacturing and the energy sector. A further parent company, TECOM Investments, has integrated all the technology, communication and research branches by being the head of several free economic zones, including Dubai Internet City, Dubai Media City (DMC) and Dubai Knowledge Village. In addition, the Dubai Group and Dubai International Capital were founded as

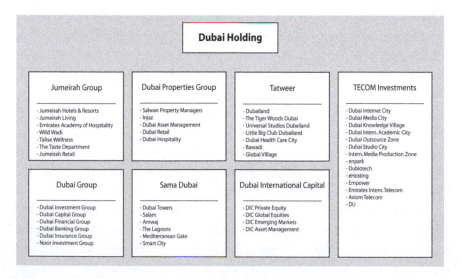

Figure 3.2 The structure of Dubai Holding after its foundation.

umbrella organizations that cover mainly investment and insurance companies. Last but not least, two real estate companies, Dubai Properties and Sama Dubai, were launched in order to develop real estate projects in Dubai itself and abroad. Although the DDIA was taken over by Dubai Holding, most leading positions within the private holding were given to former leaders of the DDIA. Consequently, Mohammed Abdallah Al Gergawi became the chairman of Dubai Holding, which established itself as the most important developer of Dubai's economy beside a second recently founded holding called Dubai World.[32]

The new holding Dubai World was founded in 2006 after the restructuring of the Ports, Customs & Free Zone Corporation (PCFC), which was founded in 2001 as an umbrella organization covering the Jebel Ali Free Trade Zone and the DPA. Because of its remaining public functions, the DPA, which had already been founded in 1991 as a public institution, did not become part of the holding Dubai World despite the fact that it was financially independent and profit-orientated, unlike other companies that joined the new holding such as, for example, Dubai Maritime City and, most importantly, the real estate giant Nakheel. In its peak time, the Dubai World conglomerate covered over thirteen different economic sectors with a focus on the maritime sector. The former chairman of the PCFC, Sultan Ahmad Bin Sulayem, was also appointed as new head of the board of directors of the new Dubai World group. Furthermore, he remained the chairman of the companies Nakheel, Dubai Ports World (DPW) and Jebel Ali Free Zone Authority (JAFZA) within the holding. In addition, he was put in charge of the semi-public DPA and thus gained an important governmental role.

However, he was not the only case of appointment to a leading position within the private and public sectors as both Al Gergawi (DH) and Al Abbar (Emaar) were appointed to important functions within Dubai's government in addition to their chairmanship of private corporations. While Al Gergawi became Minister of State for Cabinet Affairs, the position of the general manager of the DED was given to Al Abbar. Consequently, all three became important members of the Executive Council and thus some of the politically most influential stakeholders in Dubai.[33]

The Executive Council was founded in 2003 to create development plans for Dubai and decide on the phrasing and implementation of new laws. The deputy chairman of the Executive Council is the uncle of Sheikh Mohammed, Sheikh Ahmad Bin Saeed Al Maktoum, who was appointed as the president of the Civil Aviation Department. Furthermore, he has been in charge of the airline Emirates as chairman of the Emirates Group. Apart from Al Abbar, Al Gergawi and Bin Sulayem who have already been mentioned, there were eleven other appointed members of the Executive Council including Khalifa Mohammed Al Khalafi, the general manager of the Lands Department, and Qassim Sultan Al Banna, the director general of the Dubai Municipality (DM), who were very decisive figures during Dubai's most crucial development period between the years 2003 and 2010.[34] The decisive impact of the Dubai Executive Council on a new form of urban governance can mainly be explained by its high level of integration regarding private sector protagonists and their corporate interests. Thus, the main focus of any decision-making was the initiation of extensive property-led development via mega projects transforming Dubai to both an emerging investment hub and an important service hub with a high level of regional and global connectivity.

One major consequence of this privatized form of governance has been a minor administrative authority of the DM caused by its loss of responsibility for all of the urban area due to the newly initiated holdings, which have been run as private companies and not as public institutions. Therefore, the urban development has been mainly determined by the decisions of the main corporations with the permission of Sheikh Mohammed as the last authority. The DM itself was reorganized into five sectors, namely, the Corporate Service Sector, the General Service Sector, the Environmental and Public Health Services Sector, the Health Service and Environmental Control Sector and last but not least the Planning and Engineering Sector.[35] However, all central development decisions and initiatives originated from Sheikh Mohammed and his main economic leaders. Thus, the governance of Dubai has been largely formed by corporate interests and thus the main objective to stimulate accelerated urban growth. This new model of corporate-driven governance led to both a reduced number of key stakeholders with access to a highly efficient decision-making process and a more and more decentralized form of local urban management.

But despite its reduced impact on a holistic level, the DM has retained its urban planning responsibility in certain areas. The Planning and Engineering Sector was subdivided into six different departments, namely, the Planning Department, Survey Department, GIS Department, Building Department, General Projects Department and Architectural Heritage Department. The Planning Department was authorized to deal with land allocation and zoning ordinance, particularly in the case of housing areas for local citizens. Its main function is to formulate and periodically review the general planning regulations. It was also put in charge of reviewing and implementing the urban area structure plan and designing zoning plans per administrative area.[36] While the Planning Department has been in charge of land use planning and building permission, the independent Road and Transport Authority has been responsible for developing the general road network and public transport projects, which has highly affected the development of new residential areas since mega projects have occupied most infrastructural capacities.

The Planning Department operates on the basis of the five-year strategic plan of the DM. There are three main general strategic directions of the urban planning section. The first involves complying with the existing rules and legislation that govern urban development concerning both projects and institutions. The second involves general planning development, including conservation projects related to architectural heritage wherein the planning is particularly focused on the development of existing communities, the supply of infrastructure and the provision of residential plots for citizens. The last main strategic direction is the creation of a suitable legislative environment, including the maintenance of regular updates to the planning zoning ordinance and ensuring the efficient supply of public services.

The zoning ordinance is one of the biggest responsibilities of the DM and was built on three kinds of plans with different time frames; there are the Dubai Emirate Strategy Physical Plan (1993–2050), the Dubai Urban Area Structure Plans and the Five Year plans for the Dubai Urban Area. Although the Planning Department has retained its function as the main public urban planning institution of Dubai, it lost its planning influence on most of the urban area, which has become occupied by large-scale real estate projects of the various holdings and their developers (Figure 3.3). Consequently, the role of the Planning Department has been limited to mainly manage the core urban areas, surrounded by the extensive new developments of semi-public holdings.

In summary, the transformation of Dubai's urban governance from a centralized administrative type to a cooperate-driven model of urban governance began in the 1990s, when the Emir Sheikh Mohammed became responsible for the economic development of the Emirate. One of the first consequences of this transformation was the foundation of the DED in 1992 as a governmental institution intended to create economic strategies for rapid economic growth and diversification. Furthermore, the Sheikh initiated major investments to establish new economic sectors in Dubai. Thus, tourism became a key economic sector, when hotels, beaches, cultural heritage sites, theme parks and events, such as Dubai Shopping Festival, were subsidized by the government to market Dubai as an up-and-coming tourist centre in the Middle East.

Thus, landmarks such as the Burj Al Arab have become driving forces in the creation of the image of a modern Dubai (Figure 3.4). Along with tourism and

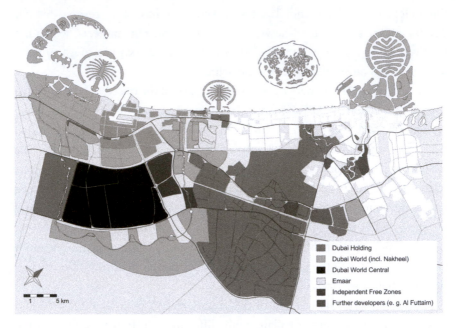

Dubai Holding
Dubai World (incl. Nakheel)
Dubai World Central
Emaar
Independent Free Zones
Further developers (e. g. Al Futtaim)

Figure 3.3 All urban areas managed by major holdings in Dubai.

growing international attention, many other economic sectors such as financial businesses started to develop. Other important factors include the relocation of many companies to Dubai due to liberal policies including tax-free environment, less bureaucratic burdens, as well as Dubai's important geopolitical location between growing global markets, and the availability of relatively cheap energy, labour and modern infrastructure.[37] This attraction of many new economies led to a growing interest in investment in real estate, which was expected to rapidly gain value as a result of economic growth, subsequent migration and thus exponential demand. Consequently, property-led development was perceived as a major catalyst for accelerating further economic diversification.

Although the legal process of opening the real estate market to foreign investors took several years until 2002, many projects were already announced and were in the process of realization.[38] While the first freehold properties were predominantly residential developments, there was an early attempt to use the growing investment possibilities to create specialized business parks, such as DIC and Dubai Media City, in order to encourage rapid economic diversification as well as a successful branding of real estate projects. Consequently, more companies were founded and subordinated under the umbrella of two new holdings, Dubai Holding and Dubai World. While the real estate developers Dubai Properties and Sama Dubai became part of Dubai

Figure 3.4 The Burj Al Arab hotel tower in Dubai.

Holding and Nakheel joined Dubai World, Emaar has remained independent due to its specific historic roots and partnership structure.

Since the beginning of the twenty-first century, a relatively small number of leading businessmen, including the chairmen of Dubai Holding, Dubai World and Emaar, run a large part of Dubai under the supervision of Sheikh Mohammed from a mainly business-oriented perspective, which led to an enormous growth and speed in property-led development between 2004 and 2008. This joint venture between the ruler and the private sector is profoundly dependent on the fact that most un-built land legally belongs to the royal family. The result has been an increasingly diminishing influence on the part of the DM and its Planning Department on the overall urban development due to the large-scale distribution of land to cooperate holdings.

While the DM has remained in charge of the implementation of the urban area structure plan within the already existing built areas, more recent developments are being planned individually by each major real estate company.

In many projects, one master developer creates a master plan of the development and many further sub-developers execute the project under his supervision. In order to guarantee rapid development, the infrastructure is usually developed for the whole project by the master developer and a less bureaucratic procedure of building permissions has been established through a system in which initial approval is granted by the master developer before being passed on for approval by the DM as well as other authorities such as, for example, the JAFZA, which allocate building permits within their areas.

This more decentralized style of urban management has been a substantial factor in the exponential growth and profound transformation of the former urban structure. In this context, it could be argued that Dubai's rulers can claim to have initiated one of the fastest building sites in human history and an embodiment of a new concept of a city governed as a profit-oriented company. This form of cooperate governance, with few restrictions and burdens for the single investor in combination with a powerful Emir and the context of recent globalization tendencies, led to great potentials to ignite a new scale of property-led development and subsequent economic diversification.

While Dubai launched its first freehold property project in 1999, most other real estate markets in the Gulf have only officially opened their markets after major political reforms between 2002 and 2004. In the Kingdom of Bahrain, the reorganization of the ministries under the king's cabinet and the Crown Prince Salman Al Khalifa led to the founding of the EDB in 2002, which gradually implemented a new regulatory basis to enable property-led economic diversification strategies, which mainly focused on coastal areas. Gradually, the EDB became a driving force within urban governance by establishing several new committees such as the Urban Development and Housing Committee, which was put in charge of a large housing development, currently known as Northern City Islands.

In Qatar and Abu Dhabi new laws were introduced in 2004 to enable a freehold property market, limited to particular areas. Furthermore, new authorities were launched, such as the Urban Planning Development Authority in Qatar and the Abu Dhabi Urban Planning Council, to effectively coordinate major urban development projects. In this respect, Dubai's model of initiating semi-public holdings or project-related public–private partnerships to develop government-owned land, which in many cases had to be reclaimed along the coasts, has been copied in Gulf capitals but at a smaller physical scale. In comparison to other public–private alliances in property-led economic development strategies worldwide, the particular constellation of rulers as political leaders and main

CEOs of holdings led to the most efficient decision-making processes as well as a natural underestimation of future challenges for consolidating the various new developments due to a rather limited overview of the impact of rapidly initiated projects.

This new form of urban governance has had a large impact on housing supply in all Gulf cities. The initiated economic development strategies have been rooted in general hub visions and open real estate markets. The result was an increasing rise in land prices and construction costs, which led to an inevitable shortage of affordable housing for both local and migrant populations. While local citizens have still been relying on government support, such as the distribution of land, affordable loans and housing projects, the rapidly increasing foreign population has been dependent on small- and medium-sized developers who were building compounds in suburban areas and highly dense blocks in inner-city areas. Only around 10 per cent of the migrant population has however been able to afford the rapidly rising rental rates in exclusive mega projects along the waterfronts, which thus often remained investment entities.[39]

In the past housing has been characterized by three types of markets: suburban housing for locals, the compounds for higher-income expats and the inner-city apartments for lower-income groups. Yet, the new property-led development dynamics led to an extensive migration and an increasingly diversified housing market. As a result, at least five major housing markets can be identified today: the suburban housing for locals, the exclusive freehold properties in mega projects, the compounds within urban peripheries, the highly dense housing blocks in downtown and transition zones and the housing for labourers in industrial areas and outskirts. The surge in land prices is the direct result of both the high level of land occupation by freehold property projects and the increase of housing demand due to migration. The new form of urban governance focusing on igniting property-led development strategies can thus be viewed as the primary reason for rapid growth and extensive migration resulting in the rising shortage of affordable housing in Gulf cities.

New restructuring tendencies within governance

Since the global financial crisis in 2008, the new form of cooperate urban governance, as it was introduced and implemented since the end of the twentieth century in the Gulf region, has witnessed its first major challenge in coordinating an economic diversification strategy during a period of insecure investment and rising doubts on the general development path of Gulf cities.[40] Due to the scale of newly launched urban developments, any loss of momentum and shrinking growth rates led to a major threat for any investment. Thus, various mega project initiatives were put on hold. This significantly affected the overall perception of Gulf cities as rather fragile entities dependent on a thriving financial sector rather than on the expanding size of the newly established economies. While tourism, trade and transit have remained the most important pillars for justifying a property-led development in the Gulf, the remaining wealth on fossil fuels and the subsequent investment potentials have become both the only reason for preventing an entire economic collapse in 2008 and the most fragile dependency on sustaining growth rates in future. The rise of emerging migrant cities for millions has been a direct result of highly efficient procedures within local urban governance and the prospect of remaining oil and gas resources enabling the continuous development and maintenance of urban structures. However, the newly established cities have been questioned regarding their overall sustainability due to their major crises in mediating between the ongoing growth dependency and spatial consolidation in the form of integrated rather than fragmented urban structures.[41]

Housing has therefore become a main indicator of the increasing gap between an economic development strategy aiming for fast and extensive investments rather than focusing on initiating a demand-driven pattern fuelled by local and migrant communities willing to settle. After a period of reforms to enable large mega projects, which were not guided by any central plan, governments became more aware of the necessity of an overall and highly reliable legal framework to ensure the integration of basic urban qualities and an effective housing supply. The main challenges can be outlined in terms of the high level of urban fragmentation and sprawl due to the move of medium-income groups to urban peripheries for more affordable rents, the over-occupied apartments in downtown and industrial areas and the high maintenance costs of exclusive projects, particularly along waterfronts, and the increasing housing shortage for local populations.

These challenges suggest that the recent form of urbanism led to the highest possible costs for governments to maintain cities due to inefficient urban structures and the continuous need for new infrastructure as well as the remaining responsibility to secure housing and services for a growing number of local populations. Due to the speed and scale of urbanism in the Gulf, neither transport-oriented development nor integrated housing strategies have been successfully implemented. Consequently, urban development patterns followed a rather undifferentiated version of property-led development, which was not limited by any major regulatory frameworks or the prior condition of sufficient local infrastructural supply.

As discussed in Chapter 2, the time of the breakout of the international financial crisis was accompanied with a new approach in the Gulf region to finally formulate and introduce holistic development visions to address the overall question of future Gulf cities. In 2008, for instance, Qatar's rulers published the Qatar National Vision. In the following years a new planning framework, known as the Qatar National Master Plan, was elaborated and gradually implemented.[42] A few years later, the former Urban Planning Development Authority was moved under the umbrella of the Ministry of Municipalities and Urban Planning, which was recently restructured as the Ministry of Municipality and Environment. This tendency of reorganizing and reinstating a centrally controlled spatial planning process is rather common as a reaction to earlier growth-oriented strategies. Thus, a central planning unit has been initiated within the ministry to coordinate the most crucial planning decisions and to enable the development of the main infrastructural grid.

The new emphasis on infrastructure development as precursor of new dynamics rather than perceiving mega projects as the main drivers of urbanism can be seen as a direct and positive reaction to the newly emerging urban realities of increasing traffic congestion and housing shortages. By distinguishing macro-planning frameworks, such as the Qatar National Development Framework, and municipal urban administration via the Municipal Spatial Development Plans, a decision-making structure has been established re-acknowledging main regulatory frameworks. This was followed by a more detailed local implementation approach from district to district. One part of the new frameworks will be a new 'National Housing Strategy' to address the urgent requirements of sufficient housing supply, particularly for national citizens.[43]

Qatar's urban governance has furthermore launched new affordable housing projects in the form of public–private partnerships with Barwa, the country's major real estate developer since 45 per cent of its shares are owned by the Qatar Investment Authority.[44] These alliances with the private sector can still be found in all Gulf countries. Nonetheless, while in the past affordable housing for migrants was the main responsibility of small-scale developers within transition zones and suburban peripheries, the rising housing demand and land prices have led to severe shortages that governments needed to step in. In Qatar, Barwa thus developed Barwa City as a mass housing compound in the South of Doha to meet the rising need of migrant workers and their families for more affordable housing.

In other countries, such as the Emirates of Dubai and Abu Dhabi, new urban renewal strategies were launched in certain districts in order to keep deteriorating areas attractive for medium-income migrants and new policies were implemented to force developers to integrate a certain percentage of affordable housing.[45] In Abu Dhabi, the affordable housing policy was implemented in 2016 and nineteen developers subsequently signed the new agreement, which also includes a new property database and thus more transparency. According to the new policy, at least 20 per cent of the overall gross floor area in multi-unit residential buildings should be developed as middle-income rental housing. Rental prices are set to a maximum of 35 per cent of the average total household income and will be reviewed and adjusted on an annual basis and each unit needs to be rented for a period of at least ten years.[46]

The various initiatives of urban governance to supply housing for low- and medium-income migrants have still remained rather limited and their overall impact is still considered uncertain. In general, the major focus of housing strategies can still be found in the attempt to meet the needs of local citizens rather than migrants. As in the past, governments have remained involved in supplying land, affordable loans and social housing projects. The Northern City Islands project in the Kingdom of Bahrain was an initiative of the Ministry of Housing to supply more than 3,000 housing units to Bahraini families. Various partnerships with the private sector have been initiated to develop these newly reclaimed islands offering a total of around 4,100 housing units.[47]

In the Emirate of Dubai, the government launched the Mohammed Bin Rashid Housing Establishment, which is a governmental authority with proclaimed corporate characteristics aiming at providing housing to local citizens. This includes the granting of residential lots, governmental houses as well as providing housing loans. The Abu Dhabi Housing Authority was established in 2012 and has been similarly involved in launching housing programmes and initiatives to meet the needs of local citizens. In Qatar, the Governmental Housing and Building Department of the Ministry of Finance is involved in developing policies of governmental housing as well as their management and maintenance. Despite all property-led development dynamics and a large increase of the statistical wealth of all nationals, a large percentage of the local population has not been able to benefit from recent developments as investors, landlords or any other major stakeholder. The low rate of participation in the private sector is another major indicator for local populations, which have remained dependent on public subsidies and thus on governments heavily involved in supplying housing.

In summary, it can be stated that the recent attempt to regain government control regarding urban growth and housing supply led to a juxtaposition of old and new forms of urban governance. The cooperate alliances of governments and semi-public holdings led to a quick decentralization of urban management enabling fast growth rates but despite an abstract central control, no overall legal framework coordinated spatial development patterns towards a needed level of integration. Thus, speed and scale of urban developments led to fragmented patchwork structures made of mono-typologies lacking basic infrastructural supply and services. In parallel, the investment pressure, fuelled by the increasing need for regional investment havens as well as the optimistic perspectives on the remaining wealth on oil and gas, led to rapidly increasing land prices in all accessible areas. The supply-driven development model of real estate-dependent growth dynamics thus led to a shortage of housing in various market areas. Particularly, lower-income migrant groups witnessed a rapid imbalance and rental rates higher than 40 per cent of their average income. This caused a widespread move of guest workers and their families to outskirts, which contributed to severe traffic congestions and one of the highest ecological footprints worldwide.

The recent dynamics of deteriorating downtown areas and the rapid decrease of living standards of low- to medium-income groups led to new initiatives to guarantee the overall housing supply. The new tendency of regulating a previously deregulated system of property-led development is a clear sign for a third reconfiguration process of urban governance in the Gulf (Figure 3.5). This intervention was a direct consequence of increasing threats originating from the lack of local urban consolidation and the global financial crisis. Recent developments in Gulf cities reveal both their large economic vulnerability and the remaining need of governmental involvement to regulate, shape and guide real estate markets.

Cooperate governance permitted both the self-management of major mega projects and the frequent building violations of previously implemented zoning regulations. The result has been extensive migration-driven urbanism and the transformation to emerging service hubs, but the costs of this rapid paradigm shift from welfare settlements to boomtowns can be mainly found in the form of the loss of control leading to unprecedented dependencies on government funds and thus an overall reassessment of the chosen development model. The deregulation of market monopolies has proven to be incapable of generating a

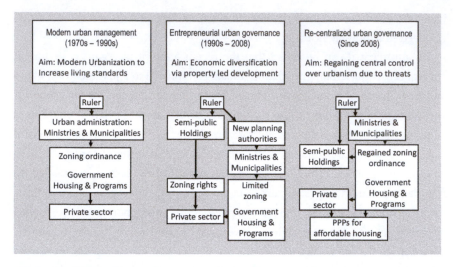

Figure 3.5 The third reconfiguration of urban management and governance in the Gulf region.

healthy environment, in which housing demand is driving a quick diversification of supply. Instead, investment was stimulated without questioning a rather decisive question of property-led development strategies: Who will be the end-user and thus potential final investor of newly built real estate?

Conclusion

The top-down decision-making process in all emerging Gulf cities has been mainly responsible for defining the new organizational structure including the decentralization and privatization of urban governance. The main decision-makers within overall governance interact on two main levels: the definition of the subordinated public administration and the initiation of semi-public holdings or project-based public–private partnerships. The main problem has however been the widespread phenomena of few and competing dominant stakeholders, which are often less supervised and controlled by any holistic framework and are thus self-managed entities with large impact on spatial developments. Thus, private business interests can often dominate urban governance, which is particularly evident in real estate and infrastructure projects. The resulting urban landscapes display a high deficit of consolidation and a market, which has become detached from the actual needs of a rapidly changing urban society. All these tendencies can be witnessed in major Gulf cities, which experienced the highest growth rates fuelled by the remaining perspective of continuous oil and gas revenues.

The fast transition from a central management of urban development, mainly driven by the main aim to enable and sustain a high living standard of local citizens, to a new form of entrepreneurial governance initiating economic diversification processes has led to very particular real estate markets challenging the overall supply of suitable and attractive housing for all income groups. The main aim of initiating a new form of governance via holdings as new and decisive stakeholders for economic diversification strategies has always been the establishment of Gulf cities as major service hubs to sustain future wealth. The strategies implemented have however led to both an unprecedented period of rapid growth and a subsequent period of uncertain developments causing governments to realize actual costs and dependencies.

Regional investments led to a quick rise of freehold property projects and an inherited process of speculative tendencies including a fast turnover of properties. Dubai's real estate sector, for instance, has attracted 22,834 investors from 136 countries (Figure 3.6).[48] This foreign investment has developed a market, which is focused on either maintaining the property's value for future sale or regaining the initial investment via comparatively high rental rates.

Figure 3.6 The exhibition of sold properties in a mega project in the Emirate of Dubai in 2008.

This has led to the phenomenon of exclusive projects with rather high vacancy rates since only high-income tenants can afford to live in these properties and increasing occupancy rates due to shared apartments and compound villas. While high-income groups have not grown in a speed needed to match the supply of exclusive properties, lower-income migrant workers have had to accept shared accommodations or homes in the urban periphery. Despite some significant price drops of real estate since 2008, the new role of properties in Gulf cities as major investment opportunities in the region has not led to an overall readjustment to the actual needs of neither the various social groups nor the envisioned knowledge economies.[49]

Thus, the core challenge of urban governance in the Gulf can be identified in terms of bridging the gap between the perception of cities as attractive investment markets due to continuous growth perspectives and the actual function of cities as places connected with dynamic local economic developments and thus the complex and diverse needs of emerging multicultural societies. Therefore, the major questions of governance can be summarized as the following: How can growth be managed and limited in an environment, which is relying on fast growth due to competitive markets? How can infrastructural supply be enabled in all areas to balance and coordinate spatial developments as well as enhance integration? How can affordable housing be feasible for investors if land prices have reached new heights?

One current answer to these three urgent questions has been the attempt to reintroduce central planning via new holistic frameworks and the enhanced authority of major semi-public infrastructure developers, such as the Road and Transport Authority in Dubai or Ashghal in Qatar, to define overall spatial development patterns. The main factors for this shift towards recentralizing governance can be found in both the increasing traffic congestion, which has become a major threat for any economic growth, and the increasing demand of developers and investors to secure property values after the financial crisis and the attached uncertainties. The resulting form of governance has been a hybrid between maintaining the general need to increase growth rates and the new emphasis on legal frameworks and infrastructural networks to enable a parallel consolidation of built structures. This often-contradictory path of managing urbanism is rooted in both a global competition to establish successful hub cities and a rather particular structure of Gulf societies built on a large percentage of temporary migration and thus the natural absence of any civil control from below.

As one main consequence, a large number of both local citizens and medium-income migrants and their families settling long-term will rely on government support for housing supply. Thus, the two most crucial social groups for future economic development are currently not sufficiently served by the real estate markets leading to overall doubts about the entire vision of recently pursued diversification strategies in the Gulf. Future governance needs to seek new answers to the question of how to enable the integration of a private-sector-driven supply of affordable housing. And as in the case of the overall vision of future hubs, the core issue of this challenge is the undefined role of migrants in developing these competitive hub cities. The missing long-term investments of most migrants in properties are rooted in the lack of citizen rights and thus the general perception of Gulf cities as temporary working places rather than actual homes.

The Gulf region represents a unique example of top-down initiated diversification and development strategies built on expanding real estate markets without any critical mass of potential buyers as actual end users of properties. Properties thus became a major new trading commodity of large investors leaving behind urban landscapes built on images rather than any linkage to an emerging society settling and getting rooted in the actual place. This basic dilemma will lead to governance as a continuously adjusting form of managing Gulf cities from a purely entrepreneurial perspective. Thus, the housing supply of locals or important migrant groups can be regarded as inevitable expenses of a cooperate model aiming to attract continuous international investment rather than generating gradually growing local investment enabling consolidated housing markets.

Notes

1   Ashok Bardhan and Cynthia A. Kroll, 'Globalization and the Real Estate Industry: Issues, Implications, Opportunities', *Sloan Industry Studies Annual Conference*, Cambridge (April 2007).

2   Jamie Peck and Adam Tickel, 'Search for a New Institutional Fix: The after-Fordist Crisis and the Global-Local Disorder', in A. Amin (ed.), *Post-Fordism: A Reader* (London, 1994).

3   Andy Merrifield, *Dialectical Urbanism: Social Struggles in the Capitalist Society* (New York, 2002).

4   Harvey Molotch, 'The City as a Growth Machine: Towards a Political Economy of Place', *American Journal of Sociology*, 82 (1976), pp. 309–32.

5   David Harvey, *Social Justice and the City* (Athens, 1973).

6   Michael Keating, 'Governing Cities and Regions: Territorial Restructuring in a Global Age', in A. Scott (ed.), *Global City Regions* (Oxford, 2001).

7   Mihalis Kavaratzis and G.J. Ashworth, 'City Branding: An Effective Assertion of Identity or a Transitory Market Trick?' *Journal of Economic and Social Geography*, 96/5 (2005), pp. 206–514.

8   Saskia Sassen, 'Locating Cities on Global Circuits', *Environment and Urbanization*, 14/1 (2002), pp. 13–30.

9   Aerni, 'Coping with Migration-induced Urban Growth'.

10 Oleg Golubchikov and Anna Badyina, 'Sustainable Housing for Sustainable Cities: A Policy Framework for Developing Countries', SSRN (2012).

11 UN Habitat, *Governance*, 2017. Available at: www.unhabitat.org/governance/ (accessed 6 May 2017).

12 Fox et al., *Globalization and the Gulf*.

13 Wiedmann, *Post-oil Urbanism*, p. 8.

14 Scholz, *Die Kleinen Golfstaaten*, p. 77.

15 Hakim, 'Revitalizing Traditional Towns and Heritage Districts'.

16 Fromherz, *Qatar: A Modern History*, p. 41.

17 Ashraf M. Salama and Florian Wiedmann, *Demystifying Doha: On Architecture and Urbanism in an Emerging City* (London, 2013), p. 26.

18 Mohammed N. Al-Nabi, *The History of Land-use and Development in Bahrain* (Manama, 2012).

19 Al-Hathloul, *The Arab-Muslim City*.

20 Horst Reichert, *Die Verstädterung der Eastern Provinz von Saudi-Arabien* (Stuttgart, 1978), p. 46.

21 Ibid., p. 110.

22 Al-Hathloul, *The Arab-Muslim City*.

23 Scholz, *Die Kleinen Golfstaaten*, p. 78.

24 Al-Nabi, *The History of Land-use and Development in Bahrain*.

25 Ministry of Housing, 'General Report on Housing and Urban Development in Bahrain', *Istanbul: The United Nations Conference on Human Settlements – Habitat II*, City Summit (1996).

26 Abdul A. Gafoor, *Islamic Banking and Finance: Another Approach* (Delhi, 2009), p. 4.

27 Florian Wiedmann, 'Real Estate Liberalization as Catalyst of Urban Transformation in the Persian Gulf', in M. Kamrava (ed.), *Gateways to the World: Port Cities* (London, 2016), pp. 157–82, p. 166.

28 Heiko Schmid, *Economy of Fascination. Dubai and Las Vegas as Themed Urban Landscapes* (Stuttgart, 2009), p. 80.

29 Wiedmann, *Post-oil Urbanism*, p. 47.

30 Ibid., p. 48.

31 Schmid, *Economy of Fascination*, p. 125.

32 Wiedmann, *Post-oil Urbanism*, p. 49.

33 Schmid, *Economy of Fascination*, p. 129.

34 Ibid., p. 131.

35 Government of Dubai, *Dubai Urban Development Framework* (Dubai, 2007).

36 Wiedmann, *Post-oil Urbanism*, p. 48.

37 Davidson, *Dubai: The Vulnerability of Success*; Mike Davis, 'Sand, Fear and Money in Dubai', in: Davis, M. and Monk, D. B. (eds), *Evil Paradises: Dreamworlds of Neoliberalism* (New York, 2007), 49–67.

38 Habib Al-Mulla, 'Legal Aspects of Real Estate Ownership in the UAE', in Cross Border Legal Publishing (ed.) *Dubai Property Guide* (Dubai, 2004), pp. 63–6.

39 Florian Wiedmann, Ashraf M. Salama and Hatem G. Ibrahim, 'The Role of Mega Projects in Redefining Housing Development in Gulf Cities', *Open House International*, 41/2, pp. 56–63.

40 Davidson, *Dubai: The Vulnerability of Success*.

41 Florian Wiedmann, Ashraf M. Salama and Velina Mirincheva, 'Sustainable Urban Qualities in the Emerging City of Doha', *Journal of Urbanism*, 7/1 (2014), pp. 62–84.

42 General Secretariat of Development Planning, *Qatar National Vision 2030*.

43 General Secretariat of Development Planning, *National Development Strategy 2011–2016*.

44 Barwa, *About Us*, 2017. Available at: www.barwa.com.qa/en/AboutBarwa (accessed 6 May 2017).

45 Nadeem Hanif. Amna E. Khaishgi and Michael Fahy, 'Affordable Homes Plan a Good Fit for Dubai', *The National*, 2017. Available at: www.thenational.ae/uae/government/20170313/affordable-homes-plan-a-good-fit-for-dubai (accessed 6 May 2017).

46 Abu Dhabi Urban Planning Council, *About Us*. Available at: Middle Income Housing Policy. www.upc.gov.ae/mirh.aspx?lang=en-US (accessed 6 May 2017).

47 Ventures Onsite, '3800 Houses Being built in New Northern Town of Bahrain to Address Shortage in Northern Governorate'. Ventures Middle East. Available at: www.venturesonsite.com/news/3800-houses-being-built-in-new-northern-town-of-bahrain-to-address-shortage-in-northern-governorate/ (accessed 6 May 2017).

48 *The National*, 'Dubai Real Estate Had a Sluggish Year of Fewer Trades and Turnover', 14 January 2017. Available at: www.thenational.ae/business/property/dubai-real-estate-had-a-sluggish-year-of-fewer-trades-and-turnover (accessed 6 May 2017).

49 Lucy Barnard, 'Dubai Property Prices Will Reach 2008 Levels, Raising Worries of Another Bubble', *The National*, 10 February 2014. Available at: www.thenational.ae/business/industry-insights/property/dubai-property-prices-will-reach-2008-levels-raising-worries-of-another-bubble (accessed 6 May 2017).

4

Mega projects: A catalyst for migrant urbanism

Since the 1990s globalization has ignited a fierce competition between emerging cities in certain geopolitical locations in the Global South to successfully enter established networks of capital flows.[1] As discussed in the preceding chapters, local governance has been increasingly challenged to introduce new development visions and plans to transform capital cities of previous welfare states into competitive hubs attracting the relocation of companies and the attention of international investors.[2] One key requirement for the successful implementation of these visions is the development of state-of-the-art infrastructure to increase the connectivity of cities via airports and ports. Another key pillar commonly implemented is the launch of mega projects followed by the liberalization of local markets that inevitably needed to attract more involvement of the private sector.

Subsequently, real estate markets and particularly housing markets have witnessed rapid growth during the first years of liberalization.[3] The resulting construction boom is in itself a significant factor guiding economic growth and diversification due to extensive employment within construction-related sectors including financial sectors and other required advanced producer services.[4] The migration of the requisite international workforce has led to new economic structures and dynamics rooted in property-led development dynamics. In many cases, the newly emerging cities are dependent on the continuous growth of investment interests. Mega projects are hence important catalysts due to their decisive role in enhancing the demand on real estate.[5]

The Emirate of Dubai and the Kingdom of Bahrain were the first pioneers to follow the vision of establishing service hubs in the Gulf region by opening local markets and by accelerating growth resulting in extensive migration. In both cases, the main reason for the new development strategies was shrinking oil and gas revenues since the beginning of the 1970s. The first free trade zones were established in Manama and Jebel Ali during the 1980s. During the 1990s, rulers recognized the potential of initiating a construction boom by permitting foreigners to invest in local real estate. Due to concerns regarding affordable housing for local populations, freehold property markets for foreign investment were only introduced at the end of the twentieth century, which led to developments of unprecedented scale and speed documented in various construction superlatives.[6]

Thus, it can be argued that the recent urbanization in emerging Gulf cities has been dominated by growth strategies rooted in real estate, which has been redefining economic, demographic and spatial development patterns.[7] Rising land prices, new forms of urban governance and an extensive migration have led to completely new urban morphologies reflecting the immediate consequences of rapid urban growth. Harvey Molotch argues that cities worldwide became growth machines mainly driven by the link between the established global financial system and liberalized land ownership rights.[8] Real estate has thus become one of the top commodities facing few restrictions regarding short-term investments. The rise and bust of recently ignited construction booms became a widespread phenomenon affecting local developments worldwide. The fragility of this development strategy was particularly evident during the international financial crisis in 2008, which has had a significant impact on property prices.[9] Thus, the extensive trade in real estate in the context of an increasingly intensified flow of international capital has created a new basis for emerging cities and their regional networks, in which each city's objective is to become a major host of international service sectors and intermediate economies while playing key roles in initiating and managing urban growth.[10]

One important characteristic of contemporary urbanism in most Gulf cities is the very specific role mega projects have played in promoting both economic growth and a reinvention of the cities' identities.[11] The initiation of freehold property markets in combination with ambitious economic development visions as future global trading, finance and tourism hubs has fuelled one of the largest building sites in human history.[12] Speed and scale of developments can only be compared to emerging cities in China, which is a remarkable fact considering the comparatively small number of local populations, the missing hinterland and the desert environment. While in 1950 around 400,000 inhabitants lived in small settlements along the Gulf coast, today more than seventeen million inhabitants live in eleven cities, with an overall share of more than 60 per cent foreigners.[13] The still remaining wealth on fossil fuels in combination with a fortunate geopolitical location and a worldwide unique governance structure within city states led to substantial urban agglomerations reaching more than four million inhabitants in the United Arab Emirates.

Since the largest share of new immigrants has been directly or indirectly engaged within the construction sector, the population growth has become highly affected by turbulences in real estate markets. While the remaining wealth of fossil fuels has prevented an economic collapse during the financial crisis, the development was severely affected due to the discontinuation of a large percentage of real estate projects, particularly new mega projects.[14] This chapter places emphasis on mega projects and the associated development patterns in Dubai and Manama to highlight the prime parallels of how the initiation of migrant cities as international hubs has led to a new dependency on images of growth and success.[15]

Dubai as pioneer of event urbanism

At the dawn of the twenty-first century, the Emirate of Dubai achieved rapid global awareness when its rulers introduced a new strategy to promote the Gulf region by establishing tourism and trade including the liberalization of local real estate markets for regional and foreign investors. The first steps towards this decisive transformation from a regional trading centre to an emerging city on a global stage were already initiated during the 1990s. The Dubai Shopping Festival, launched in 1996, created a new trend of expanding local retail markets by attracting regional tourists and thereby benefiting from an entertainment vacuum in the entire region. Successively, Dubai reinvented itself as an emerging attraction for shopping and leisure, which was accompanied by various mega projects. Heiko Schmid described this as the initiation of an 'Economy of Fascination', which can be best compared to the phenomenon of Las Vegas in the United States.[16]

The construction boom led to a period of rapid urban expansion, with the total urban area of Dubai increasing at a rate of more than 3 per cent per year. The population grew from 370,788 in 1985 to 862,387 in 2000.[17] This was due to a huge influx of expatriate migrants, who constituted about 53 per cent of the total population at the end of the twentieth century.[18] In 1999, the construction of the Burj Al Arab hotel was completed and along with it the beginning of a new era of iconic landmarks in Dubai. The Burj Al Arab and other landmark projects, which were often funded by government investments, became key elements of a new marketing strategy to brand Dubai as an emerging futuristic hub in the Middle East and thus as the new capital of the Arab world in the twenty-first century. As discussed earlier, an important factor for this ambitious vision and direction in development was the entrepreneurial foresight of Emir Mohammed bin Rashid Al Maktoum. This suggests that Dubai's economic strategy of developing itself as a key service centre was originated through the vacuum of leisure and entertainment, especially when looking at its neighbours: the two large conservative countries of Saudi Arabia and Iran.[19]

Consequently, Dubai began to initiate new free trade zones and became the first of the Gulf States to officially open the local real estate market to foreigners. The consequence of this new strategy was an unexpected surge in investment in the development of freehold properties for foreign investors in distinct areas in inner-city districts as well as on the outskirts. In order to cope with the increasing investment pressures in developments being carried out, the old centralized urban management structure of one municipality allocating building permits according to the Structure Plan of 1993 had to be changed to a more decentralized and flexible approach.[20] This led to a significant change in urban governance wherein real estate companies and their holdings, which were typically public joint stock companies, played a new role as the main developers shaping Dubai as an agglomeration of mega projects.

While in 1999 the 'Emirates Hills' project marked the beginning of the freehold property markets in Dubai, the new mega projects have quickly adapted to new requirements instead of only focusing on suburban greenfield projects. During the following years properties were sold to foreign investors on a limited basis on lease for ninety-nine years.[21] Although these early projects contradicted existing laws in the UAE, under which only locals could possess property, they became the precursors to many subsequent developments in the entire Gulf region. The first project of this kind that attracted more widespread international recognition was the 'Palm' by Nakheel, which was proposed in 2001 and developed over the following years with overall completion in 2010 (Figure 4.1). The project consisting of a palm-shaped island on the coast in Jumeirah constituted a new benchmark in real estate developments sold as freehold properties. The Palm was a new landmark demonstrating the future possibilities of property developments in the Gulf by using large-scale forms as pictorial branding for successful marketing.

Furthermore, new free trade zones were either planned or built to increase economic diversification and to attract future investors. In 2001, the free trade zones of DIC and Dubai Media City were established as new economic sub-centres of Dubai. Both 'cities' were constructed within an area accommodating

Figure 4.1 The construction of the Palm Jumeirah in Dubai.

many new developments in Jumeirah, which became the first large-scale city extension in the new millennium including a large number of residential mega developments. A characteristic of the new free trade zones has been their branding as 'cities' within the city, where each has its own particular theme and specialization in an economic sector such as, for example, ICT, media, health care or higher education. In many cases, however, the economic vision of establishing new cities was mainly launched to advertise integrated residential real estate projects, which usually cover a large percentage of the entire development area. While this phenomenon of developing new mega projects as cities was not originally invented in the Gulf, the specific characteristics have led to new forms and dimensions of this kind of urbanism. In this context, the key mega projects located in New Dubai should be underscored.

The case of New Dubai

Various key mega projects have been developed in Dubai's Western Jumeirah district, which is also known as New Dubai. In comparison to other Gulf cities mega projects in Dubai are the product of an intense development period of more than twenty years and are thus more diversified. The Emirate of Dubai has a rather significant role as a pioneer of the new development model and as a testing ground of various new project types in terms of market dynamics. The collection and comparison of all key data for each mega project, such as the projected population, the number of housing units, the basic land uses and the built typologies, can offer insights into the extent and magnitude of these developments. Furthermore, the new master-planning efforts from the DM were evaluated regarding the general role of the Jumeirah districts and the multitude of mega projects.

The New Dubai district in Western Jumeirah became the first address for residential freehold property developments after the Emirates Golf Club was founded in 1988 and several hotels including the Burj Al Arab were built during the 1990s along Jumeirah's coast. The new district extension is located at the Western coastline in a distance of around 20 kilometres from the old centre at the Dubai Creek. The district is part of the main growth corridor along Sheikh Zayed Road towards Jebel Ali and the Emirate of Abu Dhabi (Figure 4.2). The convenient location and already existing infrastructure supply prompted the developer Emaar to build its very first freehold property project, known as Emirates Living, an agglomeration of various themed suburban projects including Emirates Hills (Figure 4.2).

Over the course of the following years the Emirates Hills project was expanded through several developments including the Springs, the Meadows, the Lakes, the Views and the Greens into one large residential development, which is home to approximately 40,000 people. The whole area is about 12.3 square kilometres and is predominantly occupied by two-storey villas.[22] Apartment buildings were built within the projects the Views and the Greens as well as within several smaller projects in the north of the development. In the case of Emirates Hills, the master developer Emaar has built the basic infrastructure and provided freehold properties in the form of undeveloped large-scale plots of about 40 × 100 square metres, which have been designed and constructed individually by each individual investor. Most areas of the neighbouring projects were developed by the master developer and by constructing a reduced set of different types of villas. The special feature of Emirates Living is the vast area of un-built land in the form of more than twenty artificial lakes and a golf course occupying more than 35 per cent of the entire development. Additionally, instead of an orthogonal road network, an ornamental layout was chosen for the developments, creating an individual structure with winding streets highly isolated from any public access.

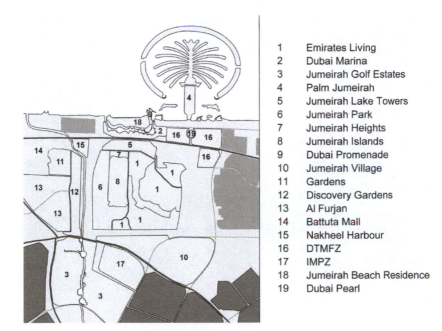

1	Emirates Living
2	Dubai Marina
3	Jumeirah Golf Estates
4	Palm Jumeirah
5	Jumeirah Lake Towers
6	Jumeirah Park
7	Jumeirah Heights
8	Jumeirah Islands
9	Dubai Promenade
10	Jumeirah Village
11	Gardens
12	Discovery Gardens
13	Al Furjan
14	Battuta Mall
15	Nakheel Harbour
16	DTMFZ
17	IMPZ
18	Jumeirah Beach Residence
19	Dubai Pearl

Figure 4.2 The mega projects in New Dubai.

Apart from these suburban housing projects, which have been designed as semi-gated communities, several new 'free economic zones' have been developed to create business areas close to the new suburbs. In 2000, Dubai Internet City (DIC) was established as the first free zone in Jumeirah providing optimized business opportunities for international technology, software and Internet companies such as HP, Microsoft, IBM and Siemens. In 2009, more than 1,200 companies were already settled in DIC.[23] In addition to DIC, the company TECOM, which was established as a subsidiary of Dubai Holding to invest in the knowledge-based economy, launched Dubai Media City (DMC) in 2001. In 2003, TECOM initiated the development of Dubai Knowledge Village (DKV) as part of the overall free zone conglomerate represented by the Dubai Creative Clusters Authority (DCCA) (Figure 4.3). Various residential projects such as large compounds with villas and low-rise apartment buildings in addition to few residential towers have been integrated in these developments. The free zone is situated between Sheikh Zayed Road and the coast with an area in the southeast covering about 350 hectares to allow for future expansion. In the centre of the conglomerate, the construction of the project Dubai Pearl has been started on a circular area to form a commercial centre and a residential complex of connected high-rise buildings to house approximately 29,000 future residents and visitors.[24]

Figure 4.3 The Dubai Knowledge Village.

A bypass leading from TECOM's DIC to DMC forms the starting point of one of Dubai's important landmarks – the Palm Jumeirah. A 300-metre-long bridge leads to the beginning of the artificial islands, which are shaped in the form of a palm with a 2-kilometre-long trunk and sixteen fronds protected by an 11-kilometre-long crescent functioning as a breakwater. In addition to a monorail, which runs from the crescent over a bridge and down the trunk to the coast, an 800-metre long tunnel at the top of the palm connects the crescent to the palm. Since 2001, more than 92 million cubic metres of sand was required to create the whole landmass on an area of about 550 hectares, which has added about 78 kilometre of new coastline. Since 2009, 1,400 villas and 20 multi-storey apartment buildings provide approximately 2,500 housing units. The entire project covers an area of 5 × 5 kilometre and consists mainly of luxury freehold properties and thirty-two hotels and resorts.[25]

In addition to the growing number of residential units on the Palm project itself, it has attracted new housing projects along the coast offering views to the artificial islands. One of these developments is Emaar's Dubai Marina, a conglomerate of residential high-rise buildings along one of the largest man-made marinas in the world. Since 2003, the project has been developed in different stages on an area of around 400 hectares for more than 100,000 future residents.[26] In the year 2014 Dubai Marina housed 28,361 inhabitants, which is an indicator for a rather high vacancy rate in spite of several tower projects still under development.[27] After a 3.6-kilometre-long artificial channel was dug, the first residential towers were built in the east of the project as well as the promenade along the marina. Most of the towers have an average height of between 130 and 200 metres and are generally designed as freehold properties offering various sizes of apartments for the upper real estate market. About nine high-rise buildings are currently being developed with a height of over 300 metres, including the 516-metre-tall Pentominium.

Between the coast and Emaar's Dubai Marina, a second residential high-rise development for about 30,000 residents was completed by Dubai Properties in 2007 – the Jumeirah Beach Residence includes 36 residential towers and four hotel towers spreading along its 1.7-kilometre long shoreline (Figure 4.4).[28] The third and second largest development of a high-rise conglomerate in Jumeirah is Nakheel's Jumeirah Lake Towers stretching over an area of 180 ha on the opposite side of Sheikh Zayed Road along the Dubai Marina. The whole development is known as the first mixed-use free economic zone of Dubai, including 79 towers, which predominantly are residential towers for more than 60,000 people and

Figure 4.4 The Jumeirah Beach Residence.

office towers for more than 120,000 working visitors. The towers with thirty-five to forty-five floors are clustered in groups of three, surrounded by four artificial lakes covering an area of about 18 ha. In the south of the project, Nakheel has developed a smaller high-rise project called 'Jumeirah Heights' offering about 2,300 residences within four high-rise buildings and six multi-storey apartment blocks.[29]

The project Jumeirah Heights not only marks the end of what is currently Dubai's biggest high-rise agglomeration but is also designed to be part of another signature project of Nakheel in Jumeirah – the Jumeirah Islands. The 300-hectare development consists of forty-six clusters of man-made islands surrounded by artificial lakes. The 736 villas have been developed in different sizes to attract various investors. Along the borders of this development Nakheel has launched the project Jumeirah Park, which includes 2,000 villas and about 10 apartment buildings in the centre on an area of more than 350 ha. Three different architectural designs and nine different sizes of villas have been developed for the entire project.[30]

Most development sites of the nine mega projects in New Dubai have been developed since the beginning of the new millennium. All projects in New Dubai aim for the upper real estate market with rents exceeding AED 100,000 per annum. Today, it is estimated that there is an oversupply of 40 per cent in this segment leading to high vacancy rates in many developments in New Dubai.[31] All projects combined have been designed for an expected total population of around 275,000 future inhabitants. The built area, excluding the main highway infrastructure, is covering approximately 29 square kilometres, which is leading to a rather moderate average urban density of less than ninety-five inhabitants per hectare (Table 4.1) when fully occupied. In comparison, New Dubai is about half the size of Manhattan Island, where around 277 inhabitants reside per hectare.

Based on the mega projects in New Dubai three distinctive new typologies can be distinguished: (1) the waterfront development in the form of reclaimed islands, (2) the waterfront high-rise clusters and (3) the suburban mega compound (Figure 4.5).

While waterfront suburban projects and their private beach access are mainly the result of land reclamation patterns and restrained infrastructural opportunities to build higher densities, the tower developments along the coast are the result of rapidly increasing land prices. The majority of towers have however led to very limited access to sea views. The residential tower clusters are often supplied with a variety of leisure spaces, such as integrated marinas,

Table 4.1 The key facts of the nine mega projects in New Dubai (as envisioned in 2008)[32]

Project name	Developer	Total area (km²)	Expected population	Urban density (residents per hectare)	Development type	Typology
Dubai Marina	Emaar	4	100,000	250	Residential, retail & leisure	High-rise
Jumeirah Beach Residences	Nakheel	0.17	30,000	1,765	Residential, retail & leisure	High-rise
Jumeirah Lake Towers	Nakheel	1.8	60,000	333	Residential & commercial (offices)	High-rise
Jumeirah Heights	Nakheel	0.6	6,000	100	Residential	High-rise
Jumeirah Park	Nakheel	3.5	6,000	17	Residential	Low-rise
Jumeirah Islands	Nakheel	3	2,000	7	Residential	Low-rise
Emirates Living	Emaar	12.3	40,000	33	Residential	Low-rise
DIC and DMC (DCCA)	TECOM	3.5	2,000	6	Commercial (free zone) & residential	Mixed
Dubai Pearl	Al Fahim Group	0.1	29,000	2,900	Residential & commercial (offices)	High-rise
Total		28.97	275,000	95		

Figure 4.5 The three main types of mega projects in New Dubai.

beaches, malls and promenades. This high level of diversity in functions and scales – that is, in consumption and leisure spaces – is based on both the average income of residents and tourist attraction. The supply of social infrastructure is often very limited. Thus, it is observed that there is a severe lack of support functions such as schools within and in proximity to waterfront tower clusters due to missing regulations and high land prices in areas reserved for exclusive projects.

The latest new phenomenon is the development of large-scale themed suburban gated communities. The development sites of these communities can occupy large areas of many square kilometres and their monotonous typologies of attached and detached dwellings as well as low-rise apartment blocks mainly differ from each other due to ornamental road grids, which are used to create individual spatial patterns. This has however led to rather detached and introverted residential areas. Subsequently, neighbourhood centres and social infrastructure have been developed in disperse locations depending on land availability rather than on a clear strategy to create integrated and accessible sub-centres for services and support facilities. In some large-scale projects certain leisure spaces, such as golf courses, water features and small malls, have been integrated to enhance the general attractiveness.

The previous discussion points out that the recent mega projects have led to new urban landscapes, which are defined by new housing typologies and their spatial distribution. The emerging island projects have led to a variety of suburban settlements on reclaimed land with limited access and a high level of exclusivity. In parallel, large-scale themed suburban mega projects have been launched towards inland along the urban periphery of former urban centres. The coastal transition zones are typically occupied by extending agglomerations of residential tower developments, which are the direct consequences of high land prices and already existing infrastructural supply. And finally, new themed mixed-use developments, which are often initiated as free economic zones along strategic growth corridors, integrate various residential typologies as either short-term housing supply depending on the demand on commercial projects or as exclusive but often isolated freehold property projects benefiting from the overall branding of developments as new cities within the city.

Notably, these development types have mainly been a result of project initiatives by semi-public holdings as well as the increasing investment pressure of the private sector. Today these developments are accommodating a growing migrant community of expatriates with medium to high income. The architecture of these developments has been designed following international building standards rather than responding to climatic constraints or any regional cultural preferences. While in the past urban densities and land use distributions were centrally administered by one planning department, the mega projects are usually the result of a certain decentralization process permitting large-scale developers, who are usually semi-public entities, a certain level of authority regarding master plans and hardly any regulation regarding the integration of social infrastructure or affordable housing.

The result has been an island-development approach following the general trend of developing stand-alone 'mega' compounds rather than integrated and cohesive new urban areas forming districts and neighbourhoods. Thus, while the urban landscapes have been diversified by the various mega projects, there has hardly been any spatial reinvention of a new form of urbanism integrating living, working and leisure. A high-rise tower thus often functions like a vertical compound rather than as an opportunity to develop a new level of integrated public spaces and services. Thus, the only actual social meeting points are provided in either an indoor environment in malls or through a small number of promenades along the coast, or scattered but hardly accessible green areas.

Liberalized real estate markets in Bahrain

Before recent development tendencies resulting from mega projects and a liberalized real estate market can be discussed, an overview of the various aspects of the economic and political aspects of urbanism should be presented. Although the economic diversification of Bahrain had started earlier than in many other Gulf States, the decline of oil prices in 1986 had a major impact on the fall of the country's GDP, thus proving that it was still reliant on the fossil resource at that time. Most of Bahrain's production industries, including the aluminium industry, depended on cheap energy. Bahrain's economy was seriously affected by Iraq's invasion of Kuwait, which led to major costs in the military sector and thus to a huge loss of public investment in infrastructural and industrial developments. In particular, joint industrial and infrastructural projects between Gulf States were either reduced or cancelled so that instead of a project volume worth about US$2.6 billion being carried out, only about 27 per cent of this volume, about US$700 million, was developed during the 1990s.[33]

Apart from the attempt to diversify the industry of the country through public investments, economic development driven by the private sector became more important. One example of the growing privatization is BALEXCO, a company founded in 1977 by public investments, over 60 per cent of which was sold to private investors during the early 1990s after it had been transformed into a stock corporation. While in the mid-1990s the privatization of Gulf Air failed due to increasing financial problems and dependency on public subsidies, the private sector did carry out essential infrastructural projects such as a new energy plant. Furthermore, new privately owned companies such as Bahrain Leisure Facilities Company, Bahrain Gulf Course Company and Al Jazira Tourism Company were instituted to establish the tourism industry in Bahrain. As an industry tourism was mainly kick-started by the construction of the new King Fahad Causeway connecting Bahrain to the Eastern Province of Saudi Arabia. In 1994, more than 5.2 million people crossed the causeway, including an increasing majority of shopping and leisure tourists.[34]

Since 2006, the Bahrain International Circuit and the annual Formula 1 race have led to wider regional and global awareness about Bahrain as a travel destination. In addition to the development of its tourism sector, Bahrain's role as an offshore banking centre has become increasingly important for its economic diversification. Towards the end of the 1990s, about forty-seven offshore banks with an overall capital of about US$67.9 billion existed in Bahrain. Furthermore, the number of local commercial banks grew rapidly, and more than thirty-two companies sold their shares in the local stock market, which was introduced in 1989. To attract more regional and international investors, the government decided to found Bahrain Development Bank in 1991, which provided low-priced loans and venture capital. In addition, the Bahrain Marketing and Promotion Bureau was introduced to support companies establishing their headquarters in Bahrain in addition to supporting a public programme since 1993 involving tax concessions, a reduction of costs regarding rent and electricity and subsidies in the case of the employment of Bahrainis. A further major change in Bahrain's economic development was the permission to found companies fully owned by foreign capital.[35]

While Bahrain's economic development was focused on increasing business possibilities for foreign and regional investors, a significant share of the local population did not actively participate within these new economic sectors. Apart from limited public investment in the education of the local population, the speed and scale of new developments called for an immediate need for highly educated, mostly foreign, employees. In order to reduce the negative impact on the local Bahraini population, several government programmes were launched to integrate the local workforce into the expanding private sector. Unlike in other Gulf countries, such as Qatar and Kuwait, the local population of Bahrain has been receiving fewer government subsidies, forcing many to accept low-paying jobs. The continuously increasing living costs in addition to the general demand for more political rights and participation have led to public demonstrations and social unrest.[36]

After the death of the Emir Sheikh Isa in 1999, his son Sheikh Hamad became ruler of Bahrain and initiated a major change in the country's political system. In 2002, the state of Bahrain was proclaimed a constitutional monarchy, and the re-establishment of an elected parliament led to a certain degree of public participation. In the following five years the population grew from about 672,000 people to more than 1,046,000 in 2007, mainly caused by the immigration of around 250,000 guest workers whose share in the overall population increased from about 38 per cent to almost 50 per cent.[37] This major growth was the direct consequence of newly introduced strategies to stimulate local real estate markets. This rapid rise of a construction boom in Bahrain was majorly affected by residential real estate since Bahrain's cities were conceived as ideal dormitory satellites for middle- to high-income expats engaged in the Eastern Province of Saudi Arabia and as holiday homes for wealthy Saudi citizens.

At the beginning of the twenty-first century almost the entire territory of Bahrain was turned into a free zone offering a low tax environment, making it one of the most cost-effective locations in the GCC. In addition, there was no law that forced companies to assign a certain number of shares or to engage a mediating agency. This liberalization led to the private sector's growing interest in Bahrain, particularly regarding the rapidly emerging real estate market between 2002 and 2008. Since 2002, the development of the mega project, known as Bahrain Financial Harbour, has been the embodiment of a new approach to re-establish Bahrain as a financial capital in the Gulf. While the real estate market was already open to GCC nationals by 1999, a 2003 law allowed foreigners to buy freehold properties and thus to receive a self-sponsored residence permit.[38]

The new legal situation and the general investment climate have led to a construction boom in the form of various residential mega projects, mainly on reclaimed land in the north and close to the urban centres. One of the first freehold property developments has been Amwaj Islands in the northeast of Muharraq, which was announced in 2002. In the following years, the private sector launched several other mega projects on reclaimed islands such as Reef Island and Bahrain Bay along the waterfront of Manama and the Durrat Al Bahrain development in the south of the main island (Figure 4.6). Beside the coastal developments, the freehold projects Al Areen and Riffa Views were launched in the inland. These developments were designed by a master developer

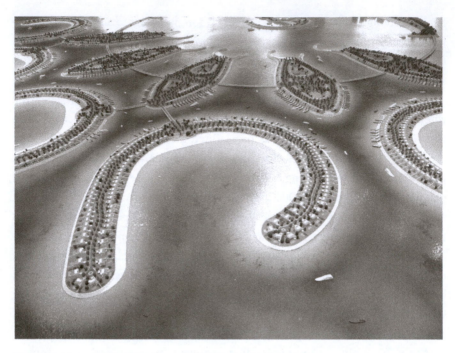

Figure 4.6 A model of the Durrat Al Bahrain development.

of a private investor group or a semi-public holding and are typically made up of mixed-use projects with integrated commercial districts, leisure facilities and hotels in addition to a large percentage of residential use.

Parallel to these master-planned projects, zoning plans for certain urban areas, such as the reclaimed coastal districts of Manama, known as the Seef district, the Juffair district and the Seafront district, were modified to permit the development of freehold property developments. Based on the new regulations, multi-storey buildings and high-rise ones were built to make the available land as profitable as possible. The consequent verticalization of the built environment has been an indicator of the profound change of urbanism in Bahrain, which has been increasingly dominated by real estate investments. In addition, new landmarks, such as the World Trade Centre Bahrain and the Bahrain Financial Harbour, were intended to consolidate and stimulate the post-oil economic sectors via landmark architectural statements.

While in previous decades most aspects of urban planning had been the responsibility of a single ministry, the decision to move the Planning Directorate in 2002 to another ministry and an increase in master-planned projects based on case-by-case decisions led to the decentralization of urban planning in Bahrain.

Due to increasing pressure from developers and real estate investors, the state's existing zoning plans were adjusted to accommodate growth rates and new development preferences. Based on Resolution No. 27, which was approved by the Council of Ministers in 2005, developments were less restricted regarding land use, maximum construction ratio and building height. The highest densities are permitted in areas with the type 'Investment Building B-A' (Figure 4.7), the construction ratio of which can be as much as 1,200 per cent of the total plot area, which is comparable to downtown Manhattan.[39]

The major share of developed real estate is located on reclaimed land along the northern and eastern shoreline of Bahrain's capital, Manama. In addition to the development of many former empty plots within the central business district along the King Faisal Highway in the north, the new centres of construction have been around the Seef district in the north-west and Juffair in the south-east. Because of the very fortunate infrastructural supply provided by the main highways leading from central Manama to the causeway to Saudi Arabia, several shopping malls have been constructed in the Seef district. Thus, many banks and office buildings have relocated to this district, which was built on land that was reclaimed in the 1980s to create a new suburb. Because of the US Navy Base and the migration of many foreign guest workers in recent years, the Juffair district has witnessed a fast development of multi-storey apartment buildings

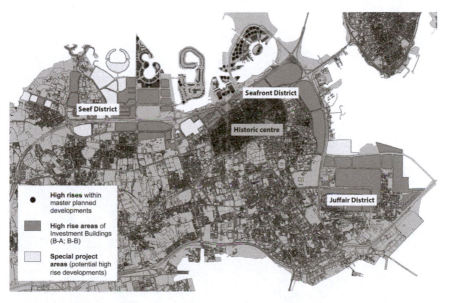

Figure 4.7 The distribution of zones in Manama permitted to be developed as Investment Buildings.

and compounds. In 2007, the main property transactions by non-Bahrainis were carried out by Saudis with an overall share of 52.9 per cent followed by Kuwaitis with 21.4 per cent.[40]

The recent development trend of focusing on new urban areas has led to the reclamation of about 170 ha in the Seafront district, about 140 ha in the Seef district and about 80 ha in the case of Juffair since 1998 (Figure 4.8). The overall urban area of Manama has expanded by more than 15 per cent from around 2,700 ha to almost 3,100 ha. A further consequence of the recent construction boom has been an exponential increase in land prices, which has contributed to less investment in old parts of Manama due to low profit expectations. All in all, there has been a clear shift and transformation of urban development towards increasingly densely built areas along the coast in addition to reclaimed island projects with a remaining high percentage of around 40 per cent of un-built land in the old urban areas of Manama.[41]

As in the other Gulf States, the international financial crisis of 2008 has had a drastic impact on local developments in Bahrain. While before the outbreak of the crisis the annual growth rate of the real estate sector reached 24.7 per cent in 2007, the value of residential freehold properties decreased more than 25 per cent

Figure 4.8 The extensive land reclamation and construction in Juffair.

in average in 2010.[42] In 2013, investment in real estate remained below 50 per cent of its preceding peak in 2007.[43] Combined with social unrest in recent years, the investment climate has profoundly changed, leading to cancelled or delayed developments. The fast rise of the construction boom and the abrupt crisis display the increasing dependency between economic stability and a flourishing real estate market. Growth expectations have been merely a consequence of speculative incentives, which, however, heavily rely on a stable environment to avoid major setbacks as in the case of Bahrain between 2008 and 2013.

Thus, it can be stated that mega projects have introduced new opportunities for upper-income groups in Bahrain, including new consumption worlds and waterfront housing, which has become a representation of social status in Gulf cities. The needed diversification of housing, which was previously mainly dominated by suburban villas, has however not led to an enhanced urban identity and efficiency in the case of single districts and urban spaces. In most cases developers have labelled housing projects as new communities rather than integrating needed infrastructure and public spaces to establish the basis for future communities. The lack of affordable housing schemes has furthermore contributed to social segregation and a rather fragile environment of exclusive projects and mass housing relying on future economic growth to avoid a complete challenging of their existence as displayed in the recent financial crisis.

A comparative discourse on two pioneers

Gulf cities face various challenges to develop a sustainable form of urbanism in a region that is witnessing increasing competition regarding new economic sectors. Thus, on the one hand, liberalization strategies and mega projects, as first introduced in Dubai and Bahrain, are needed to establish growing hubs while, on the other, diverse, efficient and attractive urban environments are needed to become sustainable metropolises. In both cases recent urban development strategies have led to rapid urban growth fuelled by emerging real estate markets. While in Dubai the local population has become a minority of around 10 per cent, the native share of Bahrain's population shrank from over 80 per cent to less than 50 per cent over the last ten years. However, it is important to put these figures into perspective as a large majority of guest workers are employed on construction sites and will leave after the completion of their short-term contracts. In both cases, however, cities are built for a new form of socio-economic reality, which is dependent on future migration.

The main parallel between Dubai and Bahrain is the fact that, in both cases, local oil and gas revenues have not been sufficient to contribute to economic development since the 1970s and after the first modernization period. Subsequently, rulers in both countries initiated alternative economic strategies to secure future prosperity. While Bahrain was one of the first offshore banking centres, Dubai became a major regional trading hub since its first economic free zone was launched in Jebel Ali. Simultaneously, both countries discovered tourism to be a major factor in their economic diversification during the 1990s. The newly launched Shopping Festival in Dubai and the construction of a causeway between Bahrain and Saudi Arabia led to a new chapter of local economic development driven by the expanding need for leisure in the region. The expansion of regional airlines in combination with large-scale tourism resorts attracted the rising interest of investors and thus the pressure to liberalize local markets.

The major differences with respect to the impact of the recent construction boom in Dubai and Bahrain are mainly rooted in their particular political circumstances and social realities. While the Emirate of Dubai is part of the United Arab Emirates with Abu Dhabi City as the capital, the Kingdom of Bahrain has become dependent on Saudi Arabia regarding its economic development as well as its domestic concerns. The divide between Bahrain's rulers and a large share of Bahrain's population is historically rooted, and in the course of the recent outbreak of the 'Arab Spring', social unrest demanding for the end of monarchy led to a major intervention supported by GCC allies. Due to the existing inequity and lack of political rights, the consequently missing social stability has become a key factor weakening Bahrain's position as a regional investment hub in recent years. As a result, real estate developments have been mainly driven by local, Saudi and Kuwaiti investment interests.

In contrast to Dubai, semi-public holdings and their real estate developments in Bahrain are rejected by a large percentage of the local population. The newly emerging urban landscapes of high-rise agglomerations and artificial islands are often seen as antithetical to local culture and values. Thus, major projects are limited to areas that can be directly accessed by the main highway network, and certain measures have been taken to develop gated and luxurious resorts detached from old urban areas. This has led to a highly segregated urban landscape in Bahrain displaying the conflict between the minority leading social classes and the majority of the population left out of the current development dynamics. One particular aspect has been the focus of new development areas along the coast due to the existing land ownership rights leading to less than 5 per cent of coastline, which can be accessed by the public.[44] In contrast to

Manama's old urban districts, Dubai's downtown areas such as Bur Dubai and Deira have witnessed a gradual upgrading process. Strict physical planning by the DM and continuous public investment in infrastructure have prevented the deterioration of Dubai's historic centre and ensured less isolation between old and new urban areas as can be witnessed in Manama.

While Dubai's real estate markets have been diversified by the various interests of investors, Bahrain's real estate sector can be best described as conventional since it is mainly focused on medium-sized residential properties in the form of apartments along the coast in addition to exclusive villa developments on reclaimed islands and scattered commercial developments. One similarity is the use of iconic shaped islands to attract the attention of investors and the general verticalization of certain districts due to rising land prices. The general scale of development sites in Bahrain is, however, reduced due to the limited size of project sites and the formation of relatively small semi-public real estate holdings with less investment capacity.

In both Dubai and Manama, new urban typologies such as residential high-rises and island projects have led to the overall transformation of urban morphologies. The redefinition of urbanism due to stimulated real estate markets has led to a new chapter of local urban development trends. While the scale of Dubai's real estate markets has never been reached in Manama or in any other Gulf city, most other GCC governments followed the general approach of liberalizing markets to attract foreign investment, extending public land via reclamation and founding semi-public holdings as developers. Real estate projects became the most important factor in redefining the image of Gulf cities, replacing the stereotypical dullness of oil cities resulting from monotonous urban typologies with a modern globalized vision in the form of emerging skylines and themed urban landscapes. Early landmark projects, such as the Burj Al Arab in Dubai, introduced a new city-branding strategy to attract global media attention. However, while in Dubai the new model of urban governance has completely reformed and replaced former conservative structures, cases like Bahrain display an increasing conflict between newly initiated development visions and the continuing social and economic realities on the ground.

The import of Dubai's strategy of rapid urban growth has led to increasingly severe division of urban and thus economic structures in Bahrain and other Gulf cities. The deterioration of certain urban areas and the lack of infrastructural supply will further increase inequity in cases like Bahrain where historic conflicts between social groups have remained. The segregation and isolation of new developments will exclude a large share of the population and the liberalized local real estate market has thus become a catalyst for an increasing gap between income groups in a fragile political environment. The capital accumulation in real estate in the Gulf in recent years has yet to be seen and analysed critically in terms of its impact on social, economic and environmental sustainability. Short-term speculative interests have turned cities into growth machines with hardly any long-term perspectives of consolidating economic growth within real estate independent sectors. Overrated growth potentials have led to high land prices, which are currently preventing a transformation from supply-driven to demand-driven development patterns. Thus, most tenants have to accept a limited variety of properties, increasing rental costs and low construction standards as well as a lack of integrated services, which diminishes the general liveability and thus attractiveness of Gulf cities.

The existing pressure on sustaining urban growth to prevent the collapse of real estate prices is mainly based on the fact that most economic sectors are directly or indirectly dependent on the construction boom. Today, it is difficult to predict how the real-estate-driven form of contemporary urbanism in some Gulf cities will transform into a new stage of consolidation. In contrast to most of its neighbours, Dubai launched its model of real-estate-driven urban growth after its establishment as a main regional trading, tourism and finance hub. The imitation of its growth strategy and the increasing competition between Gulf cities to establish post-oil economic sectors to sustain urban growth will inevitably lead to major crises of real estate markets. This can be caused, for instance, by social unrest, infrastructural collapse, lack of public investment liquidity and severe environmental problems.

Real estate can thus be identified as a conflicted catalyst of urban transformation and economic diversification in the Gulf, resulting in the phenomenon of 'instant migrant cities' based on speculative incentives rather than on developing knowledge economies leading to urban consolidation. While Dubai might be able to completely recover from the first severe real estate crisis of 2008 and preserve a dynamic real estate market due to its role as a major regional hub, several cities, including Manama, are expected to face a variety of challenges to prevent the scenario of a non-recovering real estate bubble and subsequent long-term economic recession.

Conclusion

Real estate has become one of the most favoured commodities in Gulf cities. While trading pearls led to first port cities in the nineteenth century, trading oil and gas led to expanding cities with one of the lowest average urban densities worldwide. The recent trading with real estate as part of mega projects has led to a diversity of themed worlds inviting for leisure and consumption, but hardly integrating any sense of community and neighbourhood. The exponential real estate prices have furthermore led to a continuous increase of rental rates leading to an enhanced social segregation and the coexistence of high vacancy rates and over-occupied properties, particularly in the case of more dated projects. Both the under-occupation due to high rental prices and the over-occupation due to single migrants sharing apartments or villas have led to disparities from area to area and thus often to insufficient infrastructure supply.

The new role of real estate as investment opportunity in Gulf cities has attracted both regional and global attention and has thus undoubtedly led to a diversification of local economies. In 2013, the Gulf Organisation for Industrial Consulting (GOIC) estimated that only the building materials sector's investments were around US$34.5 billion, which was equal to 9.3 per cent of the total industrial investments. The sector employed nearly 234,000 workers in all GCC countries (17 per cent of the overall industrial workforce) and operated 2,741 plants (17.5 per cent of the total factories).[45] These figures document the large share of how construction industries have become important indicators of not only economic growth but also growth dependencies. Thus, the GOIC also states that GCC construction industries heavily rely on the continuous revenues of oil and gas exports to finance major infrastructure projects. The price drop of crude oil by more than 50 per cent since 2014 has resulted in a new price environment and thus fiscal deficits. However, large financial buffers and low debt levels in most Gulf States would enable further investments in infrastructure to sustain urban growth.[46]

The dependencies between construction industries and oil and gas revenues can still be considered highly significant, as a recent report pointed out, 'The GCC has some way to go before it becomes really diversified. It scored 38% in 2012, which is below all other regions and well below the global average of 58%.'[47] While the UAE scored highest with 57 per cent, it also benefited from investments in local trade and tourism and thus indirectly from regional oil and gas revenues. The reinvestment of these revenues in building new cities for millions stems from a clear development vision for an economic transformation towards service centres. While the initiation of these city projects has instantly diversified local economies due to the need for advanced producer services, such as financial sectors, which are usually related to construction and urban growth, another dimension is the enhanced regional and global connectivity enabling emerging hubs rooted in trade, tourism and transit.

In general, the implemented property-led development strategies in the Gulf can be understood as important incentives to become connected hubs and thus integrated markets. Three main pillars of this particular strategy need to be distinguished: First, ports and airports including major new airlines have established the required global and regional connectivity. Second, free trade zones and liberalized real estate markets have been launched to attract investment. Third, mega projects in the form of real estate and international events (e.g. sports) have reshaped the image of Gulf cities as tourism destinations and centres for leisure and major business opportunities. The speed and scale of developing these new hub cities have only been possible due to the still remaining oil and gas wealth in the region and the geopolitical location, which enabled the access to labourers from South Asia as well as the opportunity to attract skilled workforce from the wider Middle East and worldwide.

In many ways, it can be argued that the established economies rooted in trade and transit between global markets would require significantly smaller settlements than currently developed. But the ignited construction boom led to new market dynamics within major urban agglomerations, which heavily rely on further investment. The main reason for this dependency can be identified in the rather recent development of these cities and the continuous exchange of their migrant populations. The vision of emerging knowledge economies, which can sustain these migrant cities would require social and economic consolidation. In many ways real estate has diversified local economies, but at the same time it has led to growth dependency, which is contradicting the original vision to establish well-connected and self-sustained markets. Instead of promoting the bottom-up growth of small-scale entrepreneurialism, sizeable holdings and their mega projects have dominated spatial and economic development and thus emphasized the segregation of urban landscapes instead of integrating an important balance between local economic development and global connectivity.

As Saskia Sassen pointed out, the rise of cities has been the consequence of a major structural transformation rooted in information and communication technologies since the 1980s.[48] The new advanced producer services rooted in highly concentrated information and inter-human interaction led to service hubs within rapidly expanding global networks. In many ways, urban developments in the form of mega projects and events were first indicators of the growing significance of certain cities in the developed world. Thus, all major global cities witnessed the rise of new landmark projects representing the prosperity and concentration of highly complex activities within emerging intermediate economies. In parallel, however, many social groups could hardly be integrated, and new socio-spatial inequalities have been observed worldwide reflected by the increasing quantity of poorly paid jobs in lower service sectors and the replacement of lower-income groups due to gentrification tendencies.

The concentration of populations in well-connected cities has however led to new densities enabling rapid knowledge and information exchange resulting in the phenomenon of urban manufacturing, which has become an essential driver for a long-term diversification and consolidation of urban economies in developed countries. The enhanced initiatives of inhabitants to gain their share of the concentrated economic activities led to highly complex networks, built on creativity and innovation. Today, these urban manufacturing networks are perceived as important but hardly measurable assets, which have been challenging urban governance worldwide to integrate their needs. The Gulf region, in comparison, has been a very particular phenomenon, where mega projects have been initiated as drivers for economic transformation rather than as a consequence of already established intermediate service economies. Subsequently, the impact of these mega projects on economic development has mainly been further growth dependency in construction-related sectors as well as tourism and international trade.

While mega projects had a significant impact on the overall perception of Gulf cities as potential hubs during the first years of the construction boom, the enhanced media attention has also highlighted the main contradiction of these new developments. Mega projects have only been possible by employing cheap construction workers from developing countries and most emerging service sectors, such as retail and tourism, have become highly dependent on foreigners and their comparatively moderate salary expectations. Thus, urbanism in the Gulf has become overnight a representation of new tendencies within globalized capitalism and the demand for new and rapidly growing consumption centres in highly controlled environments. The state-of-the-art infrastructure and the strict top-down control have enabled a rather particular decentralization and privatization, which resulted in entities managing big shares of urban developments without being responsible for any social concerns. Mega projects have formed the core of all these semi-public holdings and attracted the large share of attention while implicitly representing a new form of urbanism built on spectacles and speculative tendencies rather than consolidating and diversifying local economies.

Notes

1   Jonathan V. Beaverstock, 'World City Networks 'From Below': International Mobility and Inter-city Relations in the Global Investment Banking Industry', in P. Taylor, B. Derudder, P. Saey and F. Witlox (eds), *Cities in Globalization* (London, 2007), pp. 50–69.

2   Ibid.

3   Saskia Sassen, *The Global City. New York, London, Tokyo* (Princeton, 1991).

4   Cohen, *The New International Division of Labor.*

5   Neil Brenner, 'Between Fixity and Motion. Accumulation, Territorial Organization and the Historical Geography of Spatial Scales', *Society and Space*, 16 (1998), pp. 459–81, p. 460.

6   Davidson, *Dubai: The Vulnerability of Success.*

7   David Harvey, *The Condition of Postmodernity* (Oxford, 1989).

8   Molotch, 'The City as a Growth Machine', p. 309.

9   Michael Gerrity, 'Dubai Property Correction Overshadowed by 5-Year Supply Mismatch', *World Property Journal* (8 June 2015). Available At: www.worldproper tyjournal.com/real-estate-news/dubai-uae/dubai-property-report-2015-phidar-advisory-dubai-residential-research-report-condo-prices-in-dubai-jesse-downs-914 2.php (accessed 3 December 2017).

10 Jonathan V. Beaverstock, Richard G. Smith and Peter J. Taylor. 'World City Network: A New Metageography?', *Annals of the Association of American Geographers*, 90 (2010), pp. 123–34, p. 123.

11 Fox et al., *Globalization and the Gulf.*

12 Elisabeth Blum and Peter Neitzke, *Dubai ein Zwischenbericht über die derzeit größte Baustelle der Welt* (Stuttgart, 2009).

13 The World Bank, *Population Data*, 2017. Available at: www.data.worldbank.org/country (accessed 3 December 2017).

14 Bertrand Renaud, 'Real estate Bubble and Financial Crisis in Dubai: Dynamics and Policy Responses', *Journal of Real Estate Literature*, 20/1, pp. 51–77.

15 Ashraf M. Salama and Florian Wiedmann, 'Perceiving Urban Liveability in an Emerging Migrant City' *Proceedings of the ICE - Urban Design and Planning*, 169/6 (2016), pp. 268–78.

16 Schmid, *Economy of Fascination.*

17 Wiedmann, *Post-oil Urbanism in the Gulf.*

18 Michael Pacione, 'City Profile: Dubai'. *Cities*, 22(3), pp. 255–65.

19 Mike Davis, 'Sand, Fear and Money in Dubai', in M. Davis and D. B. Monk (eds) *Evil Paradises: Dreamworlds of Neoliberalism* (New York, 2007), 49–67, p. 50.

20 Ahmed Kanna, *Dubai: The City as Corporation* (Minnesota, 2011).

21 Davidson, *Dubai: The Vulnerability of Success*, p. 129.

22 Emaar, *Emirates Hills*. Available at: www.emiratesliving.ae/en/about/communities/emirateshills.aspx (accessed 3 December 2017).

23 Dubai Internet City, *Who We Are*. Available at: www.dic.ae/who-we-are/#get_intouch (accessed 3 December 2017).

24 Dubai Pearl, *Project*. Available at: www.dubaipearl.com/about (accessed 3 December 2017).

25 Nakheel, *Palm Jumeirah*. Available at: www.nakheel.com/en/communities/palm-jumeirah (accessed 3 December 2017).

26 Emaar, *Dubai Marina Waterfront*. Available at: www.emaar.com/en/what-we-do/communities/uae/dubai-marina/ (accessed 3 December 2017).

27 Dubai Statistics Authority, *Population 2014*. Available at: www.dsc.gov.ae/Publication/Population%20Bulletin%20Emirate%20of%20Dubai%202014.pdf (accessed 3 December 2017).

28 Dubai Properties, *Jumeirah Beach Residence*. Available at: http://www.dp.ae/about-dubai-properties (accessed 3 December 2017).

29 Nakheel, *Jumeirah Heights*. Available at: www.nakheel.com/en/communities/jumeirah-heights (accessed 3 December 2017).

30 Nakheel, *Palm Jumeirah*.

31 Michael Gerrity, 'Dubai Property Correction Overshadowed by 5-year Supply Mismatch', *World Property Journal*, 8 June 2015. Available At: http://www.worldpropertyjournal.com/real-estate-news/dubai-uae/dubai-property-report-2015-phidar-advisory-dubai-residential-research-report-condo-prices-in-dubai-jesse-downs-9142.php (accessed 3 December 2017).

32 Wiedmann, *Post-oil Urbanism in the Gulf*, p. XX.

33 Scholz, *Die Kleinen Golfstaaten*, p. 83.

34 Wiedmann, *Post-oil Urbanism in the Gulf*.

35 Scholz, *Die Kleinen Golfstaaten*, p. 84.

36 Ute Meinel, *Die Intifada im Ölscheichtum Bahrain* (Münster, 2002).

37 Ben-Hamouche, 'Manama: The Metamorphosis of an Arab Gulf City', p. 187.

38 Maher Al-Shaer, *Real-Estate Developments for Economic Growth: Significance and Critical Role of Real Estate Developments in the Kingdom of Bahrain* (Saarbrücken, 2013).

39 Wiedmann, *Post-oil Urbanism in the Gulf*, p. 126.

40 Oxford Business Group, *The Report: Bahrain 2008* (Oxford, 2008), p. 145.

41 Ben-Hamouche, 'Manama: The Metamorphosis of an Arab Gulf City', p. 200.

42 Oxford Business Group, *The Report: Bahrain 2008*, p. 143.

43 Oxford Business Group, *The Report: Bahrain 2013* (Oxford, 2008), p. 29.

44 Gareth Doherty, *Paradoxes of Green: Landscapes of a City-State* (Berkeley, 2017), p. 56.

45 Virginie Clemancon, 'GCC Building Materials Industry Set to Be Challenged by the Emerging Trends in 2015', in *Deloitte GCC Powers of Construction*. Available at:

www2.deloitte.com/content/dam/Deloitte/hu/Documents/Real%20Estate/hu-real-estate-gccpoc2015-publication-eng.pdf (accessed 3 December 2017), p. 64.

46   Ibid.

47   Ernst & Young, *Digging Beneath the Surface: Is It Time to Rethink Diversification in the GCC*. Available at: http://www.ey.com/Publication/vwLUAssets/ey-is-it-time-to-rethink-diversification/$FILE/ey-is-it-time-to-rethink-diversification.pdf (accessed 3 December 2017). p. 6.

48   Sassen, 'Cities Today: A New Frontier for Major Developments', pp. 53–71.

5

New housing typologies and urban consolidation

Urban consolidation is widely identified as one of the key challenges for policy makers worldwide, since the integration of land uses and appropriate urban densities are preconditions to enhance economic activities and to reduce the waste of energy as well as to reduce traffic congestion and the resulting pollution.[1] As in most cases worldwide, fragmentation processes in the Gulf are mainly rooted in car-based urbanism and the associated suburban sprawl, which was promoted by various industries and by the general perception of privatized neighbourhoods surrounded by gardens and gates as the highest form of a modern living standard.[2] The result has been an expanding urban periphery and the dissolving clear borders between countryside and cities.[3] The urban fragmentation was further enhanced by new highway grids and the phenomenon of shopping malls contesting the historic downtowns as main retail centres.

Any suburban sprawl is the result of car-based urbanism enabling low-rise housing patterns. The first suburban settlements were direct consequences of the problematic and highly dense urban conditions in industrial cities in the nineteenth century.[4] During the 1950s, suburban typologies rapidly gained an important economic role by advertising the general idea of individual freedom as well as the need for safe surroundings and investment opportunities for inhabitants.[5] The resulting suburban landscape and its conflicted urban conditions including social isolation and shrinking spatial diversity have led to major academic resistance, particularly since the 1960s.[6] Most protesters underlined the scientific notion that suburban areas can lack the development of functioning neighbourhoods due to the restricted walkability and the widespread lack of integrated public spaces or services and thus everyday urban encounters and economic activities.[7] This was mainly caused by a large percentage of suburban areas defined by residential land use and a high quantity of private properties resulting in an increasing number of boundaries.[8]

In contrast to suburban sprawl in Western cities, suburban developments in the Gulf were not the result of any previous industrialization and dense urban patterns but the direct consequence of Western planners being responsible for preparing plans to guide the first modern urbanization period during the middle of the twentieth century.[9] Thus, the idea of 'Garden Cities' in the desert were imports, which were quickly adopted as new standards by both public policies and the preferences of local populations.[10] Like most predominantly suburban settlements, Gulf cities became mainly structured by a hierarchical road grid and a functional division of land uses.[11] The geometrical structure of these grids has led to rationalized and repetitive areas and even cul-de-sacs were used to enhance the privacy of neighbourhoods.[12] The main highways have emerged as barriers cementing the isolation and thus fragmentation of each area.

In many cities worldwide, it can be observed that once a certain scale of urban sprawl has been reached, the move of businesses and services towards the urban periphery can be investigated.[13] This phenomenon can also be studied in all major Gulf cities. In many cases, former residential buildings along main access roads have been reused as small office buildings, social facilities or shops. The scattered distribution has however hardly led to any integrated edge cities along the urban periphery, which has mainly been defined by rather mono-functional dormitory settlements and large-scale shopping malls.

As discussed in Chapter 1, two major phases of housing dynamics and urban transformation can be distinguished during the first decades of modern urbanization in Gulf cities leading to rather distinctive urban structures: first, the arrival of the rural local population and the political objective to improve living conditions of all national citizens instigated the development of single-family detached homes resulting in low-rise residential areas in the urban periphery[14] and second, the widespread move of a large part of the local population from central districts to these new suburban areas. The newly built road grid in city centres led to an extensive demolition process of traditional neighbourhoods, which often consisted of historic courtyard houses.[15] This second phase of development led to first multi-storey apartment buildings, built to accommodate international migrants, mainly from developing countries.[16] The result of this modern urbanization was an increasingly overcrowded downtown area surrounded by a sprawling low-rise periphery.[17]

Both recent investment and migration patterns have created new urban conditions challenging sustainability.[18] The initiation and accommodation of fast urban growth during a development peak in 2006 and 2007 has only been possible by a continuation of car-based urbanism.[19] Any development of a comprehensive public transit system as basis of new settlements would have significantly slowed down housing supply. Until now, only the Dubai Metro, which has been launched in 2009, can be mentioned as a certain attempt to integrate public transit on a larger scale.[20] Today, increasing traffic congestion endangers future growth perspectives in all Gulf cities and thus major planning interventions are needed to reconfigure recently built areas.[21] This chapter therefore aims to explore which typical housing patterns can be observed and how they are impacting spatial fragmentation to identify key challenges for policy makers, planners and architects. The authors therefore focus on three major districts in Bahrain's capital Manama and another three districts in Qatar's capital Doha representing all current housing typologies and urban transformation tendencies.

Manama's three urban expansions

Since the 1990s, Bahrain's capital Manama has been expanded by adding three major districts along the shorelines in the North and East.[22] These districts are known as the Seafront district, Seef district and Juffair district. According to GIS surveys, carried out by the authors in 2010, the Seafront district is stretching more than 3.2 kilometres along the northern coast covering a reclaimed area of around 1.8 square kilometres containing Manama's Central Business district, which has been built between the historic city centre and the shoreline.[23] Its current expansion areas in the north are three master-planned developments, namely, Bahrain Financial Harbour, Bahrain Bay and Reef Island, which together add an extra 1.4 square kilometres of reclaimed land to the Seafront district. It is furthermore expected that many of the currently un-built plots in the older parts of the district will be developed over the coming years in accordance with the new guidelines permitting higher built densities. All in all, the size of the overall area, available for development in the Seafront district, is around 59 hectares, of which at least 60 per cent can be developed with new high-rise projects. The recent completion of two residential towers in the western part of the district marked the beginning of a new housing trend in Manama's main business district.

While the Financial Centre, which is the first development phase of the Bahrain Financial Harbour project, has already been completed, around 33 per cent of the total gross floor area of more than one million square metres will be developed as residential. The remaining area will be mainly occupied by the commercial buildings of the Financial Centre, the Commercial East and the Commercial West.[24] All the residential projects comprise around ten towers with up to fifty floors, including the three towers of the Villamar project, which will offer around 900 apartments.[25] The Financial Centre has the highest construction ratio within the Bahrain Financial Harbour and the average plot ratio of the Bahrain Financial Harbour will be twice the density of the old urban areas of the Seafront district.

After the completion of a reclaimed area of more than 80 hectares to the east of the Bahrain Financial Harbour, the construction of Bahrain Bay covers an area of around 44 hectares. This development consists of two islands that form a man-made bay surrounding an oval island in the centre. Apart from the development area of these three islands, more than 20 hectares is needed for the construction of an outer ring road. Bahrain Bay's total gross floor area is expected to be around 1.45 million square metres spreading on a total developable lot area of just around 20 hectares. Thus, the development will be one of the most densely built urban areas in Bahrain. Around 60 per cent of the developed area will be occupied by residential units consisting of apartments. Most future residents will be accommodated in the high-rise-developments and in a project named Raffles City, which will contain a gated and lower-density neighbourhood along the inner bay.[26]

In the West of the Seafront district the construction of the Reef Island project has been carried out on an area of around 58 hectares. While the residential projects will constitute about 80 per cent of the total developable lot area, the remaining share will be occupied by hotels and commercial use. More than 90 per cent of the around 1,300 housing units are apartments within 8- to 10-storey apartment buildings (Figure 5.1). The villa developments will offer just 114 units along private beaches. However, about 43 per cent of the total lot area of Reef Island is occupied by these two-storey villas due to their large average lot size of 1,400 square metres. Thus, only around 2 per cent of Reef Island, which will be one of the most exclusive residential developments in Bahrain, will consist of green public spaces. Similarly, to the neighbouring Bahrain Financial Harbour and Bahrain Bay, the main goal of the developer of Reef Island was to develop freehold properties for the upper end of the real estate market. Thus, in addition to a high standard of security many leisure facilities have been integrated. Due to the large low-rise residential area, the average built density of Reef Island is rather moderate.[27]

While the three master-planned projects along the coast will add more than one million square metres of developable gross floor area to the Seafront

Figure 5.1 The Reef Island project.

district, the undeveloped plots within the old part of the district between King Faisal Highway and Government Avenue offer a developable area of more than 300,000 square metres. In addition to these reclaimed and un-built areas, there are plans to replace the shops and warehouses at the Central Market. In general, the new developments have doubled the built area in the Seafront district during less than ten years. In contrast to the mega projects, Bahrain Financial Harbour, Bahrain Bay and Reef Island, whose development has followed approved master plans with detailed building regulations, there has been no analogous planning for the entire Seafront district.

A general zoning plan has defined the size of the buildings for each developable lot in addition to several further requirements regarding construction, such as the provision of parking spaces. According to the current zoning, 82 per cent of the district area can be developed with Investment Buildings Type B-A, which means the permission to develop residential, commercial or administrative buildings.[28] Consequently, the district area, which is mainly occupied by commercial and administrative buildings, has begun to transform into a mixed-use area with an increasing number of residential developments. In addition to the increase in the number of residential buildings in the old area of the district, all three waterfront developments have a high percentage of residential projects. While residential use accounts for around 33 per cent of the developable area of the Bahrain Financial Harbour, it accounts for more than 60 per cent of the gross floor area of Bahrain Bay and about 80 per cent of Reef Island. Consequently, the previously commercial and administrative Seafront district will turn into a mixed-use urban centre with up to 41 per cent of the urban area occupied by residential developments.

The expected development of residential projects in the Seafront district, where only a few hundred apartments have been previously integrated, will increase the population of the district to a maximum of approximately 70,000 future residents. Due to high land prices, the Seafront district has become one of Bahrain's prime locations for exclusive real estate developments targeting the upper end of the freehold property market. The subsequent high rental prices will turn the district into a residential area for upper-income groups mainly consisting of foreign guest workers. Apart from foreign tenants, a significant share of apartments is expected to be bought by GCC nationals, such as Saudis, who often visit Bahrain for business or leisure. To attract these very particular future residents and property investors, the projects must integrate a high standard of security and privacy in addition to leisure and shopping facilities. While the low-rise projects on Reef Island will be gated communities, all the Seafront district's residential towers will be guarded individually. Its location in the centre of the business district and its short distance from the causeway to Saudi Arabia and the causeway to the airport in Muharraq make the Seafront district attractive for upmarket real estate.[29]

In future, the biggest challenges will be the development of links between the different urban areas and the creation of an adequate infrastructural backbone, particularly regarding the expansion of the road network to meet the demands of the population's high dependency on the car and increasing urban densities.[30] The rapidly growing number of vehicles has led to heavy traffic congestion within certain district areas such as, for example, the Diplomatic Quarter, where the densely built environment is giving rise to increasing congestion and a lack of parking space. Furthermore, King Faisal Highway is threatened by growing traffic jams due to its function as a main access road linking the new mega projects as well as connecting the main island with Al Muharraq and the causeway to Saudi Arabia. Manama's Seafront district is a typical example of the current urbanism in Bahrain and in the Gulf, which is on the one hand characterized by rapid urban growth due to foreign investments and on the other hand an evident lack of comprehensive regulation to establish integrated developments.

Apart from the Seafront district, the Seef district has witnessed a rapid transformation during recent years. At the time when the Sheikh Khalifa Bin Salman Causeway to Saudi Arabia was developed during the 1980s, a new area of more than 5 square kilometres was reclaimed in the north of Sanabis to compensate Bahraini citizens who had lost their land due to the construction of new highways. Although the area has been subdivided and basic infrastructure was provided, very few developments were built in the following decades. At the end of the twentieth century, two residential areas in the west along the borders of the old fishing village Karbabad and in the south covered an area of around 50 hectares. These residential areas were built according to the guidelines of the first land-use plan, which divided the area into two large residential areas on each side of a central commercial area stretching from north to south.[31] While the residential areas were restricted to low-rise dwellings, investors could build medium-rise commercial buildings in the centre of the Seef district. However, most of the district remained undeveloped during the following decades due to a lack of investment interest.

After the Jidd Hafs Governorate was dissolved in 2002, the Seef district became part of the Capital Governorate and thus an urban expansion area of Manama. Since the completion of the King Fahad Causeway to Saudi Arabia, Bahrain's shopping tourism was gradually increasing, which led to the development of several shopping malls. At the same time the introduction of the freehold property market marked a significant turning point for the development of the Seef district. Its fortunate location and accessibility has led to a growing interest from the private sector to develop commercial and residential projects. Thus, despite the initial zoning plan, which envisioned the district as a suburban area with a medium-rise commercial centre, the Seef district has recently begun transforming into one of Manama's major business districts and fastest growing development areas. Subsequently, additional land has been reclaimed in the east to establish a direct link to the Seafront district.

As well as the shopping malls along the highway the main commercial centre of the Seef district is in the northern part, where most of the thirty-two high-rise buildings are located. There are currently more than 100 completed buildings in the northern district area, which includes commercial developments such as the 47-storey Al Moyyad Tower (Figure 5.2). Due to previous restrictions on the maximum number of floors, the current average height of all multi-storey buildings is between eight and ten floors. While commercial buildings either contain banks or telecommunications companies, residential developments are mainly leased to foreign guest workers with higher incomes.

Today, only around 30 per cent of the developable lot area has been developed. In the east, a new developable area of around 77 hectares has been recently reclaimed. Thus, the total developable area of the Seef district has almost doubled.

Figure 5.2 The fragmented urban development in the Seef district.

Because of different zoning in the past and the slow development of the Seef district during the 1980s and 1990s, many old buildings, mainly villas, interrupt the built environment, which is becoming more and more dominated by new high-rise projects. According to the current land-use plan the zoning of most developable areas in the north of the district has been changed from exclusively suburban residential zoning to mid-rise or high-rise investment buildings that can be developed as both residential and commercial freehold properties.[32]

Apart from its function as a centre of financial and telecommunication business, five large-scale shopping malls have turned the Seef district into Bahrain's main location for shopping. Furthermore, many expatriates working in the Eastern Province of Saudi Arabia are choosing to live in the Seef district due to Bahrain's more liberal society. Thus, despite recent economic problems in the real estate sector, a large-scale waterfront project is still being constructed, known as Water Garden City, and many new tower projects have been launched. The widespread development of these high-rise projects is in clear contrast to the initial plan to develop low-rise suburban areas. Consequently, the previously designed and partly built infrastructure has become more and more insufficient. Most high-rise projects integrate multi-storey car parks on their first floors to meet regulations (Figure 5.3). This policy however led to a decreased quality in the built environment and the additional building height has created higher densities. In general, the lack of public spaces has become a major threat to the development of the Seef district, which has emerged as a rather scattered urban landscape consisting of new high-rise projects that do not respond to their built surroundings.

Figure 5.3 Residential tower with integrated car park.

The third major urban expansion of Manama is known as the Juffair district, named after a former fishing village. Historically, the area has gained a significant role due the construction of the port Mina Salman, which was developed on reclaimed land in the south-east of Juffair in 1962, and the relocation of the US Navy to a former British military base at the end of the 1970s.[33] Furthermore, the district's development into a preferred residential area of expatriates was caused by the establishment of the first free economic zone in the south of Manama and convenient accessibility thanks to Al Fateh Highway, which was completed at the end of the 1980s. One of the first official zoning plans of the Juffair district was prepared in the course of the master plan of Manama from 1988, which included the basic road network in the form of Shabab Avenue. At the same time as the early infrastructure development during the 1980s, one of Bahrain's most prestigious modern landmarks, the Al Fateh Mosque, was built opposite Al Qudaybiyah Palace. During the 1990s several additional areas were reclaimed. It is characteristic of land reclamation in Juffair that rather small areas were gradually reclaimed instead of reclaiming one large cohesive area.

Between 2003 and 2008 the area of Juffair was expanded from 2.6 to more than 3 square kilometres via further land reclamation. The gradual process of reclaiming new plots has caused the current patchwork-like appearance and the transforming geometric form of the coastline. Today, Juffair's total lot area, which has been developed since the 1970s, is around 2 square kilometres, of which around 40 per cent is built. All in all, there are more than 900 completed residential buildings in Juffair, of which more than half are low-rise dwellings in compounds in the east of the district. The remaining buildings are multi-storey apartment buildings and high-rises. All residential buildings occupy more than 84 per cent of the developed lot area.

In recent years, thirty-seven exclusive residential high-rise developments were added to the Juffair district. These projects are representative of a new trend of luxury real estate projects sold as freehold properties. While the previous approach was to develop properties that were intended to be leased mainly to companies, to the US military or directly to guest workers, the new developments particularly target investors from GCC countries, who would often use apartments as holiday homes. As luxury residential developments, all projects provide certain services and integrated security or leisure facilities such as twenty-four-hour-guarded lobbies, indoor and outdoor pools, health clubs and even cafes and restaurants. In some cases, there are special facilities such as theatres, spas and mini-supermarkets.

Since the US Navy Base was one of the main factors that led to the real estate boom in Juffair between 2001 and 2008, landlords are often dependent on tenants from the US Navy and its employees. After a minor incident, where there was an attempt to attack US soldiers, a new regulation was implemented in 2005 stating that any building can only have a maximum of 25 per cent of its apartments occupied by US Navy personnel due to security concerns.[34] This major change led to an increasing demand for new developments and thus a lower occupancy rate. Thus, despite higher rents, costs have been increasing due to high letting agency fees. Furthermore, there is a competition between relatively new buildings offering luxury residential units. In general, the average rental prices have significantly increased. The result of the enhanced rental prices has been the relocation of lower-income tenants to more affordable districts. Today, only few apartment buildings were specifically built to house labourers in the lower end of the service sector (Figure 5.4).

In addition to be the home of the US Navy, Juffair has become an attractive residential area for the staff of companies working in the business centres of the main island or the industrial areas in Sitra and the south of Al Muharraq. This has made Juffair Bahrain's most intensely concentrated area of expatriate residents with middle incomes. In recent years, the biggest challenge of landlords and investors in Juffair has been the relocation of tenants to the Seef district due to the proximity to the business centre in Manama. This particularly concerns

Figure 5.4 Labour housing in Juffair.

employees of the financial and telecommunications sectors. Moreover, real estate projects in new and less populated areas such as Amwaj Islands are further increasing the real estate competition in Bahrain. Thus, many of the former tenants of properties in Juffair, such as Gulf Air staff, have relocated to other districts due to better facilities or more convenient accessibility. Another major threat to the future of real estate in Juffair is that it is still dependent on tenants from the US Navy, whose relocation and future scale cannot be predicted.

A further threat to Juffair's development is a growing lack of infrastructure, service facilities and public spaces. While the retail strip in the south along Shabab Avenue has been growing continuously in recent years due to restaurants, coffee shops and retail outlets, the development of public squares, parks and pedestrian zones has been completely neglected. One small playground is currently the only public green area in the oldest part of the district, where it was established by the district's very first zoning plan from the 1980s.[35] Furthermore, walking in the district is difficult due to partly unpaved walkways and inefficient waste

Figure 5.5 The urban realm between residential tower blocks in Juffair.

collection, which has led to cluttered sidewalks and thus a growing population of stray dogs and cats. Another reason for the decreasing quality of the built environment is the short distances of sometimes less than 5 metres between multi-storey buildings causing shaded and badly ventilated areas due to the fact that the initial physical planning of the district was done for low- to medium-rise buildings (Figure 5.5). The change in the former zoning plan involving the permission to construct high-rise buildings has led to an insufficiency in infrastructural capacity, particularly regarding the road network. Similar to the Seef district, recent high-rise projects integrate multi-storey car parks with up to six floors. This is leading to a pedestrian-unfriendly urban environment and hardly any potential to integrate other uses.

The spatial transformation of Manama

The general trend of reclaiming new land along shorelines for new developments has led to the reclamation of about 4 square kilometres since 1998. Thus, the overall urban area of Manama has expanded by more than 15 per cent to

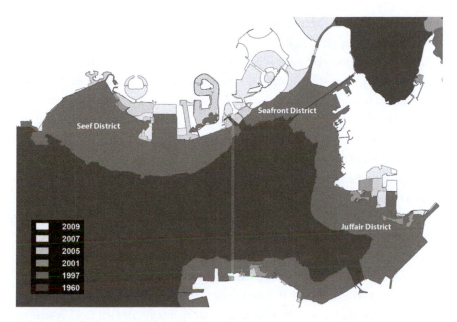

Figure 5.6 The historic land reclamation in Manama.

almost 31 square kilometres (Figure 5.6). A further consequence of the recent construction boom has been an exponential increase in land prices, which has again contributed to less investment in old parts of Manama due to low profit expectations. All in all, there has been a clear shift and transformation of the urban development towards more and more densely built areas along the coast with a still high percentage of around 40 per cent of un-built land in the old urban areas of Manama. In general, three preferred housing typologies can be distinguished in the form of densely built tower blocks, exclusive waterfront towers and low-rise dwellings in gated environments.

While in the north the Seafront district and the Seef district have turned into mixed-use urban areas with large commercial projects and a growing number of residential developments, some areas such as Juffair are mainly residential, with residential projects occupying up to 90 per cent. In the case of the Seafront district, the area was almost exclusively occupied by administrative and commercial buildings until recently, when the first residential towers were completed. In future, many residential areas will be part of the three master-planned developments along the coast, where the developments are occupied to a large extent by residential projects. In comparison to the Seafront district, which is turning into a mixed-use urban centre due to current residential developments, the Seef district, which was previously designed to be mainly a residential area, has become more and more attractive for the relocation of companies and shopping malls.

Thus, the previous land-use division of residential and commercial areas has recently begun to transform in the north of Manama. The mix of land uses has been less restricted or controlled due to a general zoning plan that permits investors to develop most areas according to their choice of residential or commercial projects. The consequence has been a concentration of specific uses or certain kinds of developments in particular locations. Examples are the cluster of shopping malls in the Seef district due to the proximity of the causeway to Saudi Arabia or the vast amount of residential tower projects in Juffair due to the proximity to the US Navy Base. Thus, despite overall mixed-use tendencies on a macro scale, many district areas have remained rather mono-functional reflecting the urban past and remaining car dependency. In contrast to the rezoned urban expansion areas, the three waterfront projects integrate commercial services along public promenades. But despite the growing integration of commercial and leisure facilities, there has been a big lack of accessible social facilities because of increasing land prices and missing regulations.

Apart from a lack of social services, very few areas have been reserved for the development of public spaces, such as parks and promenades along shorelines. While the Seafront district has around 20 hectares of green area in the form of a large seaside park, which is however difficult to be accessed by pedestrians, there is only around 1.5 hectares of public spaces in the Seef district and just one public playground in Juffair. Furthermore, in contrast to the integration of semi-public promenades within the three master-planned developments along the coast, there has been no plan to develop public promenades along the shorelines in Juffair and Seef. This is mainly because of ongoing land reclamation and various landowners who prefer to sell seaside lots to private investors.

In addition to the lack of development of public spaces, the development of utilities and road networks has not kept pace with the rapid construction of real estate, particularly in the case of urban areas where the zoning plan has recently been changed and now permits the development of much higher built densities. The ring of highways along the coast, which links all the current development areas, has become more and more congested with traffic because of both the fast population growth and missing public transit alternatives. The lack of parking spaces led to the common phenomenon of using un-built land or sidewalks as improvised informal parking sites. And new building regulations led to integrated multi-storey car parks in the case of tower projects resulting in rejective environments for pedestrians.

Based on the current zoning plan, most of the developable areas along the coast can be built with high-rise projects with construction ratios of 750 per cent and in some cases even 1,200 per cent of the lot area. Consequently, more and more commercial and residential high-rises have been developed. While in the Seafront district including the Diplomatic Quarter more than 30 towers have been built, there has been the development of around 73 high-rise buildings in the Seef district and around 241 of these buildings in Juffair. At the beginning of the construction boom the average building height was about ten floors, which is almost half the average height of recent projects. More than 75 per cent of all current developments are occupied by residential use, leading to an urban density increase to approximately 150 to 200 residents per hectare in Manama's new urban expansions. In comparison to the old urban area of Manama that has an average urban density of around fifty-three residents per hectare, the newly developed areas will become some of the most densely populated areas in all of Bahrain. According to the authors' calculations, more than 100,000 future housing units could be integrated according to current regulations and the average urban density could thus increase to more than 300 residents per hectare in all expansion areas (Figure 5.7).

Most of the recently developed real estate projects consist of luxury apartments with comparatively high average rental rates. Due to these high rents most of the new areas have been populated by expatriates with middle and high incomes. Thus, in addition to the increasing social segregation of income groups, there

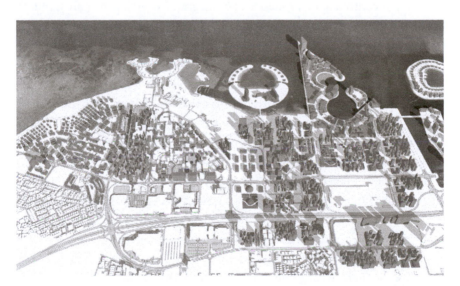

Figure 5.7 A simulation of potential future developments in the Seef district.

has been an ongoing segregation between local and migrant populations. To attract high-income groups there has been an increasing number of projects offering sea views and integrated leisure facilities. Furthermore, most luxurious residential developments are designed to be gated communities, for example, the villas on Reef Island or the various compounds in Juffair. In the case of residential high-rise buildings, guards guarantee the safety and exclusivity of the residences. In addition to the trend of integrating amenities, there has been a growing competition to outshine rival developments by designing landmark architecture with building heights beyond fifty floors.

In contrast to the construction of competing high-rise projects and a more and more densely built urban environment, clear guidelines have been implemented in the form of separate master plans for the Bahrain Financial Harbour, Reef Island and Bahrain Bay. In addition to specifying the maximum developable ground floor area, the master plans of these projects, which were designed by individual master developers, include clear restrictions on building heights and uses. Consequently, these master-planned developments follow certain intentional urban design standards introduced by worldwide renowned planners, such as Skidmore, Owings & Merrill or Atkins. However, despite the detailed planning of these island developments, there has been a lack of comprehensive planning regarding any response to adjacent developments and the former urban area. Thus, the main waterfront of Manama is composed of three individually designed projects with clearly defined borders and thus they do not contribute to a cohesive and integrated overall urban area. In fact, they are developing into rather exclusive residential areas with few integrated commercial developments such as shopping malls or office towers.

The recent construction boom led to the enormous urban growth of Manama, where around 20 per cent of Bahrain's development area is located. Because of their accessibility and connectivity, the coastal areas of Manama became more and more attractive for real estate developers and thus despite many un-built areas and obsolete buildings in the centre of Manama, the development trend has focused on the coast, leading to a large number of construction sites between the coastline and the outer ring road. The built density in the old districts however has remained rather consistent due to rising land prices and a lack of interest from investors in developing projects in outdated and rather isolated areas because of lower profit expectations. This competitive aspect of the private sector, which has taken over the main direction of the current urban development, is leading to a more and more densely built frame around Manama and the focus on newly reclaimed areas.

Hence, the view of Manama's skyline from the centre to the coast is of increasing building heights from an average of around three floors in the centre to an average of around six to eight floors in the transition zone, which was developed between the 1970s and 1980s, and finally to an average of over eleven floors along the coast where several landmarks reach heights of up to fifty floors. This transformation from the previous development trend during the first phase of modern urbanization, wherein mainly low-rise suburban areas were built along urban peripheries to the current densification along coastal areas due to the construction of residential high-rises, is one of the two main characteristics of the contemporary form of urbanism in Bahrain. The second is the development of large-scale master-planned projects in the form of man-made islands shaping and shifting both new waterfronts and urban identities.

New development dynamics in Doha

Like Manama, Qatar's capital Doha has witnessed rapid development and transformation during recent years. According to GIS calculations and a review of historic satellite images, the total residential area of metropolitan Doha almost doubled from around 109 to 198 square kilometres during a period of rapid growth between 2004 and 2017. The largest percentage of the total residential area is covered by suburban typologies (Figure 5.8). But due to new zoning regulations in previous suburban areas, the share of apartment buildings and towers increased. Furthermore, new waterfront projects were launched, adding entire districts along the Northern shoreline. The current land-use distribution reveals that almost 90 per cent of all residential areas are occupied by low-rise and the remaining 10 per cent by medium- to high-rise developments, of which a large percentage have been built during recent years. In general, three new housing patterns can be identified in the case of Doha: (1) The high-density clusters of apartment buildings in former suburban areas, such as the Al Sadd district along the C-Ring Road; (2) waterfront projects on reclaimed land, such as the West Bay district and the Pearl project along the Northern shoreline and (3) finally, large-scale clusters of compounds along growth corridors, such as the Al Waab district close by the Doha Expressway.

Since 2004, large former suburban areas in proximity to the historic cores and commercial districts have transformed into medium- to high-density neighbourhoods. In most cases, such as the districts developed along the C-Ring Road, the low-rise neighbourhoods were previously urban periphery and have

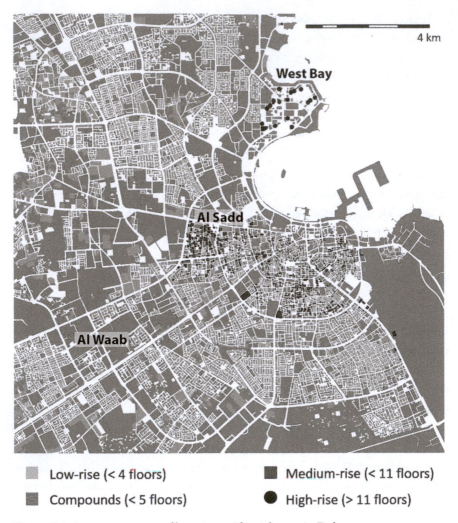

Low-rise (< 4 floors)

Compounds (< 5 floors)

Medium-rise (< 11 floors)

High-rise (> 11 floors)

Figure 5.8 Large percentage of low-rise residential areas in Doha.

gained new roles as central areas due to the continuous urban growth towards inland. The districts with newly gained centralities are transitional areas between mixed-use and commercial downtown areas and suburbs. In general, the typical housing typology is the apartment block or tower with an average height of up to eleven floors.

Similar to transforming districts in Manama, the uncoordinated development of high-density housing typologies in areas previously planned for suburban typologies has led to a rather scattered urban landscape with a lack of public realm and green areas in Doha. The low distances between buildings have restricted the supply of daylight and ventilation. The general lack of affordable housing has furthermore caused an overpopulation of these areas due to the tendency of shared apartments in the case of single migrant workers. Both the high density and the general lack of efficient public transportation led to increased traffic congestion and to a chaotic parking situation in most areas. One of the most prominent examples of a recently transformed suburban area is the Al Sadd district, which is located at a very important central junction.

Mega projects are a further development trend and can be observed along Doha's Northern coasts. They have transformed coastal lines due to continuous land reclamation and the addition of a new housing typology – the exclusive residential high-rise. While in the past high-income groups resided in villas and compounds, the exclusive waterfront projects have begun to offer an attractive alternative to the suburban lifestyle. The sea view and the integration of various amenities and services have attracted international investors to Doha. The high rents and the phenomenon of only temporarily used holiday homes led to rather moderate occupancy rates in most of these developments.[36] In addition to exclusive high-rises, most waterfront projects include other housing typologies and semi-public promenades, as well as hotel resorts to attract tourism. The West Bay district is located on a previously reclaimed area, which was originally designed as 'diplomatic quarter' to accommodate embassies and suburban typologies. Due to its prominent location at the Northern shoreline of the Corniche, many high-rise projects reshaped and redefined Doha's waterfront. Further mega projects along waterfronts can be found further north, where the Pearl island project has been built and the Lusail City was launched as new satellite settlement.[37]

The third development trend is that of the peripheral large-scale compound projects. While in the past compounds hardly exceeded beyond a certain scale, the new developments can cover areas of more than 30 hectares. These mega compounds and compound clusters integrate a variety of services depending on their sizes and are often themed and sometimes referred to as small cities within the city. Due to the general expansion of highway networks and the relatively lower land prices, a large share of the rapidly increasing housing demand has been covered by this suburban typology. Since 2004, new clusters of individual compound sites have been built, particularly in the Western urban periphery of Doha, such as the Al Waab district. Due to the infrastructural extension for the Asian Games in 2006, many new compound projects were launched, which have formed a landscape of sprawling low-rise typologies with an average building height of two to three floors offering a mixture of attached and detached dwellings behind gated walls.

In summary, the three main housing patterns have transformed Doha and its metropolitan surroundings into more complex urban landscapes. The previous monocentral structures of central mixed-use districts surrounded by a low-rise urban periphery have been modified by three main development tendencies. The urban fringes of downtown areas witnessed a rapid replacement of former suburban structures in the form of high-density apartment buildings and commercial developments. Subsequently, the new waterfront projects integrated new leisure spaces as well as high-rises as new residential typology. Finally, the continuously sprawling suburban typologies led to the phenomenon of large compound clusters in proximity to emerging edge cities. The main result of the recent spatial transformation of Doha is that the overall integration of residential areas has significantly decreased on a district scale. This lower level of spatial integration and accessibility is mainly the result of the large-scale expansion of highway networks towards the urban periphery leading to major barriers and fewer connections between neighbouring districts.[38]

Due to the new level of connectivity of all major ring roads, many commercial developments relocated from downtown areas towards C-Ring Road. The Al Sadd district has thus witnessed a rather rapid replacement of former low-rise residential buildings and has emerged as a mixed-use business centre. But despite its enhanced global accessibility, a large percentage of all inner access roads within the Al Sadd district have lost a significant share of their integration on a local scale. Despite its large-scale tower projects, the West Bay district has not evolved as an accessible business district and has remained urban periphery due to its isolated location at the end of the Corniche.[39] Subsequently, many initially planned commercial towers have been replaced by residential developments, particularly along the Northern half of the district. The Al Waab district and its cluster of major compounds has benefited from the general shift of centralities towards the Western outskirts and the expansion of the new highway grid. The Doha Expressway, in particular, has enabled many suburban areas to be rather accessible on a metropolitan scale. It however spatially divided many districts and their inner areas have become rather isolated, which has resulted in less commercial developments and services within inner district areas.

While the Al Sadd district can benefit from a highly integrated C-Ring Road, the West Bay district suffers from the absence of any highly integrated road network. Thus, the West Bay district has remained part of Doha's spatial periphery despite large-scale developments attracting movements. In addition, the modern high-rise district also suffers from a rather poor local integration with hardly any major grid enabling a clear orientation rooted in main corridors for pedestrians. The main reason for this spatial layout is the large shopping mall complex in the centre of the district, which is occupying a large percentage of central areas and which has enforced the development of a road network disabling sufficient connections and a better distribution of thorough traffic towards the district's periphery.[40]

The urban morphologies of the Al Waab district reveal a high level of accessibility due to major highways connecting the district to all major sites within Doha. The district however suffers from a rather low spatial integration on a local scale with hardly any major access roads, which can be easily reached from all areas. The compound structure has led to a clear isolation of most areas and thus a rather hindered integration of shared future services. The high dependency on shopping malls along highways rather than local neighbourhood centres is further exacerbated by the rather low urban densities.

In summary, all three districts suffer from a problematic spatial layout disabling the immediate attraction of commercial and leisure activities along integrated central corridors due to previous or still present suburban structures. Since 2004, main highways have been added or extended, leading to isolated and detached inner district areas. The contemporary road networks thus reveal a lot of long distant connections, but no sufficient number of medium links between neighbourhoods. Rapid growth and car-based urbanism have led to basic primary and tertiary road networks, but the secondary one, needed for establishing district centres, is rather absent and is the result of fast development and missing public transit.

The resulting urban fragmentation in Doha

To understand the level of urban fragmentation in Doha, general movement patterns of inhabitants need to be introduced.[41] The travel routes of all respondents to a questionnaire survey in 2013 were analysed depending on the location of their residences and subsequently mapped via GIS (Figure 5.9).[42] Due to various commercial developments along the C-Ring Road the travel distances for shopping are with an average of 6.1 kilometres the lowest in the case of residents residing in high-density transition zones, such as the Al Sadd district. The travel distance is however still rather high, which is mainly caused by the lack of walkability leading to many residents travelling by car. The favoured leisure spaces are shopping malls in the periphery, which is leading to an average travel distance of 7.5 kilometres of all interviewees in this group. Thus, the lack of integrated leisure spaces in direct proximity to these highly populated areas

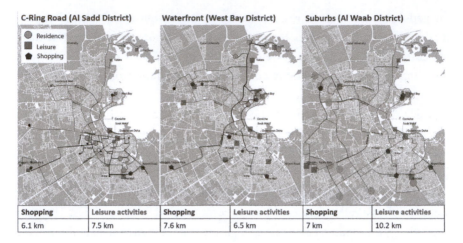

C-Ring Road (Al Sadd District)		Waterfront (West Bay District)		Suburbs (Al Waab District)	
Shopping	**Leisure activities**	**Shopping**	**Leisure activities**	**Shopping**	**Leisure activities**
6.1 km	7.5 km	7.6 km	6.5 km	7 km	10.2 km

Figure 5.9 The travel routes of questionnaire respondents residing in three differing areas.

has led to a rather frequent commuting towards the urban periphery and coastal areas to meet friends and spend leisure time outdoors.

The questionnaire respondents residing in high-rise apartments along the waterfront differ from participants residing in transition areas mainly due to the shorter travel distances regarding preferred leisure spaces. The average of 6.5 kilometres and the evaluation of the various routes have led to the conclusion that a larger share of participants are satisfied with the leisure spaces in their direct surroundings. There is however still a significant number of travel routes to big shopping mall complexes and the historic centre. The lack of affordable shopping opportunities has led to long distance commutes towards inland. Thus, in the case of shopping, interviewees commute more than 7.6 kilometres, which is the longest distance in comparison to all other resident groups.

In the case of the new compounds along the urban periphery, the overall longest travel distances can be detected. The participants residing in suburbs need to travel long distances for their commutes to favoured and frequently visited leisure spaces, such as hotels, waterfront promenades or the restored historic centre. By tracking travel routes an average travel distance of 10.2 kilometres was calculated due to leisure activities. In the case of shopping, residents must travel an average of 7 kilometres. This is a clear indication of the lack of supermarkets in most suburban neighbourhoods and the high level of dependence on shopping mall complexes.

The survey outcomes suggest that the recently built residential developments within the transition areas along the C-Ring Road, at the newly emerging waterfronts and along the suburban periphery, currently lack a balanced integration of services needed to minimize car travels. The frequent commutes for everyday shopping and leisure activities are contributing to traffic congestions and thus, a generally endangered liveability. The extension of highways and shopping mall clusters, aiming at accommodating the increasing demand, has furthermore led to a car-centred lifestyle, experiencing the city on a global rather than district scale. Thus, the main share of the highly mobile and international workforce commute far distances for everyday activities, which is a clear indication for the lack of integrated and sufficiently attractive district and neighbourhood centres.

The juxtaposition of all analysed travel routes and the overall spatial context reveals that recent urban development patterns have led to rather few concentrations of activities. The prioritization of the direct accessibility via highways has hindered the development of more integrated district centres and thus a higher diversity of frequently visited places. Thus, there is a high dependency on three major shopping mall complexes, which have replaced the historic downtown areas as retail centres and as main meeting points for all income groups. The two main public leisure spaces, frequently visited by questionnaire respondents, are the Corniche and the Souq Waqif. The overall selection of only ten main locations for leisure and shopping activities among questionnaire interviewees living in three rather differing urban areas is a further proof for the missing development of functioning district centres surrounded by neighbourhoods.

Conclusion

As in the case of all urban transformation processes, the investigations of certain development patterns can reveal various contexts as well as prospects of new tendencies.[43] Since 2004 three main housing developments and resulting urban typologies can be distinguished in Gulf cities: the high-density transition zones between downtown and suburban areas; the exclusive waterfront projects as new landmarks and homes of higher-income groups and the sprawling suburban landscape made of themed and gated compounds. Both Manama's three urban expansions and Doha's Al Sadd, West Bay and Al Waab district are important cases exhibiting the new development tendencies. All districts have been built in their present form during the last fifteen years. And all six districts share that they were previously envisioned as suburban extensions. Thus, the road networks as well as the distributed land uses and services were planned for lower urban densities. The case studies have revealed a problematic spatial layout on a local neighbourhood scale offering hardly any highly integrated and accessible corridors for resident activities in all districts. The focus on developing new highways or the expansion of existing highways, as the outer ring road of Manama, has led to an enhanced isolation of inner district areas due to the missing integration of secondary access roads.

The examined everyday commutes of inhabitants in Doha illustrate the high level of mobility of medium- and high-income groups and the preference to visit far distant locations by car. This detachment from the surrounding districts underlines the general failure of recent developments to establish integrated urban areas. The increase of commercial activities in more walkable distances is furthermore challenged by the concentration of few and far-off retail centres in highly accessible locations along major highways. This urban condition is particularly problematic in densely populated urban areas, such as the Al Sadd district in Doha or the Juffair district in Manama, where the daily traffic congestions have begun to reduce the attractiveness of these districts with high development potentials as functioning urban spaces due to appropriate urban densities. The compound clusters in the Al Waab district and in the east of the Juffair district or the gated communities on Reef Island have led to highly fragmented landscapes of disconnected patchworks rather than coherent districts, since gates and walls have prevented any identifiable centre or shared public realm.

In summary, each new housing pattern has not by itself promoted the emergence of self-contained and integrated developments. The predictable synergies between car-based urbanism and rapid urban growth led to a high level of activities concentrated in very few and scattered areas. The main challenge of contemporary urban planning in Gulf cities therefore lies in reconfiguring urban structures via transit-oriented development initiatives, which enable increased densities at key junctions and integrated instead of isolated district cores. The former car-driven urban development needs to be gradually replaced by establishing efficient public transportation. The precondition for new transit systems is however the enhanced access to inner district areas, which implies a modification of general spatial patterns. The biggest hindering factor for establishing this access is the current land ownership structure due to the suburban past. Thus, measures must be undertaken to reduce plot areas to enable an improved infrastructural supply and public spaces along key corridors. These corridors need an enhanced level of local integration to become the starting points for a new urban experience reconnected to the immediate urban surroundings.

Today, this relationship between neighbourhoods and public realm can mainly be found in master-planned mega projects and big compound developments. In these cases, the public realm has however been usually restricted to be used by higher-income groups, and it is often dominated by commercial uses. Lower- and medium-income groups have often been undersupplied with functioning district centres and integrated public spaces. The result of the recent construction boom has been an urban landscape built on scattered island projects linked with highways, in which major shopping mall complexes have gained the main role of public leisure centres. The success of shopping malls as perceived urban centres and thus major concentrations of daily activities can not only be found in harsh climatic conditions during summer months, but also in the lack of integrated urban development caused by recent development dynamics. The fast move of millions of migrants led to the phenomenon of a housing market, in which both housing shortage and investment interests led to the fast supply of housing units without accommodating all needs of future residents. New highways and shopping malls have often been the consequence of a pragmatic planning approach to accommodate fast growth instead of small-scale and integrated development patterns.

The three main tendencies of housing dynamics can be observed in all major Gulf cities. In Dubai, the fringes of Bur Dubai and Deira have witnessed a rapid development of high-density projects, while the Dubai Marina has added one of the world's biggest residential high-rise clusters along the Emirate's waterfront. Gated suburban developments can be found in many scales and forms, including the Palm project stretching into the sea or the Emirates Hills project inland. In Abu Dhabi, the cluster of downtown high-rises was extended, and the Al Reem Island added a new waterfront. In all cities land ownership, land prices and infrastructural supply were the main precursors of the urban form. And in all cities, reclaimed land and not-yet subdivided land have quickly gained the priority regarding infrastructural supply. The result has been both construction superlatives in the form of new architectural landmarks in few but highly visible locations and an increasing lack of urban consolidation enforcing further urban sprawl and car dependency.

Notes

1   James McIntosh, Roman J. Trubka, Jeffrey R. Kenworthy and Peter W. Newman, 'The Role of Urban Form and Transit in City Car Dependence: Analysis of 26 Global Cities from 1960 to 2000', *Transportation Research Part D: Transport and Environment*, 33 (2014), pp. 95–110.

2   Robert Cervero, *Suburban Gridlock*. Center for Urban Policy Research
    (New Brunswick, 1986).

3   Thomas Sieverts, *Zwischenstadt: Zwischen Ort und Welt, Raum und Zeit, Stadt und
    Land* (Berlin, 2000).

4   Hall, *Cities of Tomorrow*.

5   Peter Calthorpe, *The Next American Metropolis: Ecology and the American Dream*
    (New York, 1993).

6   Jane Jacobs, *The Death and Life of Great American Cities* (New York, 1961).

7   James H. Kunstler, *The Geography of Nowhere* (New York, 1993).

8   Melvin M. Webber, 'Order in Diversity: Community without Propinquity', in
    L. Jr. Wingo (ed.), *Cities and Space: The Future Use of Urban Land, Essays from the
    Fourth RFF Forum*, Resources for the Future (1963), pp. 23–54, p. 24.

9   Shaibu Garba, 'Managing Urban Growth and Development in the Riyadh
    Metropolitan Area, Saudi Arabia', *Habitat International*, 28 (2004), pp. 593–608.

10 Jamel Akbar, *Crisis in the Built Environment: The Case of the Muslim City*
    (Singapore, 1988).

11 Saleh Al-Hathloul and Muhammad A. Mughal, 'Urban Growth Management – The
    Saudi Experience', *Habitat International*, 28/4 (2004), pp. 609–23.

12 Al-Hathloul, *The Arab-Muslim City*.

13 Joel Garreau, *Edge City: Life on the New Frontier* (New York, 1991).

14 Pacione, 'City Profile Dubai', p. 256.

15 Christa Diener, Annette Gangler and Andreas Fein, 'Transformationsprozesse in
    Oasensiedlungen Omans', *Trialog*, 76 (2003), pp. 15–21, p. 15.

16 Salama and Wiedmann, *Demystifying Doha*, p. 30.

17 Reichert, *Die Verstädterung der Eastern Province in Saudi-Arabien*.

18 *The National*, 'Dubai Real Estate Had a Sluggish Year of Fewer Trades and Turnover'.

19 Heinz Pape, *Er Riad. Stadtgeografie und Stadtkartografie der Hauptstadt Saudi-
    Arabiens* (Paderborn, 1977).

20 Sara I. Mohammed, Daniel J. Graham and Patricia C. Melo, 'The Effect of the Dubai
    Metro on the Value of Residential and Commercial Properties', *Journal of Transport
    and Land Use*, 10/1 (2017), pp. 263–90.

21 Elie Azar and Mohamed A. Raouf, *Sustainability in the Gulf: Challenges and
    Opportunities* (London, 2018).

22 Ben-Hamouche, 'Manama: The Metamorphosis of an Arab Gulf City', p. 185.

23 Nelida Fuccaro, 'Understanding the Urban History of Bahrain', *Critique: Critical
    Middle Eastern Studies*, 9/17 (2007), pp. 49–81.

24 Bahrain Financial Harbour, *Overview*. Available at: www.bfharbour.com/ (accessed
    3 December 2017).

25 Gulf Holding Company, *Projects*. Available at: www.gfholding.com/Projects
    (accessed 3 December 2017).

26 Bahrain Bay, *Development Plan*. Available at: www.bahrainbay.com/development-plan/ (accessed 3 December 2017).

27 Reef Island, *Key Components*. Available at: www.reef-island.com/key-components (accessed 3 December 2017).

28 Bahrain Municipal Geo Explore, *Map*. Available at: www.ma-investment.gov.bh/website/discover_bah/ (accessed 3 December 2017).

29 Oxford Business Group, *The Report: Bahrain 2017: Construction & Real Estate. Sustainability in the Gulf: Challenges and Opportunities*. Available at: www.oxfordbusinessgroup.com/bahrain-2017/construction-real-estate (accessed 19 December 2017).

30 Florian Wiedmann, 'The verticalization of Manama's urban periphery', *Open House International*, 38/3 (2013), pp. 90–100, p. 99.

31 Al-Nabi, *The History of Land-use and Development in Bahrain*.

32 Bahrain Municipal Geo Explore, *Map*, 2017.

33 Al-Nabi, *The History of Land-use and Development in Bahrain*.

34 Wiedmann, *Post-oil Urbanism in the Gulf*, p. X.

35 Ibid.

36 Bertrand, 'Real Estate Bubble and Financial Crisis in Dubai'.

37 Lusail, *Lusail City*. Available at: www.lusail.com/ (accessed 19 December 2017).

38 Ashraf M. Salama, Florian Wiedmann, Alain Thierstein and Wafa Al-Ghatam, 'Knowledge Economy as an Initiator of Sustainable Urbanism in Emerging Metropolises: The Case of Doha, Qatar', *International Journal of Architectural Research: ArchNet-IJAR*, 10/1 (2016), pp. 274–324.

39 Velina Mirincheva, Florian Wiedmann and Ashraf M. Salama, 'The Spatial Development Potentials of Business Districts in Doha: The Case of the West Bay', *Open House International*, 38/4 (2013), pp. 16–26.

40 Ibid., p. 25.

41 Peter Gordon, Ajay Kumar and Harry W. Richardson, 'The Fnfluence of Metropolitan Spatial Structure on Commuting Time', *Journal of Urban Economics*, 26/2 (1989), pp. 138–51.

42 Before the travel routes of everyday activities could be assessed, questionnaires were distributed by both authors to more than twenty companies in Doha to interview migrant guest workers from various countries and cultural backgrounds. In total, around 350 questionnaires were collected. Most participants are from the Indian subcontinent (40 per cent), while the participants from the Philippines (19 per cent), Western countries (21 per cent) and the MENA region (20 per cent) have equal shares. Slightly more male interviewees (63 per cent) participated in the survey and the average age was thirty-three. The questionnaire investigated where the participants live and where they go for their weekly shopping as well as where they spend their leisure time.

43 Lewis Mumford, *The City in History: Its Origins, Its Transformations, Its Prospects* (Boston, 1968).

6

Lifestyle trends and multicultural perceptions

Over the past few decades the modern globalization process has initiated not only an increasing connectivity but also competition between cities worldwide.[1] Modern infrastructure and the gradual liberalization of markets have enabled businesses to explore the best places for their international operations.[2] To enter a major role within international networks, cities are required to establish a high level of connectivity.[3] Due to their geopolitical location, Gulf cities were increasingly conceived as potential hubs attracting economic activities within expanding regional and global networks.[4] As discussed in earlier chapters, the resulting rapid urbanization has resulted in mass migration and thus new demographic realities in the Gulf region. Subsequently, all local markets needed to react to the new demand on services, goods and housing, from shopping malls and beaches to furniture and penthouse apartments. While actual demand-driven aspects in the form of individual lifestyle preferences can be regarded as rather restricted during the first period of rapid growth due to limited capacities, a differentiation and diversification can be generally observed after a certain period, as in any other emerging market.[5]

Migration and new imported lifestyle trends have thus had a significant impact on urbanism by changing housing and general consumption patterns. This can be observed in cases of migrants from rural or urban places as well as migrants from various socio-economic and cultural backgrounds. While there is always an imperative that a low-income group automatically restricts the choice of housing and thus dictates certain living conditions, high-income groups have a wide spectrum of house types to choose from.[6] This has led to an increasing diversity of upper real estate markets, while affordable housing schemes often follow more repetitive models, mainly dictated by land prices and construction costs rather than particular demand-driven dynamics.[7] These parameters, however, are dependent on both existing infrastructural networks and current development policies promoting diversity or regulating strict building standards.

Generally, new housing typologies and thus new neighbourhoods together with their own physical characteristics can be identified in rapidly growing cities. Gulf cities have therefore been facing a recent urban transformation rooted in rising land and rental prices, new demographic characteristics and the economic realities resulting from migration and newly initiated economic centres.[8]

In recent years, research on lifestyle trends and the perceptual dimension has played an increasingly important role in understanding these urban transformation dynamics, by particularly focusing on housing preferences. Primarily, the introduction of lifestyle groups follows the need of economists to predict future demand patterns within increasingly complex urban societies. The theory of 'Sinus-Milieus'[9] is thus often used in real estate studies to forecast market potentials as well as deficits in other sectors.[10] Since modes of transport have been very limited in Gulf cities, which have led to a restriction of lifestyle choices, lifestyle trends can be studied by investigating the choices of residences, their typology as well as their location. This chapter explores the main lifestyle trends and their impact on urbanism by analysing the differing neighbourhood contexts in the Gulf region. Lifestyles are a product of individual preferences but within the limitations of existing spatial, sociocultural economic and environmental realities. Thus, the investigation of lifestyles and their relationship with urbanism develops an understanding of current development dynamics between people and places rather than following the approach to quantify market potentials and deficits. Following the introduction of four major lifestyle groups and their distinctive neighbourhoods in Gulf cities, the major differences between cultural perceptions can be examined.

Lifestyle trends in Gulf cities

To understand lifestyles and their roots, the concept of 'habitus' can be utilized. The habitus of an individual must be understood as the result of both a relatively stable disposition of knowledge or character and a more complex mental and subjective schema of perception.[11] Habitus refers to past experiences resulting in different skills, dispositions and habits, which lead to certain socio-behavioural practices. According to Pierre Bourdieu, each social class shares a certain general habitus due to similar environments and experiences. This habitus has a direct impact on each individual leading to dynamics between given structures and understandings, which have developed over generations, and new individual behaviour.[12] The habitus can thus be identified as a holistic approach towards understanding the origin of lifestyles and the result of a long-term historic evolution, which is continuously changing. This suggests that individuals need their habitus to find new solutions based on their intuition, which in his view is directly linked to societal norms. The resulting lifestyles have significant impact on how social structures and spatial development patterns evolve.[13]

In the Gulf, the recent migration and extensive internationalization of local societies has led to significant differences of how life is conceived since the habitus of most individuals has been formed elsewhere. Thus, the cultural dimension of lifestyles can be understood as the direct result of past experiences in societies, which naturally differ from place to place. The resulting behavioural patterns, such as the use of public spaces or appropriating the home environment, can vary due to various cultural perspectives. Thus, the public realm in Gulf cities and in any other places with a high level of migrant populations can be regarded as an exhibition of a multitude of spatial practices. For example, sidewalks and public squares or green areas illustrate various ways of how urban spaces in neighbourhoods and city centres can be conceived as opportunities for social interaction, engagement or individual self-expression. In Gulf cities, three main traditions are currently merging the way in which public spaces are used: the Middle Eastern Islamic tradition and its conservative nature, the Western international tradition focused on leisure and the South Asian approaches of living outdoors. This relationship to urban spaces is highly affecting desired residence locations.

While the habitus is clearly defined as a product of past experiences and mental processes, present lifestyles are also defined by contemporary social structures and the associated position of each individual. In 1970, the British anthropologist Mary Douglas introduced her 'group and grid' model.[14] According to her definition, a group implies a general boundary around a community, which is based on choice, and a grid includes the outer forces and regulations. Douglas distinguishes between four main group-grid types: the 'isolate', the 'positional', the 'individualist' and the 'enclave'. While the 'isolate' only includes social groups that have been isolated by the system, such as prisoners, and therefore hardly has any impact on developments, the 'individualist' is primarily concerned with private benefits and is therefore rather mobile and less invested in a particular place.[15] Therefore, social status and its expression play an important role in lifestyle dynamics.[16] The 'positional' is rooted in a distinct group following a clear grid-given structure and thus often supports tradition and order.[17] Finally, the 'enclave' includes all groups that refuse to participate in any given framework and follow their own structures.[18] These four fundamental types offer an enhanced understanding of currently transforming lifestyle dynamics. The diversity of lifestyles is thus highly dependent on the general social, economic and spatial structure.[19]

Mapping the preceding understanding to various communities within Gulf cities, the group-grid structure has been transforming in recent years. Until new development dynamics commenced, most local populations would have been identified as a rather positional group, which has been defined by cultural traditions and sustained by a welfare state environment. Today, emerging trends can be observed, such as an increasing behaviour of building enclaves due to extensive migration and the associated threat of cultural alienation. Since local populations have become minorities, new frameworks have often been rejected, and the special status of national citizenship has gained new importance to secure special rights.[20] In parallel, young generations have experienced a rapid internationalization and thus tendencies of a new form of individualism and self-expression can be observed in the entire region.[21] Another important factor for rising individualists within local populations has been the enormous financial success of many local citizens, who have been benefiting from fast growth rates, particularly as landlords, sponsors and investors, enabling a more international and mobile lifestyle. On the contrary, the migrant populations have been defined by three groups. While low-income labourers can be regarded as isolated social groups due to their limited possibility to make any major individual decisions, most migrants with families can be found in positional groups, in which they are aiming to sustain and develop their current positions. International experts often embrace their opportunity to work as 'individualists' in Gulf cities without ever aiming to settle long-term.

In addition to the holistic approach of understanding lifestyles as the result of the habitus as defined by Bourdieu and Douglas's 'group and grid' model, other scholars have introduced pragmatic models relevant to the way in which certain life modes that shape lifestyle trends in future can be distinguished. In essence, life modes indicate how work, family status and consumption choices mirror opportunities and aspirations with respect to how lifestyles can change in future. Three pragmatic life modes relevant to work patterns can be distinguished: self-employed life mode, wage earner life mode and career-oriented life mode.[22] This classification demonstrates that lifestyles vary based on the income level, work sector and work style of an individual.[23] While life modes can be distinguished according to the various ways in which people work, other factors such as the demographic increase and decrease of families and the associated life modes have been researched by scholars to investigate the dynamics of housing and urbanism.[24] Thus, young societies might have other preferences and needs to raise future children than older ones. Coupled with how people work and their family status, the role of leisure and consumption patterns can be identified as the third determining factor for any life mode and its future implications. While some social groups are significantly limited in their spending, others consciously choose to save their earnings or at least a portion of them. Other groups alternatively opt for a predominantly, if not solely, consumer-driven lifestyle, as already analysed and described in the late nineteenth century in Europe.[25] Urbanism is particularly affected by the various life modes due to emerging housing needs and preferences, as well as mobility choices and the most favoured centres for leisure and consumption.[26]

The life modes of Gulf populations can be characterized as less diverse due to the large share of single labourers and their circumstances without family life and limited income. Yet, the life modes of other migrant groups are dominated by work since many contracts are limited in time and engaging on a contractual basis in the Gulf region is often perceived as a temporary opportunity rather than as an actual option to settle long-term. Contrarily, local populations are rather young with large majorities under the average age of thirty years, and in many cases, governments are still maintaining certain welfare state mechanisms.[27] Their life modes are consequently family and leisure oriented. Another constellation of life modes can be found in migrant families, who have often settled in Gulf cities for several decades. Their life modes are characterized by both family life and hard work, since they have become the backbone of the lower private sector running shops and small businesses. Examples can be found in the rather diverse Indian and Iranian migrant families in Dubai. In the Kingdom of Bahrain, for example, many nationals have also been engaged in these economic sectors, while in other countries the share of national workforce within the private sector is still rather low. Thus, many governments started initiatives, such as the Emiratization programme initiated by the Vision 2021 in the United Arab Emirates.[28] In future, these programmes might have a significant impact on population structures and it can be expected that the share of nationals engaged in the private sector will increase, leading to new life modes and lifestyles.

Primarily, future housing trends are expected to be the most immediate factor transforming urbanism in the Gulf. The home environment is both a form of self-expression and an important factor impacting human perceptions.[29]

Where and how a human was raised will always affect future choices and his or her acceptance of certain conditions.[30] Additionally, the age, income level and household size will also impact the preference of certain housing types. To study the relationship between housing and lifestyles, the basic needs must first be identified. While the need for shelter can be seen as the lowest level of needs based on the simple premise of human survival, the social needs to establish a sense of belonging are followed by the individual needs of self-expression.[31] In principle, lifestyle theories are based on a complex framework that acknowledges the reality of human beings as being driven by dynamic interactive factors as well as static personal and situational factors.[32]

By and large, lifestyles have always been drivers for housing developments. Yet, the existing housing conditions have a reciprocal impact on lifestyles. Lifestyles are a product of individual and collective processes within societies and, therefore, their characteristics are highly complex. According to Bourdieu's theory, society is the product of a historic process and the organization of a society is directly linked to past experiences. This is manifested in the individual's habitus, which is rooted in cultural customs, basic needs and desires as well as social status. This abstract conception of the foundation of lifestyles in addition to the understanding of the present group-grid structure of a society provides an overview of basic social groups and their roles. The theoretical understanding of how societies are structured needs to be incorporated into an understanding of predominant life modes as basis for future potentials. These life modes can be simplified and defined by being mainly family-related, work-based or leisure-oriented.

Characterizing lifestyle trends requires an understanding of the contemporary demographic structure of Gulf cities in a given context. As highlighted in Chapter 2, up to 80 per cent of most migrant populations are from South Asia, mainly from India and Pakistan. This share is particularly high since up to half of all urban populations are labourers. Most of these labourers are male due to the large demand for workforce in construction sectors. The second largest share constitutes migrants with families having low to medium income, of which a major share has settled in Gulf cities before the recent urban transformation. While the share of local citizens has been continuously shrinking to approximately 10 per cent in certain cities, the number of higher-income migrants has more than tripled to around 10 per cent due to emerging advanced producer services. This basic demographic structure in combination with recent development patterns allows for a clear identification of key lifestyle trends, which have been impacting local urbanism.

The most dominant group, which can be identified immediately, is the work-focused group of migrants. This group includes both labourers and single guest workers whose presence is on a temporary basis to save money for their families and the return to their home countries. In addition to working in the construction sector they also work in the mainstream lower service sectors that include retail, hospitality and transportation. This group can also be found in other better-paid jobs, such as accounting, engineering and administration. Despite their limited income and their objective to save their earnings, they usually adhere to basic principles of order and thus a rather positional behaviour. This is rooted in their uncertain employment situation coupled with their Asian and Middle Eastern cultural backgrounds. Leisure time is rather reduced and is usually spent in public spaces and accessible shopping malls, where the main activity is centred on meeting friends from a similar cultural background rather than consumption. Therefore, many commercial centres and shopping malls have begun to restrict these social gatherings in their facilities, which have reinforced street life in many districts. Moreover, the lack of mobility has limited this lifestyle group to visit many places and thus surrounding neighbourhoods have a more significant impact on their urban experiences. All in all, it can be argued that more than half of the population in Gulf cities can be counted to this lifestyle group, mainly characterized by being employees with short-term contracts, limited leisure time and absence of family life.

The second largest lifestyle group is characterized by being both work focused and family oriented. This lifestyle group includes both migrants who have settled in Gulf cities for several decades and newly arriving migrant families with sufficient income whose objective is to settle for a longer period in spite of limited contracts or challenging economic circumstances. Due to the required minimum income to get the permission to move with spouse and children, most migrants meet a certain educational background and they are mainly from South Asia or the Middle East. In contrast to the single work-focused migrants with families left behind, this group often has a clear vision to settle longer term in Gulf cities. Being centred on family activities, they can be regarded as the most positional group in Gulf cities willing to face challenging circumstances to ensure long stays. These low- to medium-income groups have often been initiators of entrepreneurial activities as they play important roles in diversifying local economies. They account to up to and average of 30 per cent in most Gulf cities and their distinctive characteristic is their inner cultural networks and thus the direct exchange between already settled and newly arriving migrants. As previously indicated, an increasing share of nationals have become part of this lifestyle group, for instance second- or third-generation migrants with citizenship or Bahrain's lower-income national population.

The third lifestyle group can be found in the national populations, who have still been benefiting from earlier welfare state mechanisms and land ownership. The access to higher income has offered opportunities for an enhanced mobility and significant leisure time. Nonetheless, this group can be described as very family oriented and positional. Due to extensive migration, this group has found itself in an increasingly separate world, detached from the usual market forces that most work-centred groups are encountering. This group shares the objective of preserving local traditions and customs, as they have become a social minority. This has led to enclave tendencies and the common practice to express themselves via traditional clothes and carefully chosen public meeting points. The former land distribution for local housing developments has enabled this group to live in almost detached and almost homogeneous spaces. Most leisure time is spent in private and spacious villas where the different generations meet and interact. Local neighbourhood mosques can play a significant role within these communities. Despite their shrinking share, it has had a significant impact on urbanism, rooted not only in their neighbourhoods made of spacious villas but also in the fact that a substantial new income source has been through renting out properties, selling land or sponsorship activities. The individual economic benefits are however often perceived detached from a growing mistrust in migration and long-term growth strategies.

The fourth lifestyle group can be best described as being international and mobile. It includes both highly educated expats and nationals, who have begun to build their lives between the Gulf region and global cities, such as London or New York. This group has been benefiting from high salaries and the established connectivity permitting the required level of mobility. The Gulf region is primarily perceived as an opportunity for business but without losing ties to other places worldwide. Thus, mobile internationals are rather diverse, especially with respect to their cultural roots, but they usually belong to a senior age group made of established and experienced professionals. Their lifestyles are thus not compromised by major budget considerations and are often dominated by the demand for a certain living standard and an expression of an achieved social status. This group follows a clear individualist approach regarding leisure choices as well as family settings. While they are the smallest group of less than 10 per cent in Gulf cities, they can be considered as important drivers of new economies as well as consumption patterns (Table 6.1).

Table 6.1 The four typical lifestyle groups in Gulf cities

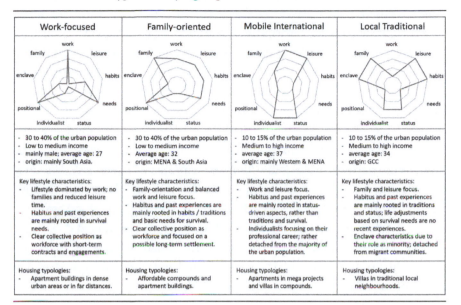

Work-focused	Family-oriented	Mobile International	Local Traditional
- 30 to 40% of the urban population - Low to medium income - mainly male; average age: 27 - origin: mainly South Asia.	- 30 to 40% of the urban population - Low to medium income - Average age: 32 - origin: MENA & South Asia	- 10 to 15% of the urban population - Medium to high income - average age: 37 - origin: mainly Western & MENA	- 10 to 15% of the urban population - Medium to high income - average age: 34 - origin: GCC
Key lifestyle characteristics: - Lifestyle dominated by work; no families and reduced leisure time. - Habitus and past experiences are mainly rooted in survival needs. - Clear collective position as workforce with short-term contracts and engagements.	Key lifestyle characteristics: - Family-orientation and balanced work and leisure focus. - Habitus and past experiences are mainly rooted in habits / traditions and basic needs for survival. - Clear collective position as workforce and focused on a possible long-term settlement.	Key lifestyle characteristics: - Work and leisure focus. - Habitus and past experiences are mainly rooted in status-driven aspects, rather than traditions and survival. - Individualists focusing on their professional career; rather detached from the majority of the urban population.	Key lifestyle characteristics: - Family and leisure focus. - Habitus and past experiences are mainly rooted in traditions and status; life adjustments based on survival needs are no recent experiences. - Enclave characteristics due to their role as minority; detached from migrant communities.
Housing typologies: - Apartment buildings in dense urban areas or in far distances.	Housing typologies: - Affordable compounds and apartment buildings.	Housing typologies: - Apartments in mega projects and villas in compounds.	Housing typologies: - Villas in traditional local neighbourhoods.

Lifestyle groups and their neighbourhoods

The extensive migration during the last twenty years led to two new lifestyle phenomena: firstly, the arrival of the new small group of highly educated workforce and the associated international and mobile lifestyle tendencies, and second, the reality of more than half of the urban population consisting of migrant employees with short-term contracts and thus without a requirement for actual contributions. The resulting multicultural but often fluid migrant population has led to a transformation of local housing markets in the Gulf, especially in capital cities. The need to accommodate a rapidly increasing workforce as well as the rising pressure of investments on freehold properties have resulted in new urban typologies, as previously discussed in the case of Manama and Doha. On the one hand, mass housing has been required on a new large scale to accommodate low- to medium-income migrants, while on the other hand, exclusive mega projects have become the actual drivers of urban growth, but only minorities have been able to afford the rental rates along new waterfronts. In parallel, the local populations and their housing needs have often been catered via the remaining coordinated land distribution in secluded areas, mainly in urban peripheries.

In proximity to the historic centres and in transition areas along urban fringes, densely built urban areas have emerged in recent years. The main housing typology has been apartment towers and blocks with an average height of up to eleven floors in city centre areas and five to seven floors in transition areas (Figure 6.1). The most common housing type is the two- or three-bedroom apartment, most of which accommodate single migrants with work-focused lifestyles. The remaining share is inhabited by migrant families that are looking for rental rates that are more affordable than those in accessible suburban areas.

Due to the widespread phenomenon of shared living, private bedrooms cover most of the ground floors with often more than 70 per cent according to comparative examination of more than 200 ground floor plans by the authors in 2017.[33] In most cases, kitchens are separate and the sitting areas are usually small. It can also be observed that daylight is often limited due to the densely built surroundings and the insufficient distances between buildings. The neighbourhood surroundings often include basic commercial services but social infrastructures, such as schools and public spaces, are very limited. The architectural style is dominated by the functional appearance of prefabricated construction elements and thus lacks general attractiveness. Additionally, the

Figure 6.1 Typical apartment blocks and towers in transition areas in Juffair, Manama.

high frequency of changing tenants has led to a neighbourhood environment hardly reflecting the need for leisure and social interaction.

While urban areas along the fringes of historic city cores have been witnessing rapid growth due to the rising interest in vertical typologies of apartment buildings, the suburban sprawl has continued. In addition to villas and town houses, an increasing number of apartment buildings and blocks have been integrated into compound developments to accommodate both work-focused and family-oriented lifestyle groups (Figure 6.2). Due to local regulations, this housing typology usually reaches an average height of two to four floors and the typical apartment reaches more than 100 square metres as the majority are three-bedroom apartments. The entrance usually leads to a small lobby and is slightly larger in size in shared living spaces than in downtown apartments. While certain amenities, such as swimming pools and gyms, are often included within the compound precincts, general commercial services and social infrastructure are usually less integrated, which ultimately leads to higher car dependency and daily commutes to shopping and leisure destinations.

Compound regulations usually permit the development of more densely built plots by constructing attached or semi-attached houses. Thus, a certain diversity of single-family dwellings can be observed. The entrance leads to a medium-sized lobby or semi open-plan living area. The proportion of private bedrooms to shared living areas is usually balanced due to the general layout of bedrooms being located on the first floor. This typology mainly accommodates

Figure 6.2 Apartment buildings in suburban areas in Dubai.

family-oriented groups with medium and high income. The design follows regional standards and conservative layouts. In most cases, kitchens are separate and small rooms for maids are integrated. Due to the size of these homes, living areas are usually not separated and thus there is no traditional *majlis*, a separate room for male visitors in proximity to entrances serving a cultural preference in the Middle East. Based on their location in suburban neighbourhoods, the compounds are usually supplied by shopping malls or small district centres.

Since the beginning of the construction boom, coastal areas have been witnessing rapid development including their extension via further land reclamation along waterfronts. Due to high land prices and generally well accessible locations, residential high-rise buildings with more than 100 floors have been built (Figure 6.3). A certain diversity of apartments from studio to penthouse apartments can be observed; in most cases, the entrance directly leads to a large spacious open-plan living area, which can cover half of the entire ground floor plan. This clearly representative space accommodates the needs of a mobile and individualist lifestyle. Access to daylight is plentiful and the orientation of sitting areas is dependent on the views to the surrounding urban or natural scenes. Spacious terraces and balconies are often integrated

Figure 6.3 Residential high-rises in Dubai Marina.

to underline the exclusiveness of this typology, which is further expressed by many in-house services and sport and leisure activities. The architectural design of most high-rise buildings is essentially influenced by Western design, expressed through postmodernist steel and glass architecture while featuring various regional or classical details. Whereas the coastal areas integrate near-by amenities and services due to a high density of hotels, social infrastructure is limited due to high land prices. Notably, there are high vacancy rates due to increasing rental rates.

In addition to high-rises, most mega projects along waterfronts include a certain range of exclusive single-family dwellings for high-income groups. With an average size of up to 500 square metres, these homes are significantly larger in area than the usual compound homes, which is a clear indication that they are not only designed but also built as potential homes of higher-income migrants. Due to their location in gated environments, they usually form linear and open developments unlike the compactness found in compound developments. These homes accommodate individual as well as family needs of both international and local communities, who can relate to a beach-oriented lifestyle (Figure 6.4). The entrances lead to a central corridor or lobby and the share of areas occupied by

Figure 6.4 Waterfront villas in the Amwaj Islands development in Bahrain.

private bedrooms is slightly lower due to the presence of open areas. The share of open-plan living spaces is thus significantly higher than that observed among typical compound homes, which is a sign of the tendency towards a modern and contemporary open layout. The integration of commercial and leisure amenities and services, such as small malls and beaches, create holiday home setups. Yet, in the majority of exclusive waterfront projects, the supply of social infrastructure is limited due to high land prices and the absence of standards or bylaws forcing developers to integrate sufficient services.

Since the rise of oil production, local populations have moved towards urban peripheries and adopted suburban lifestyles in rather exclusive environments. The resulting homogeneous neighbourhoods primarily consist of single-detached villas (Figure 6.5). The average living area within contemporary single-detached homes reaches up to 600 square metres, which is the largest size out of all existing housing typologies. The design of private houses follows the typical spatial requirements of traditional dwellings in Gulf States and the objective to accommodate large families. In addition to a main representative entrance leading to a large central lobby with stairways, a servant entrance is usually integrated to allow for segregated movements and circulation. Next to the main entrance, a private sitting area, known as *majlis*, is often included to allow the separation of male and female guests in accordance with local customs. The family living room is placed next to the dining room, which

Figure 6.5 A single-detached villa in the outskirts of Dubai.

usually incorporates a small open kitchen, while the kitchen for daily cooking is located outside of the main living areas next to the servants' and utility rooms. The first floor is commonly designated for en-suite bedrooms. In some cases, a living room is integrated to permit intergenerational, that is, extended family living under one roof. The villas usually have sufficient access to daylight despite their large ground floor area since skylights in the stairways area are often used to enhance the natural lightning. The villas are usually built in the centre of standardized plots, which are surrounded by a high wall to protect the families' privacy. The neighbourhoods integrate basic social infrastructure, but hardly any commercial services.

The mapping of all main lifestyle groups to housing typologies results in new insights of how Gulf cities have become rather segregated entities despite the significant demographic transformation and enhanced social diversity in recent years. While the local population and the associated traditional lifestyles can be easily located in homogeneous suburban neighbourhoods, the high-income migrants with a mobile and international lifestyle can usually be found along waterfronts in residential high-rises as well as exclusive compounds. The work-focused, but also family-oriented, lifestyle groups mainly reside in compounds along urban peripheries, where rental rates are still affordable, as well as apartments in downtown districts. The single migrants and their work-centred lifestyles are found in shared apartments in densely populated and built areas or in compounds and along industrial sites, where a large share of male labourers have been accommodated.

Since the spatial segregation is mainly rooted in income, the segregation of cultural groups has decreased to a certain extent. While South Asian migrants from India and Pakistan mainly dominate industrial areas, the overall sociocultural composition of many downtown districts is more diverse due to the increased migration from the MENA region and the Philippines. The compound landscapes in urban peripheries are the most culturally diverse due to a mix of international migrants from the Middle East and Asia as well as a certain percentage of Westerners in proximity to the neighbourhoods of the local population. The waterfronts and exclusive projects are accommodating a wide spectrum of international migrants with a significant presence of Western cultural backgrounds as well as the holiday homes of regional property owners. In essence, the extensive migration has led to a continuously transforming and changing multicultural society, which can be observed in certain downtown and suburban districts. The intercultural exchange has however been limited due to absence of public realm as well as the opportunities to integrate specialized businesses and services. The most significant evidence of the enormous cultural diversity of Gulf cities can often be observed in small shops, convenient stores and restaurants in relatively run-down areas catering to the needs of migrants.

Multiculturalism in the Gulf

The growth of new advanced service sectors in Gulf cities is currently dependent on a concentration of highly educated migrants. Despite their various cultural backgrounds migrants with a certain income level and educational background are generally perceived as a social force generating integrated rather than segregated forms of urbanism due to availability of leisure time and financial opportunities resulting in opportunities for social and economic interaction.[34] These assumptions have been tested in the Global North rather than in emerging cities in the Global South, such as the Gulf region, where development dynamics are often dictated by short-term mechanisms of instant urban growth rather than the long-term evolution of integrated migrant communities. In this respect, there is an increasing challenge to develop dynamic multicultural societies and to minimize segregation resulting from rapid and extensive population growth and the associated socio-spatial fragmentation.[35] The preceding discussion suggests that Gulf cities manifest an important case for exploring the various perceptions of migrants with respect to housing as it relates to needs, cultural traditions and ultimately to the city.

Due to the limited size of local populations and despite the international financial crisis, the recent economic development strategies have been reliant on continuous international migration in recent years.[36] In addition to skilled workforce from the Indian subcontinent and the Philippines, many migrants in higher economic sectors originate from Egypt and the Levant region as well as Europe, North America and Australia. The main migrant groups in Qatar, for instance, are from the Indian subcontinent constituting around half of the entire population, followed by migrants from Egypt and the Philippines.[37] All migrants from Western countries constitute only around 3 per cent. Qatar is an example of a rather high diversity of migrant groups, who arrived during the period 2003 to 2017. Today migrants from more than sixty nations reside in the small state. The main motives to relocate to the Gulf region are the high-income level in comparison to home countries, the possibility to gain working experiences in certain sectors and the provision of general security as well as modern infrastructure and services. Due to the geopolitical location and well-connected airports, Gulf cities are furthermore perceived as highly suitable for a rather mobile lifestyle. Today, economic development agencies, such as the GSDP[38] in Qatar or the ADCED,[39] have identified the importance of mid-income migrant groups for a successful economic diversification.

A key pillar for considering liveability in Gulf cities, or the quality of urban life, is an affordable, diverse and attractive housing supply in liveable surroundings as well as accessible services and an overall positive assessment of future opportunities.[40] Therefore, relevant studies need to be based on a comprehensive understanding of contemporary urban conditions and the associated perceptions.[41] The one-dimensional approach of investigating urban transformation processes needs to be extended by examining the views of various social groups and their concerns with respect to liveability.[42] The interdependencies between urbanism and individual perceptions usually result in new spatial development patterns in future.[43] Given the identified four major lifestyle trends in Gulf cities, the individual perceptions of migrants and their cultural context are important to explore. Most migrants engaged in emerging economies belong to three main lifestyle trends, either focused on family life and stability or short-term career goals or a rather mobile international lifestyle. The cultural diversity encompassed within these migrant groups has led to rather various perceptions and urban experiences despite having similar urban lifestyles. These perceptions are important indicators for aspirations of these groups to invest and settle long-term.

Multicultural perceptions in Qatar

Since 2012 the authors carried out various studies to investigate migrant perceptions in Qatar's capital Doha, which is a rather apt case study due to the scale of migration that took place in recent years.[44] Between 2003 and 2017 the population of Doha's metro region (including Al Rayyan) has increased from less than 700,000 to more than 1.6 million inhabitants, of which approximately 90 per cent are migrants.[45] The rapid growth and the ambitious plans to establish new economic sectors have led to a high diversity of migrant groups with medium to high income. In a comprehensive study conducted by the authors, more than fifty companies within advanced producer service sectors, such as finance and engineering, have been asked to participate in an attitude survey. In total, approximately 400 employees participated in the survey. Among the key issues explored, liveability related factors were key parameters in understanding participants' perceptions from various cultural perspectives. Each participant has been first asked to respond to the general information of both themselves and their current way of life, before they were asked to react with indicators on their general level of satisfaction and perceptions.

The survey was constituted in three main sections. The first part addressed the profile of each participant based on key characteristics, such as his or her nationality, gender and age as well as the length of stay in Doha. Placing emphasis on the current housing type as well as neighbourhood surroundings, the second part of the questionnaire was concerned with information on how the urban life of migrant groups is currently experienced. The third and last part tackled the way the city is generally perceived. The analytical procedure involved distinguishing four main cultural groups representing the migrant knowledge workers and key differences between these groups with respect to gender, age and periods of living in Doha as well as car ownership. In total, four key migrant groups could be identified including respondents with a European descend, mainly from the UK (17 per cent). The second group identified migrated from the MENA region, particularly Egypt and Lebanon (17 per cent). The largest group has moved from South Asia (37 per cent), mainly India, and the second largest group is from the Philippines (29 per cent).

All four groups share one important aspect that they have lived in average less than fifteen years in Doha and that they earn a medium to high income due to their professional occupation allowing them to move their families to Doha. However, it must be stated that the country of origin has a significant impact on the average salary in the case of similar working positions.[46] This is mainly based on the various perceptions of attractive salaries in the migrants' home countries and the willingness to accept the living and working conditions in Gulf cities. Respondents from India, for instance, have emphasized their very positive impression of a high level of security in Doha, while Europeans have emphasized their high salaries as their main motive to live in the Gulf region. Further analyses reveal that the average age of Europeans is the highest, which is an indicator for a large share of senior employees, who are attracted to work in Doha before their retirement. The youngest average age can be found in the case of respondents from Egypt and the Levant, which is an indicator for the general attractiveness of Gulf cities to gain working experience and better living and working conditions.

While Europeans have stayed the least average number of years in Doha, respondents from the MENA region have stayed the longest average period of almost eight years, which is a further indicator of a high share of young migrants focusing on building their lives in the Gulf. The relatively high number of years residing in Doha in the case of the Indian migrants can be attributed to the generally attractive option to stay in the Gulf instead of moving back to India, while Filipinos have the tendency of staying a few years, which can be attributed to the significant cultural differences as well as the high female percentage within this group. The lowest share of female employees can be found in the case of the Indian respondents, who are mainly hired as engineers. The most balanced share of female and male employees can be found in the case of Arab employees, who occupy a high diversity of different professions, while the significant share of senior positions in construction-related businesses explains the rather low share of female employees in the case of the European respondents group. The lowest ownership rate of cars can be found in the Filipino group, which is influenced by the high share of female employees. The highest rates of car ownership can be found in the cases of the Arab European respondents, who prefer to live in suburban areas and heavily rely on their own cars.

In the past most migrants were provided with accommodations by their employers. However, most respondents preferred to choose their own residence. In the case of the Filipino group approximately every fifth respondent has an accommodation provided by their employers, while only every tenth of the Arab respondents are living in housing units rented or owned by their employers. The relatively high share of respondents, who needed to look for an accommodation in Doha, is an important indication that the housing market for migrants is increasingly developed and that employers often prefer to offer fixed housing allowances instead of providing accommodations. One of the important findings revealed is the housing choices and preferences in terms of location and typology. In the case of the European group every second respondent has decided for a villa in a compound followed by one-third living in high-rise developments, mainly along the waterfront. Less than one-fifth of the European group is currently housed in apartment blocks in proximity to Doha's downtown areas. In comparison, approximately two-third of all Indian and Filipino respondents reside in areas along the main central ring roads. While Indians have preferred medium-rise apartment blocks, an even share of Filipino respondents resides in high-rise buildings of more than ten floors. A similar distribution can be found in the case of respondents from Egypt and the Levant, of whom every second respondent has moved to districts in proximity to Doha's downtown.

Studies about the general satisfaction and perception with respect to the relationship of their current housing conditions and that of their home country reveal that respondents have rather differing perceptions of their current residence. A significant share of complaints could be found in the case of the Indian group of respondents, of which around 20 per cent identify their housing conditions as increasingly unacceptable due to densely built and polluted downtown areas. However, the largest share of approximately half of all Indian respondents perceive their housing conditions as an improvement to their previous experiences in India. In comparison, most respondents from Europe and the Middle East cannot identify any improvement to their housing conditions, but they are generally satisfied, mainly because of the larger size of residences in comparison to home countries. The Filipino group is rather satisfied with the current housing conditions and almost half of all respondents would even identify a clear housing improvement since they have moved to Doha.

Another important indicator of a functioning supply of attractive housing is the perception of general ground floor layouts and room sizes. Most Europeans have no complaints, which is an indication of highly spacious living conditions in villas and waterfront developments. Respondents from India, Philippines and Middle East share a similar average level of dissatisfaction in the case of room sizes, particularly living rooms are identified as too small in typical inner-city apartments. The general layout of apartments is mainly criticized by Indian respondents, who have a need for separate kitchens, and respondents from the Middle East, who have a need for separated visitor areas due to regional customs. The quality of utilities and kitchens and the supply with sufficient daylight are further requirements of satisfying housing conditions. In the case of utilities mainly Europeans would identify the general quality as dissatisfying due to frequent problems of various types. Other migrant groups seem to be accepting the general standard of utilities and have a lower share of complaints. But the frequent problems with sewage, electricity and water supply can be identified as a general concern across all housing types.

With respect to perceptions of neighbourhoods and outdoor environments, only around one-third of all European respondents would identify their current neighbourhoods as pedestrian-friendly, which is both a strong indication that suburban areas, where many European migrants reside, are not walkable due to the limited integration of services and pedestrian walkways. But this can also be attributed to the high quality expected standard of pedestrian-friendly surroundings from a European perspective. Furthermore, most European respondents expressed dissatisfaction with the availability of green spaces in their neighbourhoods. The complaints about the lack of green areas can be found in the case of the Indian and Filipino respondents, which is a strong indication that their residences in inner-city areas are supplied with neither gardens nor public green areas in walkable distances. The respondents from the Middle East generally share the complaints with respect to the supply of green areas around their neighbourhoods. But they identify their neighbourhoods as walkable despite constraints, such as traffic. Indian and particularly Filipino respondents share this perception, which is an indication for the previous urban experiences in home countries and the resulting lower expectations.

Most Europeans perceive the immediate surroundings of their neighbourhoods as sufficiently safe and suitable for children. This relatively high degree of satisfaction rate can be attributed to the fact that most European respondents live in gated communities or exclusive waterfront developments. Approximately half of all European respondents however complain about a severe lack of commercial services, such as supermarkets, in proximity to their homes. This is another evidence of the very little integration of services in suburban areas. Two-third of all Indian respondents perceive their neighbourhoods as least family-friendly followed by respondents from the Philippines and the Middle East. This can be attributed to the chaotic traffic conditions in inner-city areas and the very few integrated playgrounds and social services. More than half of all Arab and Indian respondents perceive the integration of commercial services as sufficient, while every second Filipino respondent would prefer more commercial services in his or her neighbourhood. The relatively high share of dissatisfaction regarding commercial services is particularly related to the lack of grocery stores, which are mainly built as mega stores in malls and at main traffic junctions rather than small- to medium-size supermarkets equally distributed in districts.

In addition to housing-related concerns further studies conducted by the authors investigated perception of urban life, such as traffic conditions.[47] Only in the case of respondents from Western countries a large majority assesses the traffic conditions in Doha as chaotic. While only a slight majority of Middle Eastern survey participants share the opinion that the traffic experience is moderate, a clear majority perceives it as moderate and even pleasant in the case of Indian and South-East Asian respondents. This result underlines the diverse urban experiences in home countries. Most respondents rely on their own cars, while the remaining share uses taxi services and personal drivers. Public transportation services are not yet provided to all inhabitants and limited to a small selection of bus routes. Thus, respondents were asked if they would prefer public transportation instead of using a car or taxi. Due to the climatic conditions most respondents would always prefer to drive a car instead of using a metro or bus service. Only in the case of migrants with European origin a major share would rather use public transportation, which is rooted in their perception of traffic conditions as rather chaotic and even dangerous as well as their past experiences of using modern and efficient public transportation.

Another important aspect of perceived liveability in any city is how and where inhabitants spend their leisure time. The main leisure spaces identified by the survey respondents are four major shopping malls, the old historic city core, the waterfront promenades as well as various hotel complexes. In contrast to the other three groups, a high percentage of Western respondents prefer to spend their leisure time in hotels, where clubs and restaurants sell alcohol, often along private beaches. While in the case of Middle Eastern survey participants a majority prefers to spend leisure time in restaurants in the old city core, South-East Asians clearly prefer shopping malls and Indian respondents public spaces, such as Doha's Corniche or Aspire Park. Both Indians and South-East Asians perceive the distances to leisure spaces as too far from their residences, while only around one-fifth of the survey participants share this perception in the case of Middle Eastern and Western respondents due to their general access to new urban areas along the northern shoreline. Generally, it can be stated that leisure spaces are currently perceived as attractive but rare.

Additionally, respondents were asked about the general impressions regarding the attractiveness of Doha as their city of residence. While almost all Middle Eastern respondents would like to settle in Doha permanently, around half of all respondents of the remaining groups would be interested to live in Qatar beyond their initial contracts. To assess the general impressions respondents were asked how attractive they have perceived Doha on arrival and how they perceive it today. In the case of Middle Eastern respondents, no major difference can be assessed, and a clear majority shares the opinion that Doha is an attractive city. A significant shift between initial perception and current assessment can be noticed in the case of all other three groups, in which cases the share of a positive perception of Doha has increased during recent years.

More than 55 per cent of the survey participants view that Doha's most representative urban space is the high-rise agglomeration in West Bay viewed from the Corniche. This is followed by the old historic market, known as Souq Waqif. The Souq was rebuilt between 2004 and 2007 and was winner of the Aga Khan Award due to its careful restoration of historic buildings.[48] Other urban spaces such as the Pearl development, the Education City or the Museum of Islamic Art were mentioned as further urban spaces reflecting contemporary urbanism in Qatar. To get a comprehensive insight on how the urban environment is experienced by respondents, four urban spaces were identified to assess how they are perceived from multicultural perspectives.

The first selected urban space is the Corniche stretching towards West Bay due to its historic significance and prominent location (Figure 6.6). The seven-kilometre-long promenade links the old port area close by the historic city core and the modern skyline in West Bay. Since the end of the twentieth century West Bay became the main centre for high-rise projects in Doha, which was ignited by the announced move of public and semi-public institutions. In 2008 the Museum of Islamic Art, designed by the Chinese architect M. Pei, was completed on the opposite side of West Bay forming an ensemble of postmodern and traditionally inspired architectural landmarks.[49] Due to its size and position the Corniche is often perceived as the main centre of Doha despite its prime function as transition zone. All respondents are very familiar with the Corniche and in the case of each cultural group a majority perceives this key urban space as attractive and iconic. Only in the case of the South-East Asians a significant share of respondents of one-third would not identify the Corniche as iconic and around every fifth respondent does not even perceive it as attractive. Reasons are the very limited supply of commercial services, the constrained accessibility for pedestrians and the resulting exposure to local climatic conditions.

Figure 6.6 The West Bay district at the Corniche in Doha.

The second selected urban space is the restored historic market area. In addition to the Souq Waqif, the historic part of Doha is currently extended by a major development, known as Msheireb. Today the rebuilt traditional market is the only urban space where the historic vernacular architecture can be experienced (Figure 6.7). Most respondents are familiar with the urban area due to frequent visits. Most South-East Asian respondents however claim that they are not attracted to this central urban space and that they feel rather repelled to spend their leisure time in its precincts, while Middle Eastern respondents visit it frequently on a weekly basis. All other groups share the perception that it is a very important part of Doha as an attractive and iconic urban space representing the urban heritage.

The C-Ring Road along the Al Sadd district was selected as third case study representing a typical contemporary urban landscape. The ring road encircles the old downtown area and in recent years it became the main centre for office developments as well as apartment buildings. Due to the extending urban periphery the Al Sadd district became one of the most accessible and increasingly important business centres. Today a majority of companies are currently located in the area and its surroundings.[50] Thus, most respondents reside in apartments within or close by the Al Sadd district. Due to the previous restrictions on low-rise residential developments along C-Ring Road, the recent transformation to a high-density urban area has led to the impressions of a rather fragmented

Figure 6.7 The Souq Waqif in Doha.

urban structure. Thus, only a minority within each group would perceive this urban space as attractive. Particularly, respondents with a Western background assess the space as unattractive and rather unfamiliar, while Middle Eastern and Indian respondents are highly familiar with the environment and are generally rather neutral when they have to assess its attractiveness.

Another investigation focused on Doha's suburbs, which are defined by Qatari housing areas, compound developments and large-scale shopping malls. Today the most significant share of all urban settlements is covered by these suburban typologies. The most prominent examples can be found in the North of Doha in proximity to Qatar University and Education City as well as in the West of Doha in the surroundings of Aspire Zone. A large quantity of respondents is housed in compounds in these urban areas. Due to the high walls protecting both the privacy of Qatari families and compounds and due to a missing supply of proper pedestrian walkways, public spaces or integrated services, the urban periphery of Doha is generally perceived as rather unfamiliar and unattractive by all migrant groups. Respondents with a Western background are mostly repelled by the current built environment in Doha's suburbs, while Middle Eastern respondents perceive the urban spaces produced by these developments as less conflicted.

The comparison of all four urban spaces results in the observation that substantial areas and places of Doha are currently perceived as rather unattractive. While key landmark urban spaces, such as the Corniche, shape an impressive image of Doha as an emerging international and modern metropolis, the actual everyday urban environment of most respondents in suburban and downtown areas differs dramatically from this well-designed and maintained urban scene. The rapid urban growth in combination with missing regulations led to fragmented and chaotic urban landscapes with hardly any distinct identities. Although the dense built environment of central areas is in clear contrast to the low-rise urban sprawl along Doha's periphery, both urban landscapes are an expression of randomness and supply-driven approaches within local real estate markets. Doha is therefore an archetypal case of a late twentieth-century-born city in the Global South in which key spaces are overemphasized to brand a city with a globalized image, while most urban areas are perceived replaceable, repetitive and repelling.[51]

Conclusion

Today, Gulf cities reflect a significant social segregation and fragmentation due to major income differences resulting in new urban typologies. Accordingly, the differing neighbourhoods and their locations have led to a manifestation of this spatial disintegration. Furthermore, the increasing diversity of cultural groups has caused rather differing perceptions and thus some migrants are more tolerant to certain circumstances than others due to past experiences in developing countries. The largest proportion of foreign populations currently experience Gulf cities as a temporary opportunity to earn money and professional experience due to limited contracts. The frequent move of migrants has led to a housing market in which most properties are built to supply basic needs, rather than accommodate cultural particularities. This shelter-approach has led to densely populated and fragmented suburban and downtown areas that now face the major threat to turn into highly problematic districts with shrinking liveability due to missing infrastructure and architectural qualities.

Despite missing building standards, the increasing land prices have led to a significant shortage in housing supply. Today, emerging affordable housing crises can be found in the case of lower-income national populations and migrant medium-income families who have decided to settle long-term. The complex requirements regarding safe surroundings, schools and efficient mobility have made many downtown areas increasingly unsuitable for families. The move to suburbs has therefore been the logical consequence where increasingly apartment buildings have been built within compounds in far distances from urban centres to provide affordable housing. While low- to mid-income groups are struggling to find appropriate residences, the higher-income groups have the option to decide between a growing variety of exclusive projects from waterfront high-rise apartment buildings to villas along golf courses. However, this group is shrinking, and the vacancy rates of the most exclusive housing projects are usually high.

Evidently, the national population is facing a growing challenge to maintain the high housing standards, which are still rooted in the first urbanization period and the experienced welfare state conditions. Despite the common practice to still distribute land to locals and to support their housing supply via government programmes, the rising construction costs and the location of the allocated plots often prevent the development of new homes. Thus, many young families are forced to live with their parents, which led to the common phenomenon of intergenerational living.[52] In general, it can be observed that increasingly local citizens are forced to move to the free housing market and rent apartments or dwellings, where adjustments to local customs are visibly lacking.

Contemporary trends in housing reflect a very particular stage of development, in which supply- and speculation-driven dynamics are more dominant than a gradual adjustment to the lifestyle trends of a settled and consolidated multicultural society. In future, it is anticipated that the different lifestyle groups will further diversify and that local housing markets will be tested to accommodate the various needs of migrant and local populations. The long-term settlement of migrant workforce and the beginning engagement of national citizens in new economies will become important preconditions for a functioning demand-driven development and a clear reflection of a new identity of Gulf cities as integrated societies rather than as temporary shells and shelters for short-term migration.

Gulf cities can be best described as migrant cities built by migrants for future migrants, who however remain unknown. Today, most developers have not consciously adjusted their ground floor designs of new housing projects to any cultural or lifestyle preferences. The main tendency is to follow basic layouts permitting shared living and ways to reduce construction and maintenance costs. The limitation for adjusting housing designs to the actual tenants and their demands is indicative of an absence of a clear vision of a typical long-term tenant or end-user and the pressure to meet the rapidly increasing demand for new housing units. This has forced migrant communities to adjust to present conditions rather than redefining housing based on their needs and preferences.

Consequently, one of the key challenges of contemporary urban governance in Gulf cities is the development of highly inclusive urban environments offering attractive neighbourhoods to a wide range of different lifestyle trends of multicultural societies. Today, the general housing conditions are not perceived as satisfactory at several levels. All main housing typologies are frequently criticized with respect to their general design characteristics and construction standards, the poor integration of accessible services in neighbourhoods and the lack of responsiveness to certain preferences. Thus, many new tools and strategies need to be explored with respect to the way in which various housing typologies and neighbourhoods can be adjusted, adapted or upgraded. As well, the exploration of new strategic imperatives and guidance for new developments should be a priority. In future, it is anticipated that enhanced housing standards will play a decisive role in transforming Gulf cities into liveable environments for all communities and cultural groups.

Notes

1   Friedmann, 'The World City Hypothesis', p. 69.
2   Cohen, 'The New International Division of Labor'.

3 Peter Taylor, *World City Network: A Global Urban Analysis* (London, 2003).

4 Molotch, 'The City as a Growth Machine'.

5 Bardhan and Kroll, 'Globalization and the Real Estate Industry'.

6 Andrew Narwold and Jonathan Sandy, 'Valuing Housing Stock Diversity', *International Journal of Housing Markets and Analysis*, 3/1 (2010), pp. 53–9.

7 Nicole Gurran, Vivienne Milligan, Doug Baker and Laura B. Bugg, 'International Practice in Planning for Affordable Housing: Lessons for Australia', *Australian Housing and Urban Research Institute* (2007), p. 44.

8 Aerni, 'Coping with Migration-Induced Urban Growth'.

9 Sinus Institute, Profile. Available at: www.sinus-institut.de/en/about-us/profile/ (accessed 3 January 2018).

10 Maria Gröger, Victoria Schmid and Thomas Bruckner. 'Lifestyles and Their Impact on Energy-related Investment Decisions'. *Low Carbon Economy*, 2 (2011), pp. 107–14.

11 Pierre Bourdieu, *Outline of a Theory of Practice* (Cambridge, 1977).

12 Pierre Bourdieu, *Distinction: A Social Critique of the Judgment of Taste* (Boston, 1987).

13 Roland Benedikter, 'Lifestyles', in H. Anheier, M. Juergensmeyer and V. Faessel (eds), *Encyclopedia of Global Studies* (London, 2012), pp. 1076–80.

14 Mary Douglas, *Natural Symbols: Explorations in Cosmology* (London, 1970).

15 Mary Douglas, 'A History of Grid and Group Cultural Theory', *Semioticon 2006* [online]. Available at: www.semioticon.com/sio/files/douglas-et-al/douglas1.pdf ?lbisphpreq=1&file=douglas-et-al/douglas1.pdf (accessed 3 January 2018).

16 Dennis Chapman, *The Home and Social Status* (London, 1955).

17 Douglas, 'A History of Grid and Group Cultural Theory', p. 4.

18 Ibid.

19 Susan S. Fainstein, 'Cities and Diversity: Should We Want It? Should We Plan for It?', *Urban Affairs Review*, 42/1 (2005), pp. 3–19.

20 Maysa Zahra, *The Legal Framework of the Sponsorship Systems of the Gulf Cooperation Council Countries: A Comparative Examination*. Available at: www. gulfmigration.eu/media/pubs/exno/GLMM_EN_2015_10.pdf (accessed 3 January 2018).

21 Edit Schlaffer and Ulrich Kropiunigg, 'Saudi Youth: Unveiling the Force for Change', *Center for Strategic and International Studies*, 2011. Available at: www.csis-prod. s3.amazonaws.com/s3fs-public/legacy_files/files/publication/111104_Gulf_Anal ysis_Saudi_Youth.pdf (accessed 3 January 2018).

22 Thomas Hojrup, *State, Culture, and Life Modes: The Foundations of Life Mode Analysis* (London, 2003).

23 Ashraf M. Salama, 'Trans-disciplinary Knowledge for Affordable Housing', *Open House International*, 36/3 (2011), pp. 7–15, p. 10.

24 Elspeth Graham and Albert Sabater, 'Population Change and Housing across the Lifecourse: Demographic Perspectives, Methodological Challenges and Emerging Issues', *ESRC Centre for Population Change*, Working Paper Series, 64 (2015).

25 Thorstein Veblen, *The Theory of the Leisure Class* (Oxford, 2013).

26 Julia O. Beamish, Rosemary C. Goss and JoAnn Emmel, 'Lifestyle Influences on Housing Preferences', *Housing and Society*, 28/1–2 (2001).

27 *Arab News*, 'More than Half of GCC Population under age 25', 17 July 2012. Available at: www.arabnews.com/saudi-arabia/more-half-gcc-population-under -age-25 (accessed 3 January 2018).

28 *Prime Minister's Office*. UAE Vision 2021, 2010. Available at: www.vision2021.ae/en/ news/emiratization-efforts-private-sector (accessed 3 January 2018).

29 Clare C. Marcus, *House as a Mirror of Self* (Berkeley, 1997).

30 Lance Freeman, 'Interpreting the Dynamics of Public Housing: Cultural and Rational Choice Explanations', *Housing Policy Debate*, 9/2 (1998), pp. 323–53, p. 330.

31 Norma L. Newmark and Patricia J. Thompson, *Self, Space and Shelter* (San Francisco, 1977).

32 Glenn D. Walters, *Lifestyle Theory: Past, Present and Future* (New York, 2006), p. 3.

33 Ashraf M. Salama, Florian Wiedmann and Hatem G. Ibrahim, 'Lifestyle Trends and Housing Typologies in Emerging Multicultural Cities', *Journal of Architecture and Urbanism*, 41/4 (2017), pp. 316–27.

34 Richard Florida, *The Rise of the Creative Class: And How It's Transforming Work, Leisure, Community and Everyday Life* (New York, 2002).

35 Leonie Sanderock, *Towards Cosmopolis: Planning for Multicultural Cities* (Chichester, 1998).

36 Sulayman N. Khalaf, 'The Evolution of the Gulf City Type: Oil and Globalization', in J. W. Fox, N. Mourtada-Sabbah and M. Al-Mutawa (eds), *Globalization and the Gulf* (New York, 2006), p. 259.

37 Jure Snoj, *Population of Qatar by Nationality*. bq magazine, 2014. Available at: www. bq-magazine.com/economy/2013/12/population-qatar-nationality [accessed 10 February 2017].

38 General Secretariat of Development Planning, *Qatar National Vision 2030*.

39 Abu Dhabi Council for Economic Development, 'Sustainability – Playing a Central Role in Abu Dhabi's Economic Growth', p. 23.

40 Charles L. Choguill, 'Toward Sustainability of Human Settlements'. *Habitat International*, 20/3 (1996), pp. 5–8.

41 Marino Bonaiuto, Antonio Aiello, Marco Perugini, Mirilia Bonnes and Anna P. Ercolani, 'Multidimensional Perception of Residential Environment Quality and Neighbourhood Attachment in the Urban Environment', *Journal of Environmental Psychology*, 19/4 (1999), pp. 331–52.

42 Edgar Butler, Stuart Chapin, George C. Hemmens, Edward J. Kaiser, Michael A. Stegman and Shirley F. Weiss, 'Moving Behavior and Residential Choice: A National Survey', *National Cooperative Highway Research Programs*, Report No. 81 (Washington DC, 1969).

43 Eddie C. M. Hui, Si M. Li, Francis K. W. Wong, Zheng Yi and Ka H. Yu, 'Ethnicity, Cultural Disparity and Residential Mobility: Empirical Analysis of Hong Kong', *Habitat International*, 36/1 (2012), pp. 1–10.

44 Ashraf M. Salama, Florian Wiedmann, Alain Thierstein and Wafa Al-Ghatam, 'Knowledge Economy as an Initiator of Sustainable Urbanism in Emerging Metropolises: The Case of Doha, Qatar', *International Journal of Architectural Research: ArchNet-IJAR*, 10/1 (2016), pp. 274–324.

45 Ministry of Development Planning and Statistics, *Population and Social Statistics*, 2016. Available at: https://www.mdps.gov.qa/en/statistics/Statistical%20Releases /Population/Population/2016/Population_social_1_2016_AE.pdf (accessed 3 January 2018).

46 Gulf Migration, 'UAE: A Comparison of Average Monthly Salaries Received by Nationality Group of Workers'. Available at: www.gulfmigration.eu/uae-a-comparison-of-average-monthly-salaries-received-by-nationality-group-of-workers-in-us-selected-professions-2015/?print=pdf (accessed 3 January 2018).

47 Ashraf M. Salama and Florian Wiedmann, 'Perceiving Urban Liveability in an Emerging Migrant City', *Proceedings of the ICE – Urban Design and Planning*, 169/7 (2016), pp. 268–78.

48 Raffaello Furlan and Laura Faggion, 'The Souq Waqif Heritage Site in Doha: Spatial Form and Livability', *American Journal of Environmental Engineering*, 5/5 (2015), pp. 146–60.

49 Salama and Wiedmann, *Demystifying Doha*.

50 Mirincheva et al., 'The spatial development potentials of business districts in Doha'.

51 Neil Brenner and Roger Keil, 'From Global Cities to Globalized Urbanization', in R. T. LeGates and F. Stout (eds), *The City Reader* (New York, 2011), pp. 599–608.

52 Sharon Nagy, 'Making Room for Migrants, Making Sense of Difference: Spatial and Ideological Expression of Social Diversity in Urban Qatar', *Urban Studies*, 43 (2006), pp. 119–37.

7

The everyday urban environment
of migrant communities

Following contemporary literature various theories of everyday urbanism can be encountered.[1] It is often portrayed as the common and collective form of urbanism since it capitalizes on the day-to-day reality of life experienced by a majority with no major implication to define perfect configurations of built environments. Second, everyday urbanism is used on a conversational level since it integrates diversity and simultaneity and a certain informal flexibility. It is thus seen as a non-structuralist form of urbanism softening the relationship between the designed environment and socio-spatial practice.[2]

According to other common theories, everyday urbanism reflects life as a receptacle of all types of meanings that range from the ordinary to the extraordinary.[3] Thus, public activities in typical urban settings are investigated in the representative realms of everyday life, which has become a crucial field in current cultural discourses.[4] Instead of conceived top-down decision-making by few stakeholders, everyday urbanism is produced by the spatial practices and perceptions of communities interacting with their surroundings. In Gulf cities, the resulting diversity of these interactions can be seen as an important indicator of how everyday urbanism is currently taking place.

Everyday urbanism expresses a diversity of ethnic and cultural backgrounds and the resulting lifestyle trends of social groups. From a spatial perspective, diversity is usually expressed in mixed building typologies and uses resulting in differentiated physical forms, in which people from different social classes and backgrounds can reside and work side by side. In this context, public spaces can always be identified as places exhibiting the diversity of the working and residing communities. The relations between space diversity and collective urbanism have already been described by the writings of Louis Wirth in the 1930s.[5] Today, it is common knowledge but not always common practice that the integration of accessible public spaces can instantly lead to a variety of activities, catering different types of interaction, which are often essential for local economic development. Any discourse on diversity usually emphasizes a specific concern: either demographics and cultural backgrounds, economic opportunities or a focus on urban typologies. Everyday urbanism and its impact on urban diversity are thus often investigated by analysing key characteristics in cultural, economic and spatial terms.[6]

In the Gulf region, the current state of urban diversity is often assessed as rather limited. The recent extensive growth fuelled by regional and global migration led to limited demand-driven dynamics and long-term consolidation. In many cases, international planners and architects have defined urban developments via their plans and policy suggestions rooted in an understanding of supplying functional structures but following replaceable models. The resulting spatial conditions are thus often a direct expression of simplified urban functions rather than complex relations rooted in the various social groups and their preferences.[7] Thus, a vast majority of emerging cities share their basic characteristics in spite of the significant variety of backgrounds of their inhabitants.[8] This phenomenon of an increasing alienation between urban spaces and urban populations has often been discussed in the context of globalizing urban landscapes.[9] The relationship between inhabitants and their surrounding urban environment can be best observed in the case of public spaces, which have often remained the last domain exhibiting the creativity and resilience of social groups.[10]

To study these everyday urban environments and places of socio-spatial practice, various scientific concepts need to be introduced and discussed. These concepts emerge from disciplines and areas of interest that include environmental psychology or environment-behaviour studies, new urbanism and sociology. Within the field of environment-behaviour studies, Amos Rapoport argues that the physical elements of an environment are of direct influence on the relationships and activities that happen within them.[11] The built environment is thus both a force defining human movements and a result of the overall human spatial practice in one place.[12] The long-term relationship between residents and their surroundings will inevitably lead to a spatial expression of the social structure and eventually to a representation of their various needs and preferences as community or a group of individuals who share a substantial number of values.

Another important reference is the 'conceived-perceived-lived' triad of Henri Lefebvre. His understanding of a conceived space is rooted in conscious decisions leading to actions and thus mainly expressed in governance and all its decision-makers, who impose their notion of 'order' on the concrete world.

Perceived space is introduced as the space where movement and interaction take place and where networks develop and materialize rooted in the basic needs of all users. Third, he defined lived space as the way how people live and relate to their environment. This direct unconscious and non-verbal relationship of humans to space is represented in images responsible for place attachment and thus the rather individual and subjective notion of places. Thus, everyday urbanism is widely understood as an integrated concept rooted in the lived space and receptacle of all types of meanings that range from the ordinary to the extraordinary.[13] Lived space and its everyday environment experienced and expressed by the spatial practices of the public are often identified as oversimplified domains of daily existence but a crucial field in contemporary urban culture.[14]

In the awakening of an enhanced understanding and emphasis on lived space and the relationship between people and place since the 1960s, 'the right to the city' became an important concept, which was introduced by Lefebvre as a responsive approach to renew and even replace contemporary urban politics. Thus, it became widely used and discussed, often by political activists. Harvey's essay 'The Right to the City' reemphasized the concept of a lived space, stating that the right to the city is far more than the individual liberty to access urban resources: it is a right to change ourselves by changing the city.[15] The lived space is thus seen as a passive experience wherein the outer physical environment resonates with the inner imagination, which makes symbolic use of outer objects, retaining or rejecting them according to an arbitrary, because subjective, though often cohesive system of priorities and individual desirability.

Within a certain spatial context focal points, familiar attractions or environments can define the relationship between people and places. This can be observed in various elements of a city, such as a mosque, a graveyard and a square. The public realm of urban spaces can thus express the inner relationships between inhabitants and their built environment by being either used and appreciated or abandoned. Thus, the complex relationship between inhabitants and existing urban spaces can always ignite new development patterns, such as a newly emerging resistance to decision-making disadvantaging a major share of the public. This view was further reinforced in the environment-behaviour and community-planning literature.[16] Today, environment-behaviour studies are often carried out by the systematic examination of human behaviour as it relates to the everyday life and its spatial context.

Behavioural studies are therefore important factors in understanding urban spaces expressing everyday life or if they are imposed shells forcing users to adapt. While the absence of any street life can have various reasons, such as security concerns or introverted lifestyles rooted in cultural particularities, the actual activities can be observed and evaluated to gather in-depth insights if urban spaces are perceived as attractive or repelling. Urban spaces can thus be identified as either key centres inviting a wide range of social groups to interact leading to a directly reflected social diversity or as segregated and fragmented spaces with limited access to any major segments of an urban society and thus often abused and abandoned.[17] Behavioural studies need to be combined with an in-depth understanding of the spatial environment, its historic roots as well as its various elements to gain insights into the main factors causing complex social–spatial practice of a specific community.

Since the end of the twentieth century, Gulf cities and their public spaces in urban centres have witnessed a rather significant change due to the extensive move of migrants engaged in the commencing construction boom. The unprecedented scale of migration led to the common practice of building mass housing schemes in the form of densely built towers and blocks in historic districts and their adjacent areas. This sudden change led to the move of previously residing communities to newly built settlements in urban outskirts. This however meant a significant and currently still increasing segregation of bachelor migrants with short-term contracts and limited incentives to stay in the Gulf and a disperse and fragmented relocation of families, who already arrived during the first wave of a major international migration during the 1970s, after the foundation of all small Gulf States. This group is particularly important since many of their children were born and raised in the Gulf and are thus rather attached to their birthplaces, which resulted in investments and business initiatives.

In the following, the chapter will introduce the previous spatial settings of central neighbourhoods, which were mainly defined by the first physical planning efforts and thus a rather coordinated provision of services and infrastructure. These neighbourhoods, such as Al Asmakh and Al Jadeeda in Doha and Al Satwa in Dubai, have witnessed a significant demographic change since the end of the twentieth century and thus the behaviour of residing migrant groups is a major reflection of the current socio-spatial realities. The chapter will be concluded by a small excursion to a mega project, known as Msheireb, in Doha's historic centre, which is one of the most recent and extensive urban renewal attempts in the Gulf region. The complete replacement of an entire traditional neighbourhood has introduced another alternative route of redevelopment in most accessible locations. The anticipated future gentrification is in clear contrast to the continuous deterioration and high urban densities in downtown areas. Today, most central urban areas need to be rediscovered and redefined after they lost their former population living in traditional neighbourhoods.

Traditional migrant neighbourhoods

Since the end of the 1960s, the newly gained national independence led to rather fast incentives to implement new master plans for all major capital cities. While the national populations were catered with new housing in suburbs, the historic centres and their traditional market areas became the main residence of foreign labourers. Between these mixed-use and densely built inner-city cores the transition areas towards the outskirts were used to integrate neighbourhoods for middle-income migrants and their families, often in proximity to the newly built central business corridors stretching towards airports or ports. These neighbourhoods were often built by a mix of medium- and low-rise apartment buildings following zoning plans and integrating commercial activities in the form of ground floor shops and offices along main roads. The inner district areas were served by social facilities, such as mosques, health centres and occasionally small green areas or playgrounds. The size of the different neighbourhoods was mainly defined by the major road grid, which in many cases became a spatial barrier enhancing the introversion of inner residential areas.

In Abu Dhabi, for instance, the first master plans led to mid-sized blocks with six floors surrounded by commercial or mixed-use towers with an average height of twenty floors along the main road grid (Figure 7.1). Small parks and major cultural projects, such as museums, defined key orientation points within the rigid urban form focusing on high density and mixed uses in central areas and a quick transition to suburban surroundings. During the 1980s and 1990s, an average of 200 residential blocks were constructed every year. The strict building regulations led to rather repetitive typologies, while the efficient supply catered the increasing housing need sufficiently. These housing dynamics were initiated by the Khalifa Committee, who was responsible for distributing state-owned land to Emirati citizens and who oversaw the development of a large part of all inner-city areas.[18] Since migrant families were not permitted to buy housing units, the rental market led to a steady income basis for many Emiratis, as well as rather low building standards. During these first decades of modern urbanization, the emerging migrant neighbourhoods benefited from their central location and walkable access to shops and services. Thus, despite their rather monotonous appearances and questionable construction standards, they

Figure 7.1 The typical mixed-use blocks in the inner city of Abu Dhabi.

have often been perceived as an adequate and integrated urban form providing residents opportunities of short distances to work places and main leisure spaces.

While these central areas have quickly accommodated an increasing share of migrant bachelors sharing apartments, the adjacent areas have been built with low-rise dwellings for families benefiting from lower densities, such as the Al Zaab neighbourhood (Figure 7.2). The neighbourhood was formerly commonly known as Al Zaab Souq, where the Al Zaab family settled for generations after its migration from the Northern Emirates.[19] The district is known for its high diversity of commercial activities and migrants residing in its precinct. There is a moderate mix of old and new housing typologies offering accommodation for various income groups. Its central location is furthermore benefiting from a quick access to major business districts and the waterfront with its public spaces and leisure facilities. Furthermore, families highly benefit from integrated schools. A major mosque marks the main centre of the district, while

Figure 7.2 A typical medium-density neighbourhood in central Abu Dhabi.

smaller neighbourhood mosques express the cultural diversity of the various Islamic communities. The Al Zaab neighbourhood is an important example of a previously developed and still functioning neighbourhood, which has not significantly suffered from recent transformation tendencies yet.

Other neighbourhoods in Abu Dhabi have however already witnessed their recent redevelopment due to rising investment pressure. One prominent example has been the redevelopment of the old Central Market, which was known for its importance as meeting point and as a bazaar for lower-income groups. In 2014, a mega project, designed by Foster + Partners, has replaced the rather informal market place with an artistic modern reinterpretation of a traditional Souq, which however functions as a shopping mall.

In Dubai, the urban modernization first began in the 1950s, when the first basic electricity, communication and water infrastructure was built. Furthermore, the waterway in the Creek was developed for modern shipping and the first provisional airfield was put into operation. These early investments were made possible by the financial support of Great Britain and loans from Bahrain, Qatar and Kuwait, where oil production had already started. Apart from this external support, it was Dubai's own economic success based on its high volume of re-export (e.g. in 1950, 85 per cent of all imports were re-exported) that made the emirate one of the most important trading hubs of the region and therefore one of the most attractive locations for business.[20] Two basic factors for this successful economic development can be distinguished, namely, the attractive trading policies provided by the government and the migrant merchants with their diverse trading networks in MENA and South Asia.[21] The continuous migration from South Asia and Iran to Dubai was initially highly affected by already settled families leading to a dense exchange and entrepreneurial initiatives in form of SMEs. Although the population came to just around 60,000 inhabitants during the 1960s, Dubai was already known for its cultural diversity and international business networks, which quickly became an important factor for both economic and spatial developments.

As in many Gulf countries, the first phase of oil urbanization in Dubai was dominated by individual major developments without comprehensive central planning. Nevertheless, after the establishment of a modern public administration, a first development plan was published in 1960 by the British architect John R. Harris, which was called 'Survey and Plan – Capital City of Dubai'. This early guide plan included five major development goals. These were the provision of a road system which would be appropriate for the anticipated volume of traffic; the zoning of town areas suitable for industry, commerce, schools and public buildings; the choosing of areas for new residential quarters outside the boundaries of the existing town; the choosing of sites for school buildings, open spaces and local centres within the new residential areas and finally the creation of a town centre in Dubai.[22] In accordance with Arab-Islamic traditions, land ownership in Dubai was based on two principles – within a settlement any plot of land that had been occupied by a homestead for a long period of time belonged to the inhabitant. Elsewhere, un-built land was at the disposal of the ruler. These principles were legally applied at the beginning of the 1960s and led to considerably centralized control of urban development due to the free use of unsettled land by the ruler.[23] Inner-city areas were thus usually owned by Emirati families, who however moved to suburban locations and started to invest in residential and commercial developments leading to a quick rise of an expanding town centre in Deira and Bur Dubai including many migrant neighbourhoods.

In 1971, it was again the architect John R. Harris and his office who were engaged to develop a new master plan, the so-called Dubai Development Plan. The new plan reacted to the unexpected rapid urban development and the new financial possibilities that arose due to the beginning of oil production. The detailed land-use plan defined new residential developments and the expansion of Dubai's main centre.[24] The extensive subdivision of land led to increasing suburbanization that had a standard typology of two-storey villas. In neighbourhoods in proximity to central areas, typologies were often mixed and both apartment buildings and commercial developments were integrated. Dubai's centre initially remained at the Creek until the Sheikh Zayed Road began to emerge as the new central business district in the South. Because of its unique function and form the centre and its various neighbourhoods were mentioned in the Dubai Development Plan: 'Additionally to the support given to the economy by activities using the Creek as a facility, there is an undoubted attraction in the presence of water and of boats near the centre of the town. Both from a functional and an aesthetic viewpoint, therefore, developing Dubai should still be centred on the Creek, where marine activity continues to flourish.'[25] Within only a few years, the residences in Dubai's downtown were almost completely occupied by migrants residing in various neighbourhoods in densely built areas, such as Deira, or low- to medium-rise districts, such as Al Mankhool, in proximity to Bur Dubai (Figure 7.3).

Some neighbourhoods with moderate densities, such as Al Satwa, developed along main growth corridors as Sheikh Zayed Road in transition areas. Al Satwa is an important example of a previous traditional family-oriented neighbourhood, which witnessed a rapid demographic change since the 1990s due to the move of single migrant workers.[26] The residences were built on rather moderate plots

Figure 7.3 A mixed-use neighbourhood within Dubai's historic market district.

(15 × 15 metres) and were originally designed for Emirati communities, who however quickly moved on to more generous dwellings. The boom in many service sectors led to a significant housing shortage for lower-income groups leading to a rather quick transformation of these central neighbourhoods due to missing infrastructural capacities to serve higher urban densities in the periphery. Similar tendencies can be currently observed in Al Jafiliya and Al Mankhool. Today, Al Satwa has however become known for the most recent strategy to demolish and replace these central and accessible neighbourhoods, which mainly accommodate lower-income migrants in low-rise dwellings built in the 1960s and 1970s, with modern mega projects. The Jumeirah Garden City will replace the entire district and all its neighbourhoods. Despite its name, this garden city development will mainly consist of residential high-rises designed for upper real estate markets.

In Qatar, similar tendencies of extensive redevelopment can be found in the precincts of the historic core and its traditional markets. Doha's Al Asmakh district, for instance, is part of the original settlement area built before the extensive oil production commenced during the late 1930s.[27] The district covers an area of approximately 30 hectares and it was originally used as a residential area by Qatari communities, who however quickly moved to spacious villas in outskirts during the 1960s. The vernacular-built environment was a direct expression of the local climate and culture. The small port and the main market, known as Souq Waqif, were easily accessible for all inhabitants leading to a distinctive main road structure, which was defined by the general wind direction to enable the natural cooling of the district.[28] The building clusters were formed by courtyard houses in various sizes expressing the traditional emphasis on privacy as well as the need to use land along the coast as efficient as possible to enable access to the few water sources along the dry riverbed. While most buildings were replaced by modern developments, the small plot sizes usually prevented building heights to exceed three floors. Since the 1970s mainly lower-income migrants resided in Al Asmakh or other adjacent neighbourhoods, such as Msheireb and Al Jadeeda.

The move of migrant families to suburban districts along the ring roads, where many new neighbourhoods were built during the 1970s and 1980s, led to shared accommodations and thus the highest population densities in Doha's downtown. In some areas, the low-rise buildings were replaced by multi-storey apartment buildings as well as commercial enterprises.[29] The first zoning efforts however inhibited the spread of commercial land use, which has only been permitted along the main road grid.[30] Consequently, the inner district's residential layout was often preserved. The limited access by car also prevented higher built densities and thus a substantial part of historic buildings was kept intact. But the lack of investment in renovation and maintenance led to a state of continuous deterioration. In most recent years, mega projects, such as the Msheireb development, were launched to replace entire central neighbourhoods causing a move of thousands of single guest workers (Figure 7.4).[31] In other cases, such as Al Sadd and the adjacent districts along C-Ring and B-Ring Road, the quick replacement of former compounds and medium-rise apartment buildings with new mass housing developments led to the move of migrant families, who have often resided in these areas for more than thirty years.

In Bahrain, the master plan for the capital Manama, which was designed by the British architect A. Monroe, covered an area of about 2,340 hectares, which was about seven times the urban area in the 1950s. According to this plan, substantial areas were allocated to land that had to be reclaimed in the following decades.[32] In addition to general land use and the road grid, which included the Manama ring road, the first master plan covered the water infrastructure, electric network and proposals for the location of parks, mosques, health centres and schools.[33] Although its urban fabric of narrow and irregular streets remained

Figure 7.4 A demolition site in the historic centre of Doha.

to a large extent, most buildings were replaced by modern cement constructions. Due to the rapid increase in size of Manama's urban area, the old core of Manama constituted only about 10 per cent of Manama's total urban area. In a study made in 1987, it was observed that about 42 per cent of the centre's population was Bahraini. A lack of maintenance led to traditional buildings rapidly decaying and being replaced, thus causing a large part of the traditional urban fabric to be lost. But due to many mosques and so-called *ma'atams* still located there, the old core has remained a cultural and social centre for many Bahraini.[34] Furthermore, the migration of foreign labour into the old districts meant that the population and its density was continuously changing and growing with as many as 952 people living on 1 hectare, which is three times the average density of Manama in the late 1980s.[35]

While the master plan of 1968 estimated that about 200,000 people would live in the capital at the end of the 1990s, less than 180,000 inhabitants were counted in 1998, which meant that the densities in the new southern urban expansion was rather moderate. The main reason for this was the development of low-rise neighbourhoods and the move of many inhabitants to satellite and dormitory settlements. Apart from the expansion of old settlements such as the town of Riffa where the population increased from about 12,000 people in 1965 to about 63,423 inhabitants in 1998, the 2 new satellite towns Isa Town and Hamad Town became preferred residential areas.[36] While Isa Town was already established at the end of the 1960s and gradually expanded during the 1970s, Hamad Town was designed and developed by the Ministry of Housing after a proposal of the Physical Planning Department in 1979.[37] These new settlements mainly catered the housing needs of national communities. But due to their move, many districts in Manama, such as Adliya, transformed into multicultural neighbourhoods with a rather diverse identity. Former suburban structures have thus turned into mixed-use centres catering commerce, culture and entertainment, while being the home of migrants. Migrant families often settled in adjacent districts and benefited from the previously planned and implemented social infrastructure.

All in all, three main urban areas can be distinguished in Bahrain at the beginning of the 1990s, namely, the old city centres in Manama and Muharraq with their existing road networks, the new urban areas that followed the general land use and subdivision plans of the Physical Planning Department and the new master-planned towns and settlements in the outskirts. In addition, the small villages within the agricultural areas remained important entities reflecting the history of local communities. While many migrant families settled in lower-density neighbourhoods in the rather accessible outer districts of Manama, labourers were mainly accommodated in the old market areas or in proximity to industrial sites. In a dramatic contrast with all other Gulf cities, a significant share of local communities has remained in their old neighbourhoods and villages, which have often been swallowed by Manama's urban expansion (Figure 7.5). In some cases, however, these neighbourhoods have witnessed a rapid demographic change, such as the former Al Hoora village, where tourism, particularly from Saudi Arabia, turned adjacent sites along Exhibition Avenue into Manama's main nightlife centre. Since the turn of the centuries, many multi-storey apartment buildings have been built in high densities leading to new demographic realities in many districts due to an increasing share of migrant bachelors and a subsequent move of families.

In summary, the preceding analysis argues that neighbourhoods, planned and developed in transition areas between historic cores and suburbs during the 1970s and 1980s, were typical residences in an urban setting surrounded by mixed-use developments in proximity to main business districts. The focus on car-based urbanism restricted built densities and led to spatial barriers in the form of major road grids. But neighbourhoods themselves were often experienced as defined entities, usually in form of bigger and thus more introverted urban areas with mosques as main community centres. These neighbourhoods provided functional spaces for migrant families to interact despite often underdeveloped public spaces. The main reasons can be found in centrality, density and diversity

Figure 7.5 An old neighbourhood in Downtown Manama.

enabling daily sidewalk interaction and thus meeting grounds for various social groups. Thus, Jane Jacob's general findings of dynamic and lively urban spaces can be rediscovered in the contexts of these first migrant neighbourhoods in Gulf cities.[38] Sufficient densities and small block sizes enabled the quick access to shops, services and work places, while the mix of old and new buildings integrated various income groups. Despite low architectural and construction qualities and the lack of certain services, these neighbourhoods became the homes for settled migrant families and thus a first generation was born and raised in these places. Their recent replacement in extensive or gradual developments has led to urgent questions about the current form of everyday urbanism and future dynamics.

Contemporary everyday urbanism

Today most national populations are residing in suburban neighbourhoods, often in far distances to urban centres. Many migrants, who already settled in the Gulf before the turn of the centuries, have been experiencing a major change of their neighbourhoods due to the construction boom in recent years.[39] The rapid shift from a rather conservative welfare state, causing consolidated developments guided by technocratic processes during the first period of modernization, to emerging cities built on mass migration meant the end of previously established central and medium-density neighbourhoods. Steadily, new mass housing developments led to a shortage of social infrastructure and services. And the demolition of former residences forced many families to leave their neighbourhoods, in which they have often resided for several decades. In a rather short period of time shopping malls in outskirts have become their new centres of leisure and consumption replacing their previous routines to meet in mixed-use central areas (Figure 7.6). Thus, a rather distinctive economic environment built on the direct exchange and interaction between diverse cultural and income groups has recently begun to transform due to new demographic realities in central areas.[40]

Most migrant communities residing in these mass housing developments have recently arrived from the Indian subcontinent (e.g. India, Nepal and Bangladesh), South-East Asia (e.g. Philippines) and Middle East (e.g. Egypt, Jordan and Sudan).[41] A large percentage of these migrants only dwell a limited number of years in Gulf cities without their families and usually share accommodation, which has increased urban densities. Both the still remaining settled migrants and the continuously exchanging majority have created rather

Figure 7.6 Restaurants in a shopping mall in Abu Dhabi.

distinctive neighbourhoods and particular ways of urban life, induced by their own cultures.[42] The contemporary street life in these areas is thus an expression of a large part of the overall population of Gulf cities, who have experienced an increasing struggle to be heard and to be integrated within today's urbanism.[43] Due to short-term contracts, the frequent exchange of these communities has led to a complex urban scenario of highly populated districts with rather small incentives towards consolidation rooted in long-term housing solutions.

Various studies have been undertaken about Gulf urbanism from various disciplinary perspectives providing important insights into the relationship between various communities and the urban settings they use.[44] The everyday urban environment of migrants has recently gained new importance to identify key characteristics of a neglected and ignored aspect of contemporary urbanism in Gulf cities.[45] The recent urban transformation has led to new spatial and social contexts, in which the spatial practices of migrant communities can be observed and studied. The Al Asmakh and Al Jadeeda districts in Doha are important contemporary examples representing the current state and transformation process of urban neighbourhoods (Figure 7.7).

In recent years, various initiatives have been launched to redevelop the Al Asmakh and Al Jadeeda districts. While the approach to completely replace

Figure 7.7 A map of the inner city of Doha.

the entire districts was first followed due to the introduction of large-scale master plans, the complex land ownership due to small plots prevented the implementation of these planning efforts. In recent years, new development visions were initiated for both districts and a certain level of preservation strategies were integrated. Nevertheless, the future upgrading of the districts will inevitably lead to the move of migrant communities due to the expected rise of rental prices in central and well accessible areas.[46] Due to the narrow streets and the land ownership by a large number of different landlords, most inner district areas of both districts have however not been replaced yet by modern developments and a large amount of historic residential buildings, which are part of Doha's architectural heritage, can still be found. The lack of modern infrastructure in combination with the missing investment in the building substance led to a continuous deterioration in recent years. This deterioration is visible in the form of run-down facades as well as entire buildings, which have collapsed and cannot be inhabited anymore.

Due to the concentration of services and commercial developments along the main road grid, which provides a certain level of accessibility by car, the inner neighbourhoods have remained densely built with hardly any public realm. The main public spaces in these inner district areas can be found in the form of street corners, along pedestrian areas and in the surroundings of small mosques. Cold stores, barber shops and small cafes have settled along these sites to serve the migrant communities. Office workers hardly visit these inner district areas, and the high level of isolation led to an almost parallel urban environment within these densely built and populated neighbourhoods. This segregation has led to rather differing perceptions of the overall population regarding these residential areas within Doha's historic centre. While many labourers and other migrant groups, who have settled in Doha for decades, have been experiencing these neighbourhoods as an everyday urban space and main local identity, most high-income groups and recently arrived migrants lack any personal relation to these essential parts of Doha. The main exceptions are locals, who own properties and who associate these urban areas with their ancestors' neighbourhoods and the first phase of modern urbanization, when most commercial activities were still concentrated in Doha's historic core.[47]

According to the Ministry of Development Planning and Statistics in 2015, the number of inhabitants residing in the Al Asmakh district reached 2,086, of which almost 94 per cent are male.[48] The dominance of male residents is a clear sign for a large percentage of labourers, mainly from the Indian subcontinent, engaged in construction or in other low-income sectors.[49] In total, there are 264 low-rise buildings, of which 251 are currently used. Since there are only 432 housing units, there is a high occupancy rate and most bachelors usually share accommodation. The high urban density and the lack of living area per resident have led to a rather extensive use of the neighbourhood surroundings. The low income of residents and the lack of higher-income groups visiting the area have resulted in that integrated commercial services are reduced to minimum needs and demands. The resulting economic activities have thus led to very particular spatial conditions and a strong differentiation between main roads and back-sided inner district areas.

The explorations of the socio-spatial practices of migrant communities in these neighbourhoods provide an excellent opportunity to learn about the history and profile of the city while understanding the unique particularities of issues relevant to environment-behaviour studies and the everyday urban environment including social interaction, appropriation, flexibility and adaptability. Nonetheless, the analysis and discussions offer important insights into planning and development efforts. Since low-income groups have limited access to shopping malls and high-profile public spaces, the neighbourhood's surroundings have thus become their main public realm for any interaction and thus both individual and collective spatial experience. The high concentration of social interaction during weekends has led to the survival of many small businesses and services catering to various cultural groups based on the relatively high level of land-use integration and lower rental rates in deteriorating buildings. The overcrowded areas and the resulting lack of private spaces have however transformed these districts into a highly conflicted urban setting.

While in the past, key areas, such as Souq Najada, were important nodal points for social interaction of residents in a very suitable public environment, the rising investment interests have led to a gradual replacement of these areas by launching hotels and other commercial developments to benefit from the proximity to Souq Waqif and the waterfront promenade.[50] In essence, two opposed urban spaces are currently facing each other, which can be particularly observed in the case of the Al Asmakh and Al Jadeeda districts. While on the one hand new mega projects generate globalized images appealing to investors and tourists, the bordering historic districts have first become a place of refuge for a large figure of labourers migrating to Qatar during a short period of time leading to highly overcrowded, informal and fragmented spatial urban conditions.[51] Therefore, they are rather suitable case studies to investigate contemporary everyday urbanism.

To understand everyday urbanism and its dynamics, functional, social and perceptual attributes of the urban environment must be investigated. In the case of the functional attributes of the neighbourhoods in Al Asmakh and Al Jadeeda, land-use integration can be regarded as rather sufficient due to the earlier zoning plans permitting mixed-use developments along all main access roads and establishing the integration of basic services and commercial activities. While the general accessibility to the key areas along the main road grid can be seen as rather high, there are no iconic places or landmarks structuring the districts and leading to an enhanced orientation. Although there are various possible gathering points along main roads, the general quality of the built environment and missing landscaping elements have led to a rather limited amount of spaces, which can be immediately perceived as potential social spaces or areas for leisure activities.

By observing the general backgrounds of users and visitors, social attributes can be identified. The district currently lacks social inclusion due to the dominant share of low-income groups, particularly male bachelors from South Asia. Certain areas are furthermore inhabited by groups with the same country of origin since their sponsors are responsible for their accommodation. The 'kafala' system is rooted in both law and custom and establishes that entry for the purposes of work requires a local sponsor, who is usually engaged in the migration process.[52] As a result, many accommodations are shared by groups from the same culture and ethnicity, and according to a survey of Human Rights Watch they are often reviewed as cramped and insufficient.[53]

Since a large percentage of the migrant community only resides a limited period in Qatar, shared language and cultural backgrounds have a direct impact on spatial practice and certain places have become their main meeting points. The lack of parks, sport grounds and sitting areas has however led to a very limited number of social activities, which are primarily reduced to exchanging news, trading, visiting barber shops, drinking tea as well as gathering around mosques after prayer times. Despite the proximity to main tourist centres and cultural attractions, such as waterfront developments, hardly any tourists can be observed in the area. While there is a dominance of the male population in the district, a minor number of women and children can be occasionally observed, who however avoid most areas and use roads as transitional spaces between homes and shops.

The perceptual attributes imply the degree to which these neighbourhoods foster the users' place attachment while offering opportunities for an intensive human experience. Due to the state of deterioration and the general lack of landscaping as well as landmarks, most urban spaces can hardly be assessed as attractive environments fostering high levels of interaction and thus identification process between inhabitants and their surroundings. A main deficit in this respect is the general lack of urban spaces generating a certain degree of comfort and relaxation by being less exposed to traffic or being defined by certain urban design elements. While boundaries between more private residential and public areas along streets are defined to a certain extent, the general perception of urban safety suffers from hardly observed spaces within narrow side roads. Yet, the greatest potential can be found in areas, where historic buildings have remained.

In general, the movement and the social interaction of migrant communities in key sites can reveal important insights how public spaces are currently used and perceived. Typical sites include both public thoroughfares and street corners offering small squares as meeting points (Figure 7.8). During weekday afternoons, there is a certain tendency that small groups are gathering and waiting for their transportation pick up. These groups are typically male labourers from the Indian subcontinent, who need to wait in certain places to look for new job opportunities. These new concentrations of low-income workforce have changed the entire characteristic of central areas, which were previously

Figure 7.8 A typical street corner in the Al Asmakh district.

inhabited by more diverse migrant communities. Due to limited living areas in residences, which are mainly used for sleeping, most labourers have adopted and appropriated their urban surroundings as an important space to socialize and to relax despite all spatial deficits. Due to the lack of any purchasing power of these social groups, formerly functioning retail districts suffer from the new demographic situation.

The gatherings of large groups have furthermore led to congested areas preventing efficient pedestrian movement and access. The perceived class spatial and class or social boundaries are particularly visible during evenings, when labourers come home to rest after a long day of work, gathering in street corners to socialize with friends and acquaintances. In addition to weekday evenings, intensive social interaction can be observed on weekends. The lack of street furniture led to informal sitting groups on sidewalks and on steps across shop fronts as well as the common phenomenon of bringing furniture to the outdoors. This led to distinctive sitting arrangements rooted in the direct interaction and spatial practice of people. Furthermore, male labourers have been frequently observed to rest and sleep in corners creating a socially problematic atmosphere of a homeless and stranded community. At the same time, the weekends represent the qualities of highly integrated districts with mixed land uses. Various commercial activities were observed, such as trading goods along the street and frequent visits of small stores. The large number of low-income groups has led to a spatial economic setting of rather evenly distributed and well accessible services for everyday needs, which has led to a reasonably dynamic but very limited market.

The exploration of the socio-spatial practice of migrant communities in traditional urban neighbourhoods provides an excellent opportunity to learn about the history and profile of the city while understanding the unique particularities of issues relevant to environment-behaviour studies and the everyday urban environment including social interaction, appropriation, flexibility and adaptability. Since labourers, who are currently most residents in districts, such as Al Asmakh and Al Jadeeda, have limited access to shopping malls and high-profile public spaces, the neighbourhood's surroundings have thus become the main public realm for any interaction and thus both individual and collective spatial experience. The high concentration of social interaction during weekends has led to the survival of many small businesses and services catering to various cultural groups based on the relatively high level of land-use integration and low rental rates in deteriorating buildings. The overcrowded area and the resulting lack of private spaces have however transformed traditional urban districts into an increasingly conflicted urban setting. While in the past, key central spaces in the surroundings of old markets were important nodal points for social interaction of residents in a very suitable public environment, the rising investment interests have led to a gradual replacement of these areas by launching hotels and other commercial developments to benefit from the proximity to new waterfront developments.[54]

Consequently, all low- to medium-rise traditional neighbourhoods in central and accessible locations are currently facing major transformations. The districts have first become a place of refuge for a large figure of labourers arriving in Gulf cities during a short period of time leading to highly overcrowded, informal and fragmented urban conditions resulting in the move of previously settled migrant communities.[55] Today, these districts are facing a future transformation by the gradual development of monotonous apartment blocks or a complete redevelopment by master developers. These districts have thus become objects of investment interests leading to a new era of potential gentrification in central areas and a subsequent move of previously residing and most vulnerable migrant groups. The complete redevelopment of similar districts, such as Msheireb in Doha or Al Satwa in Dubai, can be seen as a new threat to integrate sufficient affordable housing in most central locations.[56] The top-down master-planned projects will create state-of-the-art urban environments with high rental prices for social groups with profiles dramatically different from those of current migrant groups. Thus, these redevelopment schemes may result in eliminating an important chapter of the urban history and evolution of Gulf cities, while they also offer the potentials to attract high-income groups and thus a new level of social and economic interaction in urban settings.

Mega projects and future everyday urbanism

Today, one of the most comprehensive revitalization project in the Gulf is the previously mentioned Msheireb project in Doha's historic centre, which is carried out by a subsidy of Qatar Foundation. Its 31-hectare large site is situated in the west of Souq Waqif. In 2005, the old structures, mainly built during the period between 1950 and 1970, were demolished and the approximately $5.5 billion project was launched to revitalize the old centre by establishing residences for higher-income groups, including Qatari families, offices, retail and cultural venues.[57] Due to a total gross floor area of almost 760,000 square metres, the average plot ratio is 3.1 and the maximum plot ratio reaches more than 10.0 in the south of the project, where buildings reach maximum heights of 30 floors.[58] This high built density is mainly caused by economic feasibility considerations. The planned integration of a metro station on site will make the project highly accessible. Museums, public plazas and high-profile retail venues are included to establish the project as a major centre. The state-of-the-art architectural design by various architects, including Allies and Morrison, attempts to follow the reinterpretation and reinvention of local ornaments and thus to introduce a new standard in modern but traditionally inspired architecture in the region.[59]

The Msheireb project will have a significant impact on urban morphologies including land uses, urban densities and new spatial configurations. In the case of the adjacent Souq Waqif, old warehouses and stores were completely replaced with a replicate of the historic market, which was demolished during the first modern urbanization. Along the waterfront the Museum of Islamic Art replaced 15 hectares of potential commercial projects and extended the public realm along the Corniche. The most significant morphological transformation is however expected in the case of the Msheireb project, where a wide range of new typologies and land uses are introduced. A survey based on historic photography as well as GIS data unveils that the district was previously mainly occupied by residences in traditional neighbourhoods, which made up around 60 per cent of the total gross floor area. The remaining plot area was occupied by offices, retail and light industries. Moreover, most buildings were medium-rise apartment buildings with retail and services in ground floors. Around 25 per cent of the built area was occupied by low-rise residential buildings. Based on GIS population statistics between 10,000 to 15,000 inhabitants lived in Msheireb before the district was demolished.

According to the Msheireb project's master plan the gross floor area for residential use is increased for around 30,000 square metres in comparison to the previous district. However, the residential share of the total gross floor area will decrease to around 30 per cent. Thus, the overall built density is almost doubled to 310 per cent of the total plot area in comparison to the previous district. In contrast to the former configuration, offices will occupy almost one-third of the total gross floor area, which will lead to four times more office space. Small museums and the National Archive have been integrated to underline the cultural importance of the new district. The most significant transformation can be expected from the resettlement of high-income groups. The northern part of the district and around one-fifth of the residential area is reserved for Qatari families, while the southern and more densely built part accommodates medium- to high-income expatriates. This potential move of Qatari residents in Doha's old centre is part of the idea to introduce urban lifestyles and to initiate new gentrification processes. The overall population density within the district however can be expected to drop significantly to only around 200 inhabitants per hectare in comparison to the previous average of around 500 per hectare.

The high built density of the Msheireb project is mainly caused by the gradual increase in building height from three to seven floors in the northern to twenty to thirty floors in the southern part of the project. In contrast to the previous district, where a large quantity of around 300 small-scale buildings were built side by side in dense clusters, the new development includes around 100 buildings, mainly built in large blocks. The architectural language in the previous district can be best described as a mix of functionally designed cement buildings. In some cases, traditional courtyards were integrated, which are very suitable for the development of dense clusters and narrow streets. The urban design concept of the Msheireb project integrates the courtyard principle by translating it into modern parameter blocks, which however are reminiscent of European city cores rather than traditional Islamic cities. The large share of commercial use furthermore transforms the previously residential neighbourhoods into a major retail centre. While this shift to commercial use is needed to re-establish Doha's old core as one of the main urban centres, it also implies a discontinuation of historic urban morphologies with introverted neighbourhoods surrounded by commercial activities along main roads.

The Msheireb project reconfigures the urban grid network in various ways. It is worth examining more closely the changes in spatial morphology. In some cases, surrounding districts have not been connected limiting the potential for through movement between urban areas. Further, the master plan introduces a new centrality, parallel to Wadi Msheireb Road and extending into the centrality of Souq Waqif, thus integrating the two zones. In comparing the overall existing and proposed grid conditions, it can be said that the same degree of irregularity is maintained, thus not imposing a more linear order, but retaining a familiar degree of apparent randomness. Therefore, it could be concluded that the Msheireb project exhibits sensitivity to historical patterns in its proposal, which embeds a functional contemporary grid within a background of an irregular grid, formed of smaller unparalleled through- and to-movement corridors (Figure 7.9). The project will however lead to various transformations, not only regarding the physical urban environment but also regarding social and economic structures.

Figure 7.9 A side street in the Msheireb project.

Therefore, the key objectives of revitalization projects need continuous reflection. The new initiatives undoubtedly have an increasing impact on establishing a new image of the old centre. Recent observation studies and interviews, carried out by both authors, have proven that many Qataris as well as other high-income groups are now visiting the old centre due to new attractors, such as the restaurants in Souq Waqif. Tourists, particularly business travellers, are often staying in close proximity to the old centre and are attracted to visit the new cultural and hospitality venues along the waterfront. Another main objective is to re-establish the old centre as one of the key business hubs in Doha. This objective will mainly depend on the successful implementation of efficient transportation networks to secure the accessibility of certain areas. The high increase in built density in the case of the Msheireb project will challenge the current car-based structures. Furthermore, it can be expected that the subsequent demand on housing units for upper-income groups will continuously rise in central areas. The main development challenge in this regard is, however, the fact that many surrounding urban areas are still in a deteriorating state, and existing infrastructural networks would not permit any extensive redevelopment in the near future. Moreover, the complete removal of old structures is in contradiction with the objective to secure an evolutionary upgrading process, which integrates the various aspects of conservation and modernization and ensures the integration of affordable housing.

Due to the rapid development of revitalization initiatives, land prices in central areas are steadily rising, which is expected to lead to more and more constraints for gradual urban renewal. This however endangers conservation attempts of old buildings reflecting the beginning of Doha's urbanism in the 1950s. While the Souq Waqif project has restored lost heritage from the pre-oil era, most structures built at the beginning of Doha's first modern urbanization are currently facing replacement. In addition to the loss of individual buildings, the old vernacular structures and their low-rise clusters with courtyards are in danger of being demolished. Another challenge in this context is the integration of low-income groups within the revitalization process. Grown economic networks, which often have informal characteristics, will be dissolving and many social groups are forced to give up their small shops and entrepreneurial initiatives. The overall liveability of historic centres however will profoundly depend on more cohesive and integrated developments.[60] Future everyday urbanism and thus the use of newly integrated public spaces will rely on both a variety of services and activities and diverse residences for different cultural and income groups.[61] Otherwise, these mega project schemes will turn into segregated islands, accessed from outside, but hardly responding to adjacent urban areas, where mass housing for single migrant employees will continue to replace traditional and mixed neighbourhoods. Today, the Souq Waqif redevelopment, the Central Market in Abu Dhabi and Al Bastakiya in Dubai are typical examples of reviving historic cores on a macro urban context, but with hardly any direct benefits for surrounding districts and their inhabitants.

Conclusion

Today, the major challenge of creating vital and diverse urban neighbourhoods in Gulf cities is rooted in the inner investment dynamics, which have led to a rapid increase of land prices in central areas and thus both rising investment pressure and deteriorating properties due to missing incentives to spend on maintenance and renovation. New planning regulations keep facing an increasing struggle to accommodate the high demands of enhancing maximum built densities and the reality of missing infrastructural capacities on the ground. The fragmented development of mass housing in more or less central and accessible locations has contributed to an urban environment that lacks spatial cohesion and integration. The newly launched landmark projects within historic centres have furthermore caused an increasingly complex situation of new gentrification and renewal tendencies along waterfronts or key historic sites resulting in the extensive displacement of many migrant communities. Traditional neighbourhoods, which previously accommodated a mix of migrants with differing income, are thus currently replaced by either new mega projects or a continuous development of mass housing for many newly arrived single migrant workers. This has resulted in new demographic realities and thus the end of the traditional form of everyday urbanism in most places, which has evolved since the 1960s.

Thus, contemporary urban planning in the Gulf region must respond to the emerging conflicting perceptions and values in downtown areas, which are being envisioned and planned as rediscovered cultural and commercial centres, while facing the reality of being surrounded by mass housing and an inadequate inclusion of differing communities. Urban space diversity is however highly dependent on the interaction of many social groups, resulting in dynamic marketplaces. The mediation between short-term investment interests and long-term community-driven development patterns is particularly challenging in the Gulf region due to the evident contrast between the small minority of national citizens and the rapid move of migrants with limited prospects to stay long-term. Urban spaces are consequently a direct expression of the core problem of today's Gulf cities as being the result of large-scale investments and top-down strategies with hardly any major incentive to integrate the diverse interests of settled migrant communities. The gradual replacement of traditional neighbourhoods will erase the last remaining urban spaces that will become a part of a collective memory rather than actual physical environment.[62]

Urban space diversity is seen worldwide as a precondition to overcome boundaries, and it is particularly challenging to establish in fast-growing emerging cities in the Global South.[63] The rapid globalization of the Gulf region has recently led to various rising conflicts between maintaining growth rates and enabling the accommodation of migrant communities according to their needs as well as cultural preferences. It should be emphasized that architects, planners and decision-makers in migrant cities need to adopt a high level of responsiveness to envision urban spaces attract instead of alienate the various migrant groups.[64] In this respect, the investment in state-of-the-art public spaces along mixed-use streets and the integration of diverse housing can play an important role in establishing more sustainable communities by enhancing the economic dimension and by promoting a continuous exchange between social groups.[65]

The indecisiveness of officially integrating migrant communities and their neighbourhoods in central locations has led to the reality of frequent moves resulting in an increasing spatial fragmentation. The gentrification of historic city cores via large-scale mega projects will only lead to the relocation of the problem of social segregation with potentially more social, economic and environmental risks attached. Many examples worldwide suggest that new settlements along the urban periphery deprive large communities from the essential spatial needs, namely the high level of accessibility and direct economic interaction to develop small businesses and thus to enable the opportunities of individual advancement. Subsequently, central districts have always been key urban spaces to establish and nurture both social and spatial justice. It is hoped that the remaining traditional neighbourhoods will be recognized and treated as important place typologies that shaped the memory and history of Gulf cities. While demolition and eviction notices have been issued, recent professional and academic debates may offer possibilities for fulfilling this hope.[66] Future aspirational change could then be based not only on top-down decisions but also via initiatives generated by interest groups or the local community, employing bottom-up strategies.

Notes

1 John Chase, Margaret Crawford and John Kaliski, *Everyday Urbanism* (New York, 2008).

2 Douglas Kelbaugh, 'Three Paradigms: New Urbanism, Everyday Urbanism, Post Urbanism—An Excerpt from the Essential Common Place', *Bulletin of Science, Technology & Society*, 20 (2000), pp. 285–9.

3 Henri Lefebvre, *The Production of Space* (Oxford, 1991).

4 Fraker Harrison, 'Where Is the Urban Design Discourse?', *Places: Forum of Design for the Public Realm*, 19/3 (2007), pp. 61–3.

5 Louis Wirth, 'Urbanism as a Way of Life', *American Journal of Sociology*, 44 (1938), pp. 1–24.

6 Heike Hanhörster, 'Whose Neighbourhood Is It? Ethnic Diversity in Urban Spaces in Germany', *GeoJournal*, 51 (2001), pp. 329–38; Emily Talen, *Design for Diversity: Exploring Socially Mixed Neighbourhoods* (Oxford, 2008).

7 Ashraf M. Salama and Remah Y. Gharib, 'A Perceptual Approach for Investigating Urban Space Diversity in the City of Doha', *Open House International*, 37/2 (2012), pp. 24–32.

8 Neil Brenner and Roger Keil, 'From Global Cities to Globalized Urbanization', in R. T. LeGates and F. Stout (eds), *The City Reader* (New York, 2011), pp. 599–608.

9 David Harvey, 'Contested Cities: Spatial Process and Spatial Form', in N. Jewson and S. MacGregor (eds), *Transforming Cities* (London, 1997).

10 Ashraf M. Salama, Ahood Al-Maimani and Fatma Khalfani, 'Understanding Inhabitants' Spatial Experience of the City of Doha through Cognitive Mapping', *Open House International*, 38/4 (2013), pp. 37–46.

11 Amos Rapoport, *The Meaning of the Built Environment: A Non-verbal Communication Approach* (Tucson, 1990); Amos Rapoport, *Culture, Architecture, and Design* (Chicago, 2005).

12 Henry Sanoff, 'Measuring Attributes of the Visual Environment', in J. T. Lang, C. Burnette, W. Moleski and D. Vachon (eds), *Designing for Human Behavior: Architecture and the Behavioral Sciences* (Stroudsburg, 1974) pp. 244–60.

13 Lefebvre, *The Production of Space*; Mark Purcell, 'Excavating Lefebvre: The Right to the City and Its Urban Politics of the Inhabitant', *GeoJournal*, 58 (2002), pp. 99–108.

14 Harrison, 'Where Is the Urban Design Discourse?'.

15 Harvey, 'Contested Cities: Spatial Process and Spatial Form'.

16 Henry Sanoff, *Community Participation Methods in Design and Planning* (Chinchester, 2000).

17 Ernest W. Burgess, 'The Growth of the City', in R. E. Park, E. W. Burgess and R. D. McKenzie (eds), *The City: Suggestions of Investigation of Human Behavior in the Urban Environment* (Chicago, 1925), pp. 47–62; Irwin Altman, *The Environment*

and Social Behaviour (Monterey, 1975); William H. Whyte, *The Social Life of Small Urban Spaces* (Washington DC, 1980); Jan Gehl, *Life between Buildings: Using Public Space* (London, 1987).

18 Yasser Elsheshtawy, 'Cities of Sand and Fog: Abu Dhabi's Global Ambitions', in Y. Elsheshtawy (ed.), *The Evolving Arab City* (London, 2008), p. 272.

19 Sarah Nicholas, 'Al Zaab Neighbourhood in Abu Dhabi', *The National*, 25 September 2010. Available at: www.thenational.ae/lifestyle/home/al-zaab-neighbourhood-in-abu-dhabi-1.593982 (accessed 3 January 2018).

20 Schmid, 'Dubai: Der schnelle Aufstieg zur Wirtschaftsmetropole'.

21 Pacione, 'City Profile Dubai', p. 256.

22 Eugen Wirth, *Dubai: Ein modernes städtisches Handels- und Dienstleistungszentrum am Arabisch-Persischen Golf* (Erlangen, 1988), p. 37.

23 Pacione, 'City profile Dubai', p. 260.

24 Wirth, *Dubai: Ein modernes städtisches Handels- und Dienstleistungszentrum am Arabisch-Persischen Golf*, p. 43.

25 Ibid., p. 49.

26 Khaled Alawadi, 'Urban Redevelopment Trauma: The Story of a Dubai Neighbourhood', *Built Environment*, 40/3 (2014), pp. 357–75.

27 Al-Buainain, *Urbanisation in Qatar*.

28 Abeer A. Hasanin, 'Urban Legibility and Shaping the Image of Doha', *Archnet-IJAR: International Journal of Architectural Research*, 1/3 (2007), pp. 37–54.

29 Nagy, 'Making Room for Migrants, Making Sense of Difference: Spatial and Ideological Expression of Social Diversity in urban Qatar'.

30 MMAA (Ministry of Municipality and Agriculture Affairs), *Doha inner city redevelopment, Draft Report No. 1- evaluation and review* (Doha, 1986).

31 Rosanna Law and Kevin Underwood, 'Msheireb Heart of Doha: An Alternative Approach to Urbanism in the Gulf Region', *International Journal of Islamic Architecture*, 1/1 (2012), pp. 131–47; Rosanna Law, 'The Paradox of Msheireb', *Urban Pamphleteer*, 4 (2014), pp. 8–9.

32 Al-Nabi, *Rapid Urban Expansion and Physical Planning in Bahrain*, p. 9.

33 Ibid., p. 10.

34 Ben-Hamouche, 'Manama: The Metamorphosis of an Arab Gulf City', p. 208.

35 Ibid., p. 205.

36 Al-Nabi, *Rapid Urban Expansion and Physical Planning in Bahrain*, p. 10.

37 Ibid., p. 11.

38 Jacobs, *The Death and Life of Great American Cities*.

39 Nagy, 'Making Room for Migrants, Making Sense of Difference: Spatial and Ideological Expression of Social Diversity in urban Qatar'.

40 Salama and Wiedmann, *Demystifying Doha*.

41　Andrew Gardner, Silvia Pessoa, Abdoulaye Diop, Kaltham Al-Ghanim, Kien Le
　　Trung and Laura Harkness, 'A Portrait of Low Income Migrants in Contemporary
　　Qatar', *Journal of Arabian Studies*, 3/1 (2013), pp. 1–17, p. 4.

42　Nagy, *Social and Spatial Process: An Ethnographic Study of Housing in Qatar*.

43　Andrew Gardner, 'Gulf migration and the family', *Journal of Arabian Studies*, 1/1
　　(2011), pp. 3–25.

44　Nagy, *Social and Spatial Process: An Ethnographic Study of Housing in Qatar*;
　　Gardner, 'Gulf migration and the family'; Robina Mohammad and James D.
　　Sidaway, 'Spectacular urbanization amidst variegated geographies of globalization:
　　Learning from Abu Dhabi's trajectory through the lives of South Asian men',
　　International Journal of Urban and Regional Research, 36/3 (2012), pp. 606–27;
　　Ashraf M. Salama and Florian Wiedmann, *Demystifying Doha*; Mehran Kamrava,
　　Gateways to the World: Port Cities in the Persian Gulf (London, 2016).

45　Elsheshtawy, 'Cities of sand and fog: Abu Dhabi's global ambitions'.

46　Colliers International, *Doha's Residential Market*, 2014. Available at: www.
　　colliers.com/-/media/562F03BEE6D54CA0B7BA140DF287C911.ashx?la=en-GB
　　(accessed 3 January 2018).

47　Salama, Ashraf M. and Wiedmann, Florian. 'Perceiving Urban Livability in an
　　Emerging Migrant City', *Proceedings of the Institution of Civil Engineers – Urban
　　Design and Planning*, 169/6 (2016), pp. 268–78.

48　Ministry of Development Planning and Statistics, *Census 2015*. Available at: www.
　　mdps.gov.qa/en/knowledge/Publications/Other/Census%202015.pdf (accessed 3
　　January 2018).

49　Gardner et al., 'A Portrait of Low Income Migrants in Contemporary Qatar', p. 4.

50　Rami El-Samahy and Kelly Hutzell, 'In Search of Doha's Public Realm', *Urban
　　Pamphleteer* (4), pp. 10–13.

51　Florian Wiedmann, Ashraf M. Salama and Velina Mirincheva, 'Urban
　　Reconfiguration and Revitalization: Public Mega Projects in Doha's Historic Center',
　　Open House International, 38(4), pp. 27–36.

52　Andrew Gardner, Silvia Pessoa and Laura Harkness, *Labour Migrants and Access to
　　Justice in Contemporary Qatar*. Available at: http://www.lse.ac.uk/middleEastCent
　　re/publications/Reports/LabourMigrantsQatarEnglish.pdf (accessed 3 January
　　2018) p. 7.

53　Human Rights Watch, *Building a Better World Cup. Protecting Migrant Workers in
　　Qatar Ahead of FIFA 2022*, 2012. Available at: www.hrw.org/sites/default/files/reports/
　　qatar0612webwcover_0.pdf (accessed 3 January 2018), p. 65.

54　El-Samahy and Hutzell, 'In Search of Doha's Public Realm'.

55　Wiedmann et al., 'Urban Reconfiguration and Revitalization: Public Mega Projects
　　in Doha's Historic Center'.

56　Ashraf M. Salama, 'Intervention Urbanism: The Delicacy of Aspirational Change in
　　the Old Center of Doha', *Urban Pamphleteer*, 4 (2014), pp. 1–3.

57 Msheireb Properties, *About Msheireb Downtown Doha*. Available at: www.msheireb. com/msheireb-downtown-doha/about-msheireb-downtown-doha/ (accessed 3 January 2018).

58 AECOM, ARUP, Allies and Morrison, *Development Guidelines, Phase II* (Doha, 2010), p. 65.

59 Law and Underwood, 'Msheireb Heart of Doha', p. 145.

60 Ashraf M. Salama, Florian Wiedmann and Alain Thierstein, 'People and the City: Unveiling the Lived Urban Environment of Doha', *Qatar Foundation Annual Research Forum*, AHP36, Bloomsbury Qatar Foundation Journals (2012).

61 A. M. Salama, F. Khalfani and A. Al-Maimani, 'Experiential Assessment of Urban Open Spaces in Doha', *Open House International*, 38/4 (2013), pp. 47–57.

62 Ashraf M. Salama, 'Urban Traditions in the Contemporary Lived Space of Cities on the Arabian Peninsula', *Traditional Dwellings and Settlements Review*, 27/1 (2015), pp. 21–39.

63 Susan S. Fainstein, 'Cities and Diversity: Should We Want It? Should We Plan for It?', *Urban Affairs Review*, 42/1 (2005), pp. 3–19.

64 Sanderock, *Towards Cosmopolis*.

65 Peter Jones, Marion Roberts and Linda Morris, *Rediscovering Mixed-use Streets: The Contribution of Local High Streets to Sustainable Communities* (Bristol, 2007).

66 Ashraf M. Salama, 'Intervention Urbanism', pp. 1–3.

8

Building sustainable migrant cities

This chapter introduces a discourse on future urbanism in the Gulf that is contextualized through a concise articulation of the preceding chapters. After a historic overview underlining the previous dynamics of migration and housing in the Gulf, the official development visions were discussed focusing on one future scenario, in which the local workforce will transform during a period of twenty years into a major driver within emerging knowledge economies. These publicized visions can only be understood as political declarations needed to respond to major domestic concerns regarding the high dependency on migration. While migration is increasingly conceived as a reality and the price of regional and global competitiveness, there are hardly any visions emphasizing how migration patterns might evolve from the current developing country context and a demand-driven system of migration to a more supply-driven system focusing on the long-term stay of skilled workforce. Thus, it can be stated that one core question has remained in all Gulf cities: How are migrant communities, needed for economic diversification, attracted to settle and invest, if visions and subsequent migration and business policies have been emphasizing their short-term role to build new economies rather than sustaining them?

Chapter 3 is centred on the big question of the governance reorganization in the context of the ignited rapid urban growth and the extensive housing supply. The fast transition from a public administration of urban development to a new form of entrepreneurial governance has led to high land prices and construction costs challenging the supply of diverse and affordable housing. The initiation of holdings as new and decisive stakeholders for a property-led economic diversification strategy succeeded in speeding up growth rates, while also causing many uncertainties about future economies relying on low-cost environments. The main challenge of contemporary governance is the mediation between the perception of cities as more or less secure property markets for investors and the actual function of cities as residences for all social groups. In most recent years central planning has been rediscovered via new legal frameworks and the key role of semi-public infrastructure developers to define future development patterns. Thus, the current form of governance has become a hybrid between maintaining property-led development interests and a more coordinated development of existing urban areas via new zoning plans and infrastructure investments. The continuous prioritization of mega projects has however led to enhanced deficits in many areas, particularly in the case of affordable housing and social services.

Focusing on the specific role of mega projects in emerging Gulf cities, the following chapter explores the way in which the construction boom led to rising costs of developing real estate causing major investments in luxury properties with rather high vacancy rates and mass housing with high occupancy rates due to shared apartments. Today, the Gulf region has become a new phenomenon, where mega projects have been initiated as drivers for economic transformation rather than as a consequence of already established service economies. Subsequently, the impact of these mega projects on economic development has mainly been a rising growth dependency on all construction-related sectors as well as leisure industries, particularly regional tourism. While mega projects had a significant impact on the overall perception of Gulf cities as potential hubs, the enhanced media attention has also highlighted the main contradiction of these new developments. Mega projects have only been possible by employing cheap construction workers from developing countries, and most emerging service sectors, such as retail and tourism, have become highly dependent on foreign workforce and the comparatively moderate salary expectations. Thus, urbanism in the Gulf has become overnight a representation for rapidly growing consumption centres in highly controlled environments. Mega projects attracted the large share of attention while implicitly representing a new form of urbanism built on spectacles and speculative tendencies rather than diversified and knowledge-based local economies.

After the first part of the book exploring the new visions and their historic context as well as the special form of entrepreneurial governance and the role of mega projects as development strategy, the following chapters focus on the dynamics between new built environments and their inhabitants. First, three main housing developments and resulting urban typologies were identified including the high-density transition zones between historic downtowns and suburban areas; the emergence of exclusive projects as new landmarks and homes of higher-income groups and the sprawling suburban landscape made of gated compounds surrounding the still rather segregated neighbourhoods for the local population. In summary, each new housing pattern has not by itself promoted the emergence of self-contained and integrated developments. The predictable synergies between car-based urbanism and rapid urban growth led to a high level of activities concentrated in very few and scattered areas, which have been highly connected on a macro urban level but lack any local integration. The main challenge of contemporary planning therefore lies in reconfiguring local urban structures via transit-oriented development initiatives and linked public spaces. The precondition for new transit systems is however the enhanced access to inner district areas, which implies a modification of general spatial patterns via accessible and walkable corridors.

Following the discussion and analysis of the spatial reality of recently built neighbourhoods, the various lifestyles and multicultural perceptions are explored in Chapter 6. Overall, four main lifestyle trends can be distinguished by following a theoretical framework of how lifestyles generally evolve considering the habitus, the current social position as well as differing life modes. The most dominant lifestyle group is currently formed by work-focused migrant bachelors with South Asian cultural backgrounds and their often-limited perspectives to stay in Gulf cities. Today, the average housing conditions are not perceived as satisfactory by most migrant groups and their various needs. All main housing typologies are frequently criticized in the case of their general design and construction standards, the poor integration of accessible services and public spaces in neighbourhoods and the lack of responsiveness to certain cultural preferences. Thus, many new tools and strategies need to be explored with respect to the way in which various housing typologies and neighbourhoods can be improved. Consequently, the exploration of new strategic imperatives and guidance for new developments should be a priority. In future, enhanced housing standards will play a decisive role in transforming Gulf cities into more liveable and attractive environments for all communities.

Chapter 7 focuses on the emerging conflict in urban centres and their surrounding neighbourhoods, which have been recently witnessing a major transformation due to mass housing and gentrification tendencies in rare and accessible locations. Today, traditional forms of everyday urbanism and the resulting urban space diversity are endangered due to these redevelopment tendencies and the lack of social inclusion. The mediation between short-term investment interests and long-term community-driven development patterns is particularly challenging in the Gulf region due to the evident contrast between the small minority of local citizens and the recent scale of migration. Urban spaces are consequently a direct expression of the core problem of today's Gulf cities as being the result of large-scale investments and top-down strategies with hardly any major incentive to integrate the diverse interests of multicultural migrant communities with all their roots and aspirations. The gradual replacement of historic neighbourhoods will erase the last remaining urban spaces reflecting the rich history of migration in Gulf cities and the various cultural preferences and spatial practices.

From a governance perspective the book established an understanding of the socio-spatial implications of recently introduced visions and development strategies, which all aim to establish competitive cities, but often ignore the long-term asset of any major service centre: the knowledge capital created by the urban manufacturing of small and medium entrepreneurial incentives. This bottom-up economic development however needs spaces to evolve and a community deeply invested in building lives in the Gulf rather than elsewhere. One key factor indicating healthy social conditions and thus development potentials has always been housing, which is responsible for the production of neighbourhoods and thus urbanism itself. The following conclusion of this book will span a bridge from introducing an integrated understanding of how urban spaces and their qualities are produced to a summary of all interdependent factors required for a more sustainable form of urbanism in the Gulf region.

A discourse on space production theories

A theoretical discourse on space production can provide important insights into how recent urbanism in the Gulf region has led to growing social imbalances and highly conflicted urban spaces. Despite the general focus of such a discourse to elucidate the social space and its historic evolution, the ideas of a possible sustainable form of urbanism postulate the future emergence of a matured society connected to its environment. Thus, a comprehensive framework is needed to juxtapose the three levels of space production and the contemporary understanding of sustainability: identifying the core challenges to establish sustainable urbanism, the relationship between the common triad of space production and the triadic dynamics of economic, environmental and social concerns. Therefore, core urban qualities and their interdepending factors can be identified and mapped to a holistic approach. The main aim is to understand all three realms of space production causing the contemporary urban condition and its underlying realities.

The following analysis on the theories of space production, introduced by Henri Lefebvre, is rooted in the general aim to serve the overall understanding of how urban spaces are evolving, which is the precondition for improving and changing our urban realities. Lefebvre's main theories were introduced during a period known for an emerging awareness of rising conflicts within modern urbanization. The period during the 1960s and 1970s is thus often referred to as the 'crisis of the city' due to the commencing dissolution of cities into fragmented and spreading urban entities.[1] Manuel Castells's *la question urbaine*[2] and David Harvey's *Social Justice and the City*[3] are only two examples of the growing intellectual movement dealing with the city as a projection of a capitalist society with all its inherited conflicts rooted in social inequity. The previous approach of analysing urban sociology in strict structures, of the Chicago School in the 1920s, was questioned by new dynamics and phenomena requiring new analytical frameworks and explanations. The dissatisfaction with previous models, which were mainly reflecting developments rather than identifying their roots, was furthermore fuelled by a growing intellectual discourse inspired by the rediscovered works of Karl Marx and Friedrich Engels questioning capitalism and its effects on society and its space.[4]

During the twentieth century, urban development became fundamentally dominated by the potential increase of land prices, which defined urban densities as well as the various land uses.[5] Particularly after the Second World War, urban planning was often reduced to the calculation and implementation of physical plans that enabled cities to become rationalized entities made of rectangular grids accessible by car as described by Jane Jacobs in *the Death and Life of American Cities*[6] or by Kevin Cox in the *Urbanisation and Conflict in Market Societies*.[7] The new car-based urbanism led to various conflicts in modern cities (Figure 8.1). The desire to own properties resulted in a large-scale cultural transformation and finally the beginning of postmodern consumerism.[8] Mike Davis added another important reflection on this transformation process and the resulting conflicts by exploring Los Angeles as a major example to illustrate the future path of urbanism in his book *City of Quartz: Excavating the Future in Los Angeles*.[9] In general, it can be stated that during the second half of the twentieth century, the urban question was fully explored with an emphasis on new theories that insist upon the explicit derivation of contemporary urbanization processes out of the structure of the capitalist mode of production.[10]

As a philosopher, Henry Lefebvre approached the urban question from a holistic and elementary point of view. In his two most influential works

Figure 8.1 The Sheikh Zayed Road in Dubai.

La revolution urbaine[11] and *La production de l'espace*,[12] Lefebvre introduced his main views on urbanism, its production, its evolution and its key conflicts. To tackle the actual roots of any man-made spatial development, Lefebvre followed his own dialectical understanding of how societies shape their surroundings by identifying the physical spatial practice and the mental conception of space as two dialectical poles. Lefebvre's dialectical thinking is rooted in an in-depth reflection of three major German philosophers of the nineteenth century. On the one side, Karl Marx's dialectical materialism explains modern urbanization as the inevitable result of increasing human needs and low productivity, and on the other side, Friedrich Hegel's dialectical idealism, which is rooted in understanding any built reality as a product of thinking and recognition.[13] Finally, Friedrich Nietzsche's dialectical–philosophical concept of the 'Apollonian and Dionysian'[14] is rooted in the understanding of the world from an aesthetic point of view and thus as a product of order and chaos. Lefebvre recognized all three standpoints as valid and developed his dialectical approach by integrating all three perspectives: the physical, the mental and the subjective realms of producing our spatial reality.

Lefebvre's theories of urbanism can be linked to the contemporary conflicts endangering overall sustainability in the Gulf region. While the developed world has entered post-Fordist structures with highly specialized production, the developing world has been locked in exporting resources and labour-intensive mass production serving the advanced markets worldwide. The terms of the ongoing globalization have created a new dimension of interconnection and dependencies and thus a joint struggle for sustainability. According to Neil Brenner,[15] Lefebvre's theories help to explain the challenges of controlling spatial practices due to the enormous reach of globalized capitalism. According to Henri Lefebvre, each urban space must be studied as a historic product of its society interacting with the surrounding environment. Based on his general dialectical understanding, he identified three main dimensions in the process of space production, namely, perceived space, conceived space and lived space.[16] As already introduced in the context of Chapter 7 and everyday urbanism, perceived space is produced by the spatial practice of all the users of a space due to their daily interaction resulting in complex economies, and conceived space is according to his definition the space produced by knowledge and ideologies. In addition to spatial practice and planning (intellectus), space is formed by the invisible degree of people's attachment to a certain place. He defined this subjective dimension of space as lived space (intuitus) or representational spaces, which comprise complex and often coded symbolisms.[17]

In parallel to his theory of the three dimensions that produce space, Henri Lefebvre developed his second ontological transformation of space to address the evolution of social space through human history. In the past, social space was mainly produced via direct interaction between communities and their environment, which he named absolute space. According to Lefebvre, the emergence of the open market place in Europe during the twelfth century marked the commencing end of the unity between countryside and settlements.[18] In the sixteenth century, the newly established mercantile societies developed far-reaching networks and the town overtook the country in terms of its economic and practical weight.[19] First, town planning arose and the central control of few decision-makers led to the end of absolute space, which has always been a direct reflection of a natural symbiotic relationship between settled communities, such as farmers and craftsmen, and nomadic tribes, who both carried and tolerated the special cases of leading social classes as manifested in the Greek and Roman antiquity as well as medieval Europe.[20] Until the pearl trade commenced in the nineteenth century, this absolute space could be found along the Gulf coast in the case of all oasis settlements, which were still vernacular expressions of settled farmers and fishermen and the frequent visits of Bedouin tribes residing in self-made huts along their peripheries.

Lefebvre identified the Renaissance period in Europe as the first end of this absolute space, which has always been a local phenomenon. The increasing development of trade routes and rapid population growth led to towns becoming hubs and thus places where wealth and subsequently knowledge accumulated within new layers of society are dependent on cross-regional trade rather than local, political or religious leadership.[21] Subsequently, conceived space, the space of the intellect, began to emerge and formed a new space, known as 'abstract space', named for its characteristic of reducing and dividing spatial aspects to functional and geometrical forms enabling more efficient structures.[22] Both the new dominance of towns and their spreading economic networks enabled not only industrialization in Europe but also an extensive period of global colonialization, which heavily relied on the efficient exchange of goods and knowledge, such as technological discoveries. The emerging industrial towns became a spatial manifestation of rationalized planning aiming for increased and highly efficient production but compromising the needs of workers, as Friedrich Engels discovered in England in 1845.[23] The rising conflict between social classes sparked the evolution of modern town planning and its newly discovered importance to secure housing and to avoid civil unrest.[24]

After the Second World War, enhanced progress in infrastructural development enabled rapid urbanization. Thus, the rate of urbanization between 1950 and 1960 was twice that of the preceding fifty years.[25] Both technological progress and fast urban growth enabled the rapid introduction of a highly efficient globalization built on gradual deregulation, capital flows and the subsequent international division of labour leading to extensive rural-urban migration.[26] The outsourcing of industrial production to the developing world led to the new phenomenon of global service hubs and an unprecedented accumulation of wealth resulting in modern consumerism. The global division of consumers and labourers led to the consolidation of the North-South divide, which is rooted in post-colonial structures and the established dominance of few world cities.[27] In Lefebvre's view, the end of the twentieth century marks the potential beginning of a new kind of space, which he called differential space, that is more dominated by humans' intuition rather than predefined and detached mental frameworks of decision-makers rooted in outdated ideologies. He, however, considers this synthetic evolutionary step as still being in its infancy and an inevitable part of the emerging urban revolution.[28]

This historic excursion is important to understand the main conflict between an increasingly abstract globalized system of capitalism and local regional concerns.[29] Lefebvre thus identified the crisis of the cities as 'conflicted space', which is the result of an increasingly challenged abstract space facing its dissolution due to the fact that urbanism has become the result of a 'bureaucratic society of controlled consumption' and thus disconnected from integrating all human needs.[30] This globalized 'conflicted space' within the established abstract space is being increasingly questioned with the emergence of public awareness. Collective knowledge and creativity have risen as influential factors within development dynamics by the questioning of existing conditions. Various examples worldwide suggest the potentials of participatory urbanism built on active citizens rather than passive consumers.[31] Thus, Lefebvre expects 'lived space', which he understands as the direct intuitive link between a society and its space, to become an increasingly significant factor within future urbanism.[32] In such a scenario, the collective investment of a self-discovering society will overcome the short-term interests of capital movements and the self-management of urban cells will replace top-down and technocratic decision-making. Lefebvre thus argues that the end of an increasingly conflicted urbanism is highly dependent on the proactive participation of an aware urban society.[33]

This participatory form of urbanism is however facing rather specific spatial, social and economic conditions restricting many potential transformation incentives. The introduction of the car as a preferred mode of transport during the twentieth century marked an important milestone in urban developments by making greater distances manageable and thus making the dense cities rooted in the previous form of industrialization obsolete. More significantly, the new mode of transport enabled a new economy driven by land ownership, which resulted in a complex system of capital accumulation depending on the rising financial debts of societies.[34] This new form of urbanism led to fast urban growth and the well-documented phenomenon of urban sprawl and fragmented settlements due to the division of land uses to manage extensive traffic.[35] The enhanced consumption and the resulting waste led to complex environmental challenges, whereby cities became the main destroyers of natural habitats worldwide.[36] In Lefebvre's opinion, the dominant role of conceived space within abstract space has led to the general conflict between quantity and quality due to the shrinking access of majorities to diversify and differentiate spatial developments. Furthermore, the dependency on continuous growth has become inhibiting for the sustenance and emergence of urban qualities.[37]

In this context, Lefebvre criticized modern architects, such as Le Corbusier, as followers of the main doctrine to centralize, uniform and dictate urban spaces rather than empowering participation and thus diversification.[38] The commercialization of space has created fragmented and segregated urban landscapes, which are described by Lefebvre as agglomerations consisting of either 'spaces of leisure' or 'spaces of labour'[39] wherein the role of inhabitants is largely reduced to either the consumption of space or the production of goods and services (Figure 8.2). One central argument of this book is that a

Figure 8.2 Labourers cleaning a high-rise in Doha.

new pattern of sociotechnical organization, also referred to as the informational mode of development,[40] initiated new opportunities for the perpetuation and extension of global capitalism. This global realm of capitalism has challenged and weakened the national state as a geographically defined form of governance and led to an ongoing conflict between local concerns and global forces.[41] City states, such as Gulf States, did not face any major challenge to transform from national welfare states to corporate models of governance to establish global hubs built on international migration. The main reason for a minor resistance to apply growth-oriented strategies has been the immediate financial benefits of small local populations owning, buying and selling land as well as becoming sponsors of businesses.

While Lefebvre's work focused on Europe and its urban history, his theory of conflicted space is applicable to all places, including the Gulf region. In many parts of the world, there is rather little reflection about contemporary urbanism in relation to its complex contexts in time. The emerging cities of the developing world are often witnessed as radical examples torn between extensive poverty on one side and unprecedented luxury in small enclaves on the other.[42] The rather controlled development and short-term stays of foreign labourers have enabled Gulf cities to prevent informal settlements and thus the usual displays of urban poverty and misery. The industrialization and modernization process, which was described by Lefebvre in the case of European cities, is currently evolving in developing countries in parallel and within less than half a century instead of a gradual development spread over hundreds of years. But despite the different time frames within which modern urbanization has taken place, most emerging cities in the Global South and specifically in the Gulf are exhibitions of Lefebvre's main hypotheses of how conflicted spaces evolve. Islands of spaces of leisure for higher-income minorities are surrounded by walls and gates for protection and seclusion from the crowded spaces of labour often expressed in the form of monotonous and overcrowded neighbourhoods.

The doctrine of stimulating urban growth led to enhanced waste and unsustainable structures due to fragmentation and isolation. Modern infrastructure and thus access to global networks can however only be developed and maintained in few places of the developing world, such as Gulf cities, which have become the gates for international capital flows. The emerging networks of globalization led to well-established hierarchies, in which cities must enter a fierce competition to attract investment and the headquarters of various types of international cooperation.[43] The established gates to global markets have led to a clear divide between the economic opportunities in urban areas and the increasing struggles in rural areas. The subsequent migration has fuelled the fast growth of urbanization rates in the developing world. According to Lefebvre the rising accumulation of conflicted space worldwide will eventually lead to the collective reflection of the basic dilemma of today's capitalism, in which a hierarchical globalization is facing a strengthened resistance and desire to restructure its basic foundations, which is however endangered by arising protectionism and wars. Thus, the Gulf region and its quick rise as connected junction between global markets must be studied as both dependent by-products of the rising accumulation and movement of global capital and a new experiment of a controlled and abstract space relying on continuous migration rather than settled communities. This condition has led to a highly controlled environment restricting any major social unrest by migrant populations, as well as an expected high level of fragility during crises and economic downturns.

The role of housing in producing urban qualities

The commonly used definition of sustainability was made at the Brundtland Commission of the United Nations in 1987: 'Sustainable development is development that meets the needs of the present without compromising the ability of future generations to meet their own needs.'[44] According to this definition, human settlements must primarily be in balance with the environment by reducing the waste of natural resources and pollution. Thus, any socio-economic development must be balanced in respect to environmental concerns. This rather simplistic but abstract conception of sustainability, however, is incapable of defining the key factors within the production of spatial structures and their qualities, which either enhance or endanger urban sustainability. Therefore, core qualities of urban spaces must be identified in relation to social, economic and environmental concerns. At first, all constructed spaces need to obtain the quality of diversity to evolve and adjust to the various environmental challenges so that a community can sustain its livelihood. Rooted in the diverse needs of human beings, any created space must accommodate the various requirements of a society settled in a specific location, from housing and private spaces to markets and workshops. Any economic development will lead to an increasingly complex system of dependencies and thus spatial developments.[45] This diversity is the precondition for any future growth and sustenance of a city.

The second quality is rooted in human knowledge, which is accumulating due to interaction and exchange. The empirical findings of how to improve spatial structures are mainly focused on the desire to reduce work and to gain time. The resulting quality of efficiency is usually perceived as key access to enhanced leisure time, while its key role is the empowerment of communities to use fewer resources and thus reduce their impact on the environment for future generations. Thus, environmentalism is the conscious ideological decision of any community to integrate the needs of future generations. Finally, a third quality, namely identity, needs to be introduced, which is the result of the subjective binding of any community with its surrounding and evolving space. This identification is the result of a long-term process, in which constructed spaces are experienced as nurturing instead of repelling, familiar instead of alienating and are thus open for individual development (Figure 8.3). Therefore, a social space can only be healthy if all its members can identify with the created surrounding conditions. This more general philosophical approach integrates the reality of differing cultural perceptions and lifestyles.

The three urban qualities, introduced as diversity, efficiency and identity, have clear core linkages to both the basic triad of sustainability (balance between economic, environmental and social concerns) and the triadic production of space (perceived, conceived and lived space) as identified by Henri Lefebvre. This triadic relationship is furthermore rooted in human psychology, which differentiates instinctive, mental and emotional factors shaping the personality of each individual. Consequently, any urban space is the dialectical result of the

Figure 8.3 A self-constructed fishermen hut in Bahrain.

instinctual needs and mental conceptions of a society resulting in emotional attachment or rejection. This basic theory of how urban sustainability is the product of three core urban qualities can lead to further differentiations and a better understanding of the actual role of urban governance in particular cases.[46] While functioning markets are diversifying urban environments due to complex needs, conceptions of how spaces can be rationalized will lead to more efficient structures. Finally, the factor of how communities identify and thus attach and invest in certain locations is the direct synthesis of meeting needs and reducing effort. The disconnection of rationalized spaces by social elites and the engineered exclusion of masses to create their own markets can thus be identified as the core conflict of our present form of urbanism.

As with all other urban qualities, urban efficiency is itself based on a dialectical production and thus a triadic relationship. The ideologically influenced visions of how a space within which a society operates should be structured meet the collective knowledge of all available empirical evidence resulting in the actual organization and governance of a society. Urban diversity is rooted in the dialectical movement between investment opportunities and actual movements resulting in emerging networks. This abstract concept can be translated into urbanism as follows: investors are taking the risk of developing spaces, which enables inhabitants to follow their needs leading to networks of producers and consumers and thus the economy as a whole. Thus, urban diversity is automatically shrinking if the number of investors and businesses is decreasing.

Finally, urban identity is a dialectical result of a society's intuitive experience of a space as catering and nurturing of basic needs and its familiarity regarding basic values. These perceptions are however merely subjective and thus belong to the realm of space production, defined as the 'lived space' by Lefebvre. Consequently, any urban identity can be regarded as the collective result of an identification process rooted in evolving perspectives based on images and impressions and can never be fully determined due to its fluid and changing nature.

The introduced framework of the production of sustainable urban spaces integrates the three main realms of urban qualities as well as their individual dialectical production leading to a total of three core realms, which are rooted in the basic triadic scheme as introduced by Henri Lefebvre. The framework allows for the identification of the actual dialectical production of each realm in the context of urbanism. Static and moving factors are leading to the three core determinants of urbanism, namely, the historically evolved form of governance, current business networks and the future-oriented perspectives of a society. Governance is the direct result of available knowledge and expertise as well as specific decision-making rooted in visions. Built on businesses economic structures are produced by both working and consuming inhabitants as well as specific investment decisions. And the various perspectives of a society are rooted in the collective access to basic needs and an evolving manifestation of shared values. Furthermore, the framework emphasizes the intersecting and interdependent nature of all realms. While certain cores can be identified, the reality of overlapping and integrated characteristics overweighs any simplified and definite structure due to basic dialectical connections. This aspect of any framework attempting to integrate all factors within the production of space is often identified as one of the main reasons why an intuitive approach is required to understand the dependencies of urban qualities instead of rigid definitions.[47]

The framework of urban qualities rooted in a basic philosophical theory permits the introduction of another layer due to various intersections among influential factors. The first intersection can be found in the case of the basic needs of a human being and his/her spatial practice and thus the driver of diversifying spaces. This spatial practice is therefore rather connected and related to the individual's experience of how his/her needs have been met in recent times. Accordingly, the first important pillar for sustainable urbanism is an environment, which enables all social groups to take responsibility of their own needs. This instigates the integration of both a collective diversification of spatial structures and an identification process. A second intersection can be found in the case of cultural values and the ideologically influenced vision of how an urban space should be shaped. Both realms are highly complex inner processes with usually historic dimensions. While values are collectively shared and sustained, visions can be isolated and have a clear ideological foundation. Subsequently, the second pillar for sustainable urbanism can be found in a harmonic relationship between newly introduced development visions reflecting the values of a society to achieve an overall identity as well as efficiency due to the direct implementation of new strategies and policies.

The third intersection is the complex relationship between the available knowledge of a society and its governance, how to develop urban structures and the specific investments in new developments. Any long-term investment heavily relies on a local economic development moving towards consolidation, detached from temporary market dynamics. In this respect, the third pillar of sustainable urbanism is a high level of integration of investment needs on the one hand and an in-depth understanding of how urban structures must develop to gain benefits for all inhabitants, on the other. This would strengthen both an increasing efficiency and diversity. The framework and its three pillars of sustainable urbanism offer various explorations of interdependencies within the production of urban environments and why moving towards sustainability has remained a complex challenge. The existing scientific knowledge of new solutions has proven to be a limited factor for overall change, if the direct link between communities and their inhabited spaces has become compromised. The main reason for this disconnection can be found in elitist structures, which are built on the widespread illusions of continuous consumerism on the one hand and the disillusions of ever regaining access to challenge existing structures on the other hand. This core conflict requires enhanced scientific attention instead of simply proclaiming environmentalism.

Housing is the main element of any urban environment and as such, it is produced by the same triadic principles as any human-made space. The role of housing has however transformed from being an essential and usually self-made shelter to a much more complex commodity and as such, an accumulation of capital or debt. Housing therefore reflects the dilemma of contemporary urbanism and its core conflict: quantities instead of qualities. While housing markets for diverse luxury real estate can still provide profitable returns and thus attract investment, affordable housing opportunities have been challenged, which resulted in continuous sprawl, mass housing with poor construction and design qualities or even informal solutions (Figure 8.4). The simple and often-cited doctrine of building more housing units to lower costs and to provide diverse markets has often fuelled increasing land prices and

Figure 8.4 Housing solutions along the fringes of Doha's downtown.

infrastructural deficits. While there are many policies and affordable housing schemes via public or semi-public holdings, the essential crisis has never been solved, even in the most advanced economies. Housing has become a prime commodity in global markets and as such it has become dependent on further growth.

Thus, despite the scientific awareness that further growth dependency will inevitably lead to segregated and fragmented spaces, in which working classes must secure and even enhance the value of properties, the prevention of any further collapse, such as the financial crisis in 2008, demands the continuous creation of new investment opportunities. Due to the uneven investment in few places providing capable infrastructural capacities, we have been witnessing the concentration of rapid urban growth in few places rather than a more de-central and organic development of a multitude of urban centres. Developing sufficient infrastructure has thus always been a limitation for enhanced growth rates. Secure investments in real estate are only possible in areas where the connectivity to global and regional markets has already been established. Housing has therefore become both a factor for accelerated growth rates in emerging cities and a necessity to accommodate millions arriving from smaller settlements or rural areas. Consequently, housing has become the main factor in shaping urban spaces worldwide.

The urban quality of efficiency is mainly defined by its outcome, namely the use of as little resources as possible. Housing and neighbourhoods have an important role in reducing the waste of resources; from the newest construction standards including modern building materials and technologies as well as innovative design integrating all scales. Thus, urban design matters, such as integrated services and public spaces, are equally important as appropriate ground floor plans using space as efficient as possible without compromising values and cultural preferences. While the scientific knowledge of how to build resource-efficient neighbourhoods has gradually evolved from first ideas, such as Ebenezer Howard's vision of transit-oriented settlements in the nineteenth century, to most contemporary smart city solutions, the implementation via regulations has often failed in larger scales due to the previously described capital accumulation via land ownership and the subsequent investment patterns following land prices. Thus, in most cases, solutions for more sustainable neighbourhoods have not been feasible.

In parallel, urban diversity has often suffered from modern housing developments expressing the needs of investors, rather than the complex needs of all social groups. This has always been most visible in the case of newly built neighbourhoods, in which diversity has been compromised by most repetitive design solutions, missing old building substance and mono-functional land uses, such as typical dormitory settlements. Housing must be considered as one of the most important factors in enabling diverse and resilient neighbourhoods integrating instead of isolating the different income groups to establish vibrant markets (Figure 8.5). The establishment of a diverse housing market catering

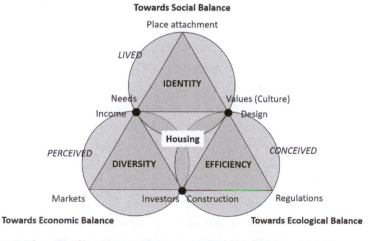

Figure 8.5 The role of housing producing sustainable urbanism.

all income groups in one location instead of disperse development patterns and segregation is a key catalyst for future economic balance and consolidation.

In many ways, the urban identity of any city is defined by the experienced quality of housing rather than few landmark projects. Thus, neighbourhoods and the immediate surroundings of any home can be considered as the most crucial spaces igniting a positive subjective relationship between people and places. Migrant cities are therefore rather particular cases, in which many new and rather differing communities meet in new environments. The imported expectations form diverse impressions and thus a rather complex process of place attachment, ideally expressed in the long-term settlement of communities and their commitment. Depending on their rights and resources the individual aspirations as well as needs and values of long-term residents will have a major impact on redefining housing developments and thus future urbanism built on neighbourhoods reflecting integrated communities.

Towards sustainable urbanism in the Gulf

Based on the theoretical discourse on sustainable urbanism and the important role of housing, several aspects need to be considered regarding Gulf cities. First, the contemporary vision of Gulf cities as emerging service hubs must be seen in the context of expanding real estate markets, which were liberalized to accelerate growth. While the geopolitical location between major global and regional markets justifies the investment in major airports, trade and tourism sectors, the recent rapid growth was mainly affected by the ignited construction boom due to investments in residential properties. Thus, a large share of migrants is currently directly or indirectly engaged in building Gulf cities rather than building new economies to sustain future hubs. During this accelerated building process, governance has quickly adopted a more corporate model built on semi-public holdings. While this has enabled a high level of efficiency to supply all required services for an ignited construction boom, it has replaced many small- and medium-sized entrepreneurial businesses, which have lost their major significance in shaping economies. Thus, many services, which are considered to become the backbone of future Gulf cities, are offered by centralized holdings dominating rather than diversifying local economies. This monopolization can cause a limited reinvestment in local developments in future.

This efficient but top-down governance of building new cities has resulted in replaceable urban landscapes and a social structure built on segregated and frequently exchanged rather than integrated urban populations. Thus, the general vision of building advanced service centres needs to be reconnected to people as main drivers of both an economic and spatial development. The current model focused on real estate led to a problematic dependency on further growth to permit affordable and attractive environments for advanced producer services and their highly skilled international workforce. Thus, Gulf cities are built on a reverse model of capital accumulation within properties, in which capital is not following the already functioning and established economies built on people and their skills. The property-led urban development must be gradually replaced, and Gulf cities need to be reinvented as small but specialized hubs within regional and global networks. Today, the current form of urban expansion has become highly problematic for a rather fragile desert and maritime ecosystem as well as a not-yet sufficiently dynamic and diverse economy rooted in cohesive and integrated societies.

Today, the environment has become increasingly polluted and exploited causing a rising threat for future liveability and sustainability in the Gulf. The high energy consumption of the region has given residents in Gulf cities a relatively high ecological footprint per capita.[48] This energy waste is caused by three main factors, namely, growing traffic, air conditioning and water production by desalination. This high waste of fossil energy resources, which are still being provided by the ongoing regional production, has led to increasing air pollution due to an exponentially growing number of cars, fossil-fuelled power plants and energy-wasting industries such as aluminium production. In addition to the air pollution caused by traffic and industry, the sea, particularly in the case of coastal regions, has suffered from salt water intrusion, untreated sewage and the impact of land reclamation. While desalination plants need more energy to meet the growing demand for water, they also produce a large amount of salt, leading to salt water intrusion in coastal areas. This increasing salinization in turn leads to dramatically increasing energy consumption to continue producing water. Therefore, water production has turned into a serious threat to the ecological balance in the Gulf.[49]

Before a potential collapse of the local ecosystem might occur, the rising costs of the recent urbanization can be expected to limit and transform current development patterns. Today, there is a clear tendency that rising land prices and the costs of essential infrastructure will reduce the previously experienced high living standards of many migrants as well as local citizens.[50] While low-income labourers have witnessed a gradual improvement of their accommodations due to improved regulations, medium-income groups, especially families, have been facing an increasing challenge to find affordable housing in central locations. Moreover, growth rates have led to an undersupply of many services, such as schools, and general infrastructure. Rising electricity costs and the high dependency on imported goods will lead to enhanced monthly expenses and thus lower consumption. Any compromised living standards can lead to the move of skilled international workforce and thus the loss of one of the foundations for competitive service economies. The recovery of expected economic downturns will highly depend on resilient social structures, built on integration rather than segregation.

Thus, the integration of migrants is one of the most important and urgent challenges of contemporary governance to build a solid economic basis on knowledge and skills rather than temporary event urbanism. While this integration will inevitably include more extensive rights to gain citizenship, the most important key is however a rising place attachment and thus emotional ties. An emerging multicultural society needs access to a big diversity of lifestyles and urban experiences. The current consumption-based approach, mainly expressed in shopping malls, cannot replace the required affiliation to a community and ideally a neighbourhood. In recent years, growing numbers of migrants from rather diverse places entered Gulf cities. Thus, according to embassies, migrants with more than seventy different countries of origin currently reside in the major capitals.[51] This form of migration has often been promoted by limiting the migration from certain countries to avoid or reduce majorities. But the lack of shared cultural backgrounds or even shared languages has created an environment of many small and fragmented groups as well as a highly level of anonymousness, suspicion and prejudices. The rather differing migrant groups can hardly be served with all their specific needs, which would require many years and ideally intergenerational growth.

In many places worldwide, migrants have however displayed their willingness to adopt new habits and thus to adjust to new environments resulting in their resourceful investment of time, skills and income. A rising share of migrants being owners of their accommodations or new regulations supporting long-term tenants would highly impact urbanism in the Gulf. The resulting consolidation would reduce overheated property markets and it would inevitably lead to demand-driven developments and a more dynamic process of urban manufacturing. This turn-around towards bottom-up dynamics, in which migrants have better access to diverse housing options and business ownership, would however require quick political actions regarding the integration of migrants and their rights. This however can only happen in most places, if the local populations have become main drivers of new economic developments. Therefore, this important step in transforming Gulf cities towards a clear expression of consolidated and integrated societies will require time. Time is however compromised by the enhanced regional and global competition and the subsequent pressure to grow markets rather than initiate markets rooted in gradual development dynamics driven by people and their needs.

The continuous pressure to attract investments has led to a problematic production of urban spaces, in which fast development is usually prioritized rather than integrating qualities. The role of architecture and urban design must be emphasized as an important dimension, in which the perceptual dimension can be changed and thus a new image of Gulf cities can ignite new dynamics. While in the past most developments have been designed as gated islands, the resulting fragmentation must be countered by a gradual redevelopment of neighbourhoods shaping cohesive and integrated districts. The introduction of public transit, such as the Dubai Metro, can only function on larger scales, if the districts can be recognized via functioning centres (Figure 8.6). A network and hierarchy of centres will always be the precondition for efficient and attractive bus routes required to supply the major transit system. Therefore, public spaces and their linkage must be designed in ways that support a clear orientation and stimulate pedestrians and cyclists. While the harsh climate during summer months might limit the use of public spaces, outdoor life has always been

Figure 8.6 The Dubai Metro.

possible during most seasons. The connected public realm is an important factor to connect neighbourhoods and thus all inhabitants.

In parallel to an extensive improvement of public spaces and walkability needed for public transit, new housing standards and major efforts in affordable housing are key factors for sustainable urbanism in the Gulf region. The quality of urban life can be dramatically improved, when both design and construction meet certain standard requirements. This however needs a major restructuring of local construction industries and design practices. In future, more construction materials need to be regionally produced rather than imported and the architectural design of most buildings must follow certain requirements. While LEED and other green building certification programmes have been introduced, their impact has been rather small due to their strict and thus expensive requirements. A gradual adjustment of general building standards would be more effective rather than rare exceptional best practices. In the case of the design appearance, architects should be more frequently challenged to enter design competitions and local municipalities need to invest in experienced district architects to define design standards for each district. Furthermore, extensive programmes are required to renew and sustain old building substance to enable the integration of diverse income groups in central areas.

The increasing crisis in affordable housing can only be solved by a major collaboration between private and public sectors. The majorities of urban populations are however migrants with temporary perspectives and thus with limited impact on housing markets regarding both quality and affordability. Subsequently, the costs of housing have been continuously rising without a sufficient integration of qualities. This reality of housing as a shelter of temporary migrants has led to a rather problematic environment, in which allocated government funds for attractive and affordable housing cannot be considered the only solution (Figure 8.7). In future, either rising income or lower land prices will enable more affordable housing in Gulf cities. Since both factors are however interconnected and most income in the private sector has become dependent on growth in property-led developments and further migration, it must be stated that a sudden adjustment of land prices would lead to a rather severe economic downturn, as witnessed during the financial crisis in 2008.

Consequently, governance must recognize and promote key economic sectors, which need Gulf cities as key hubs due to both the geopolitical location and the state-of-the-art infrastructure in the form of ports and airports. An efficient integration of this important economic basis for future Gulf cities would require an affordable and attractive environment. Thus, the major reinvestment

Figure 8.7 A public housing project in Muharraq, Kingdom of Bahrain.

of property revenues in affordable housing and public spaces must be enforced by regulations proposing long-term benefits. However, time to produce more sustainable urbanism can only be won by an emerging trust in future prosperity rather than sudden windows of investment opportunities. The current dilemma can only be solved by reconnecting places and people, whose skills and attachment will be the most important factors deciding on future Gulf cities.

Conclusion

The theoretical discourse on how urban spaces are the direct reflection of housing dynamics can be an important key to identify the core problem of any capitalist society beyond the introduction of limited practical solutions. The unequal access to wealth has led to increasingly unequal roles within societies regarding the definition of spaces. Thus, the pure approach to introduce top-down strategies for holistically solving the problem between rapid urbanization and the endangered social balance and thus environment needs to be questioned. The introduced framework of housing as a catalyst for three core urban qualities is built on Lefebvre's theories and integrates the basic triadic relationship between the main dimensions defining urbanism. In general, three conflicts can be identified endangering any sustainable development, as in the Gulf region: the divide between top-down decision-making and the values and needs of communities, the divide between consumers and masses of labourers with limited impact on developments and finally the divide between widespread speculative tendencies of investments and the implementation of long-term solutions.

These results of the introduced framework are all rooted in one main doctrine of modern capitalist societies, namely the focus on initiating further growth. While growth should theoretically be in balance with sufficient resources, the human invention of a debt-driven economy has introduced growth as necessity to validate the created capital. As a result, cities had to become growth machines attracting capital accumulation and creating complex networks of main control centres and subordinated ports.[52] This divide between global cities and ports in the developing world, which are used for industrial manufacturing and for accessing new resources, has led to a continuous North-South divide despite the officially declared end of colonialism. Current developments in the Gulf region can only be understood in this historic context. Fierce competition between cities to attract growth and thus capital has led to the three mentioned conflicts. Deregulation mechanisms were introduced to stimulate investments in emerging cities. The subsequent construction boom fuelled migration with a large majority of labourers and a small minority of high-income groups housed behind gated developments. Subsequently, most communities were obstructed from accessing the main decision-making processes, which resulted in both the danger of social unrest and a potential loss of skilled workforce as well as an increasing disillusion to ever gain a just share in defining the overall urban space.

This circle made of the perception of cities as investment opportunities rather than as homes for communities led to a shrinking identification between most inhabitants and their surrounding space. The resulting experience of spatial realities as oppressive but needed shells rather than as representations of shared values has led to a fragile foundation of many cities worldwide and particularly in the Gulf. While the new form of city making offers various opportunities, the pressure of future growth is preventing the economic integration of all social groups. The accelerated globalization has enabled the transfer of goods and labour worldwide, but its main drivers and shapers cannot be simply identified in the form of free market places. Instead, the main force of enabling complex networks with shrinking boundaries and clear hierarchies must be seen in the accumulation of investments in few locations and often-speculative tendencies. Consequently, the overall sustainability debate in the Gulf and worldwide must shift from a focus on curing symptoms to the actual core factor producing our conflicted space today: persistent social inequalities.

Thus, the main verdict of sustainable urbanism is that a rising collective awareness is requisite to challenge current global and local structures. The ongoing digitalization might enable an improved access to gain and share knowledge and thus to learn from different perspectives. The right to the city might be demanded because of this rapid knowledge exchange and increase. The currently cited scarcity of knowledge, which is emphasized using the term 'knowledge capital',[53] might be challenged through an enhanced intuitive understanding by the masses despite their limited access to education. This rediscovery of space as a collective product and a participatory process must be a major occasion to reconfigure the most dominant factors producing our built environment. As a result, no instant strategy can be introduced as a comprehensive solution of a problem rooted in the historic dominance of few decision-makers. Gulf cities have become expressions of recent globalization and urbanization tendencies and thus they must be considered as rather exposed experiments built on migration following visions of dynamic growth and central control but conveying a rising deficit in balancing short-term investment interests and long-term commitments, which however can only be achieved by empowered communities and their place attachment.

In this context, the role of architects can be regarded as rather unique in transforming places into possible starting points for resilient multicultural communities in Gulf cities. While designing spaces cannot resolve fundamental social imbalances, it can contribute to more attractive environments stimulating social engagement and enabling small businesses and their networks to evolve. Housing is the key element of urbanism and thus its design needs enhanced attention. Introducing new modular and flexible building types could provide a dynamic adjustment to changing needs. An emphasis on connected public spaces can promote walkability leading to integrated neighbourhoods and the end of gated compounds and isolated downtown areas. This spatial transformation can not only be achieved by top-down guidelines; their implementation will highly depend on an enhanced awareness of developers and investors. One possible solution is the introduction of architects engaged in municipalities or city councils, who are responsible for a more extensive coordination and communication of design choices. Another important step would be the introduction of official design competitions in the case of any major project to raise design standards and to promote an evolving culture of local architecture. Any advancement in housing and neighbourhood design on a larger scale will be a first indicator of a healthy and aware urban society.

Notes

1 Christian Schmid, *Stadt, Raum und Gesellschaft* (Stuttgart, 2005), p. 46.
2 Manuel Castells, *The Urban Question* (Cambridge, 1977).
3 Harvey, *Social Justice and the City*.
4 Schmid, *Stadt, Raum und Gesellschaft*, p. 33.
5 William Alonso, *Location and Land Use* (Cambridge, 1964).
6 Jacobs, *The Death and Life of Great American Cities*.
7 Keven R. Cox, *Urbanization and Conflict in Market Societies* (Chicago, 1978).
8 Michael J. Dear, *The Postmodern Urban Condition* (Oxford, 2000).
9 Kingsley Davis, 'The Urbanization of the Human Population', *Scientific American*, 213/3 (2006), pp. 40–53.
10 Michael J. Dear and Allen J. Scott, *Urbanization and Urban Planning in Capitalist Society* (London, 1981).
11 Henri Lefebvre, *The Urban Revolution* (Minneapolis, 2003 [1970]).
12 Lefebvre, *The Production of Space*.
13 Schmid, *Stadt, Raum und Gesellschaft*, p. 111.
14 Friedrich W. Nietzsche, *The Birth of Tragedy: Out of the Spirit of Music* (Oxford, 2008 [1872]).
15 Neil Brenner, 'Global, Fragmented, Hierarchical: Henri Lefebvre's Geographies of Globalization', *Public Culture*, 10/1 (1997), pp. 135–67.
16 Lefebvre, *The Production of Space*.
17 Ibid., p. 33.
18 Ibid., p. 264.
19 Ibid., p. 268.
20 Ibid., p. 239.
21 Ibid., p. 262.
22 Ibid., p. 361.
23 Friedrich Engels, *The Condition of the Working Class in England* (Stanford, 1968 [1845]).
24 Hall, *Cities of Tomorrow*, p. 41.
25 Davis, 'The Urbanization of the Human Population', p. 40.
26 Cohen, 'The New International Division of Labor'.
27 Friedmann, 'The World City Hypothesis', pp. 69–83; Sassen, *The Global City*.
28 Lefebvre, *The Production of Space*, p. 352.
29 Lefebvre, *The Urban Revolution*, p. 163.
30 Ibid., p. 164.
31 Merrifield, *Dialectical Urbanism*.
32 Lefebvre, *The Production of Space*, p. 399.
33 Ibid., p. 52.

34 David Harvey, *Consciousness and the Urban Experience: Studies in the History and Theory of Capitalist Urbanization* (Baltimore, 1985).

35 Hall, *Cities of Tomorrow*, p. 48.

36 Newman and Kenworthy, *Sustainability and Cities*, p. 5.

37 Lefebvre, *The Production of Space*, p. 354.

38 Lefebvre, *The Urban Revolution*, p. 161.

39 Lefebvre, *The Production of Space*, p. 383.

40 Castells, *The Informational City*.

41 Sassen, 'Locating Cities on Global Circuits', p. 29.

42 Salama and Wiedmann, *Demystifying Doha*, p. 235.

43 Sassen, *The Global City*, p. 169.

44 United Nations, *Report of the World Commission on Environment and Development: Our Common Future*, 1987. Available at: www.un-documents.net/our-common-future.pdf (accessed 10 February 2017).

45 Jane Jacobs, *The Economy of Cities* (New York, 1969).

46 Florian Wiedmann, Ashraf M. Salama and Velina Mirincheva, 'Sustainable Urban Qualities in the Emerging City of Doha', *Journal of Urbanism*, 7/1 (2014), pp. 62–84.

47 Schmid, *Stadt, Raum und Gesellschaft*, p. 111.

48 Global Footprint Network, *Compare Countries*. Available at: http://data.footprin tnetwork.org/#/compareCountries?cn=all&type=EFCpc&yr=2013 (accessed 10 February 2017).

49 Mohamed A. Dawoud and Mohamed M. Al Mulla, 'Environmental Impacts of Seawater Desalination: Arabian Gulf Case Study', *International Journal of Environment and Sustainability*, 1/3 (2012), pp. 22–37.

50 G. Lahn, 'Fuel, Food and Utilities Price Reforms in the GCC: A Wake-up Call for Business', Chatham House – The Royal Institute of International Affairs (2016). Available at: https://www.chathamhouse.org/sites/files/chathamhouse/publication s/research/Food%20Fuel%20and%20Utilities%20Price%20Reforms%20in%20the% 20GCC%20A%20Wake-up%20Call%20for%20Business.pdf (accessed 10 February 2017).

51 Snoj, *Population of Qatar by Nationality*.

52 Edward Soja, *Postmodern Geographies: The Reassertion of Space in Critical Social Theory* (London, 1989), p. 184.

53 Sassen, *Cities Today. A New Frontier for Major Developments*.

Bibliography

Abu Dhabi Council for Economic Development (2007). *The Abu Dhabi Economic Vision 2030*. Available at: www.adced.ae/sites/En/ev/Documents/Measures%20of%20Sucess.pdf [accessed 22 March 2017].

Abu Dhabi Council for Economic Development (2014). Sustainability – Playing a Central Role in Abu Dhabi's Economic Growth. *The Economic Review*, Issue 19. Abu Dhabi.

Abu Dhabi Statistics Centre (2016). *Statistical Yearbook of Abu Dhabi 2016 – Population*. Available at: www.scad.ae/en/Pages/ThemesReleases.aspx?ThemeID=4 [accessed 22 March 2017].

Abu Dhabi Urban Planning Council (2017). About Us. Available at: Middle Income Housing Policy. www.upc.gov.ae/mirh.aspx?lang=en-US [accessed 6 May 2017].

AECOM, ARUP, Allies and Morrison (2010). *Development Guidelines*, Phase II, Doha.

Aerni, Philipp (2016). Coping with Migration-Induced Urban Growth: Addressing the Blind Spot of UN Habitat. *Sustainability*, 8(8), p. 800.

Akbar, Jamel (1988). *Crisis in the Built Environment: The Case of the Muslim City*. Singapore: Concept Media Pte Ltd.

Alawadi, Khaled (2014). Urban Redevelopment Trauma: The Story of a Dubai Neighbourhood. *Built Environment*, 40(3), pp. 357–75.

Al-Buainain, Fadl A. (1999). *Urbanisation in Qatar: A Study of the Residential and Commercial Land Development in Doha City, 1970 – 1997*. Salford: University of Salford.

Al-Hathloul, Saleh A. (1996). *The Arab-Muslim City*. Riyadh: Dar Al Sahan.

Al-Mulla, Habib (2004). Legal Aspects of Real Estate Ownership in the UAE. In: *Dubai Property Investment Guide*. Dubai: Cross Border Legal Publishing, pp. 63–66.

Al-Nabi, Mohammed N. (2000). *The History of Land-use and Development in Bahrain*. Manama: Ministry of Housing.

Alonso, William (1964). *Location and Land-use*. 1st ed. Cambridge, MA: Harvard University Press.

Al-Shaer, Maher (2013). *Real-Estate Developments for Economic Growth: Significance and Critical Role of Real Estate Developments in the Kingdom of Bahrain*, Saarbrücken: LAP Verlag.

Altman, Irwin (1975). *The Environment and Social Behaviour*. Monterey, CA: Brookes/Cole.

Antoniucci, Valentina and Marella, Giuliano (2017). Immigrants and the City: The Relevance of Immigration on Housing Price Gradient. *Buildings*, 7(91), pp. 1–14.

Arab News (2012). *More than half of GCC Population under Age 25*, 17 July 2012.
    Available at: www.arabnews.com/saudi-arabia/more-half-gcc-population-under-age-
    25 [accessed 3 January 2018].
Azar, Elie and Raouf, Mohamed A. (2017). *Sustainability in the Gulf: Challenges and
    Opportunities*. London: Routledge.
Badcock, Blair (2002). *Making Sense of Cities*. London: Routledge.
Bahrain Bay (2017). *Development Plan*. Available at: www.bahrainbay.com/
    development-plan/ [accessed 3 December 2017].
Bahrain Economic Development Board (2008). *Bahrain Vision 2030*. Available at: www.
    bahrainedb.com/en/about/Pages/economic%20vision%202030.aspx#.WNJCtvnysuV
    [accessed 22 March 2017].
Bahrain Financial Harbour (2017). *Overview*. Available at: www.bfharbour.com/
    [accessed 3 December 2017].
Bahrain Information & eGovernment Authority (2014). *Bahrain Open Data Portal*.
    Available at: www.data.gov.bh/en/DataAnalysis [accessed 22 March 2017].
Bahrain Municipal Geo Explore (2017). *Map*. Available at: www.ma-investment.gov.bh/
    website/discover_bah/ [accessed 3 December 2017].
Balbo, Marcello and Marconi, Giovanna (2006). International Migration, Diversity and
    Urban Governance in Cities of the South. *Habitat International*, 30(3), pp. 706–15.
Bardhan, Ashok and Kroll, Cynthia A. (2007). Globalization and the Real Estate
    Industry: Issues, Implications, Opportunities. In: *Sloan Industry Studies Annual
    Conference*, April 2007, Cambridge.
Barnard, Lucy (2014). Dubai Property Prices Will Reach 2008 Levels, Raising Worries
    of Another Bubble. *The National*, 10 February 2014. Available at: www.thenational
    .ae/business/industry-insights/property/dubai-property-prices-will-reach-2008-
    levels-raising-worries-of-another-bubble [accessed 6 May 2017].
Barwa (2017). *About Us*. Available at: www.barwa.com.qa/en/AboutBarwa [accessed
    6 May 2017].
Beamish, Julia O., Goss, Rosemary C. and Emmel, JoAnn (2001). Lifestyle Influences on
    Housing Preferences. *Housing and Society*, 28(1–2), pp. 1–28.
Beaverstock, Jonathan V. (2007). World City Networks 'from below': International
    Mobility and Inter-City Relations in the Global Investment Banking Industry. In:
    P. Taylor, B. Derudder, P. Saey and F. Witlox (eds), *Cities in Globalization*. London:
    Routledge, pp. 50–69.
Beaverstock, Jonathan V., Smith, Richard G. and Taylor, Peter J. (2000). World
    City Network: A New Metageography? *Annals of the Association of American
    Geographers*, 90, pp. 123–34.
Benedikter, Roland (2012). Lifestyles. In: H. Anheier and M. Juergensmeyer (eds),
    Encyclopedia of Global Studies. London: Sage Publications, pp. 1076–80.
Ben-Hamouche, Mustapha (2009). Complexity of Urban Fabric in Traditional Muslim
    Cities: Importing Old Wisdom to Present Cities. *Urban Design International*, 14(1),
    pp. 22–35.

Bertrand, Renaud (2012). Real Estate Bubble and Financial Crisis in Dubai: Dynamics and Policy Responses. *Journal of Real Estate Literature*, 20(1), pp. 51–77.

Blum, Elisabeth and Neitzke, Peter (2009). *Dubai ein Zwischenbericht über die derzeit größte Baustelle der Welt.* Stuttgart: Birkhäuser Verlag.

Bonaiuto, Marino, Aiello, Antonio, Perugini, Marco, Bonnes, Mirilia and Ercolani, Anna P. (1999). Multidimensional Perception of Residential Environment Quality and Neighborhood Attachment in the Urban Environment. *Journal of Environmental Psychology*, 19(4), pp. 331–52.

Boston Consulting Group (2016). *Winning in Emerging Markets.* Available at: https://www.bcgperspectives.com/content/articles/globalization_growth_winning_in_emerging_market_cities/?chapter=2 [accessed 22 March 2017].

Bourdieu, Pierre (1977). *Outline of a Theory of Practice.* Cambridge: Cambridge University Press.

Bourdieu, Pierre (1987). *Distinction: A Social Critique of the Judgment of Taste.* Harvard, IL: Harvard University Press.

Brenner, Neil (1998). Between Fixity and Motion. Accumulation, Territorial Organization and the Historical Geography of Spatial Scales. *Society and Space*, 16, pp. 459–81.

Brenner, Neil (1997). Global, Fragmented, Hierarchical: Henri Lefebvre's Geographies of Globalization. *Public Culture*, 10(1), pp. 135–67.

Brenner, Neil and Keil, Roger (2011). From Global Cities to Globalized Urbanization. In: R. T. LeGates and F. Stout (eds), *The City Reader.* New York: Routledge, pp. 599–608.

Burgess, Ernest W. (1925). The Growth of the City. In: R. E. Park, E. W. Burgess and R. D. McKenzie (eds), *The City: Suggestions of Investigation of Human Behavior in the Urban Environment.* Chicago, IL: University of Chicago Press, pp. 47–62.

Butler, Edgar, Chaplin, Stuart, Hemmens, George C., Kaiser, Edward J., Stegman, Michael A. and Weiss, Shirley F. (1969). Moving Behavior and Residential Choice: A National Survey. *National Cooperative Highway Research Programs*, Report No. 81, Highway Research Board, Washington, DC.

Calthorpe, Peter (1993). *The Next American Metropolis: Ecology and the American Dream.* New York: Princeton Architectural Press.

Castells, Manuel (1977). *The Urban Question.* 1st ed. Cambridge, MA: MIT Press.

Cervero, Robert (1986). *Suburban Gridlock.* New Brunswick, NJ: Rutgers University, Center for Urban Policy Research.

Castells, Manuel (1989). *The Informational City.* 1st ed. Oxford: B. Blackwell.

Chapman, Dennis (1955). *The Home and Social Status.* London: Routeledge and Kegan Paul Ltd.

Chase, John, Crawford, Margaret and Kaliski, John (2008). *Everyday Urbanism.* New York: The Monacelli Press.

Choguill, Charles L. (1996). Toward Sustainability of Human Settlements. *Habitat International*, 20(3), pp. 5–8.

Clemancon, Virginie (2015). GCC Building Materials Industry Set to Be Challenged by the Emerging Trends in 2015. In: *Deloitte GCC Powers of Construction*. Available at: www2.deloitte.com/content/dam/Deloitte/hu/Documents/Real%20Estate/hu-real-estate-gccpoc2015-publication-eng.pdf [accessed 3 December 2017].

Cohen, Robert B. (1981). The New International Division of Labor, Multinational Corporations and Urban Hierarchy. In: M. Dear and A. Scott (eds), *Urbanization and Urban planning in Capitalist Society*. London: Methuen, pp. 287–317.

Colliers International (2014). *Doha's Residential Market*. Available at: www.colliers.com/-/media/562F03BEE6D54CA0B7BA140DF287C911.ashx?la=en-GB [accessed 3 January 2018].

Commins, David D. (2012). *The Gulf States: A Modern History*. London: I.B. Tauris.

Cox, Kevin (1978). *Urbanization and Conflict in Market Societies*. 1st ed. Chicago, IL: Maaroufa Press.

Damluji, Salma S. (2012). *The Diwan Al Amiri, Doha, Qatar*. London: Laurence King Publishing.

Davidson, Christopher (2009). *Dubai: The Vulnerability of Success*. New York: Hurst C & Co.

Davis, Kingsley (1965). The Urbanization of the Human Population. *Scientific American*, 213(3), pp. 40–53.

Davis, Mike (2006). *City of Quartz*. 2nd ed. London: Verso.

Davis, Mike (2007). Sand, Fear and Money in Dubai. In: M. Davis and D. B. Monk (eds), *Evil Paradises: Dreamworlds of Neoliberalism*. New York: The New Press, 49–67.

Dear, Michael (2000). *The Postmodern Urban Condition*. 1st ed. Oxford: Blackwell.

Dear, Michael and Scott, Allen J. (1981). *Urbanization and Urban Planning in Capitalist Society*. 1st ed. London: Methuen.

De Bel-Air, Françoise (2014). *Demography, Migration and the Labour Market in Qatar*. Available at: www.cadmus.eui.eu/bitstream/handle/1814/32431/GLMM_ExpNote_08-2014.pdf?sequence=1&isAllowed=y [accessed 22 March 2017].

De Bel-Air, Françoise (2015a). *Demography, Migration and the Labour Market in the UAE*. Available at: www.cadmus.eui.eu/bitstream/handle/1814/36375/GLMM_ExpNote_07_2015.pdf?sequence=1&isAllowed=y [accessed 22 March 2017].

De Bel-Air, Françoise (2015b). *Demography, Migration and the Labour Market in Bahrain*. Available at: www.cadmus.eui.eu/bitstream/handle/1814/35882/GLMM_ExpNote_06_2015.pdf?sequence=1&isAllowed=y [accessed 22 March 2017].

Diener, Christa, Gangler, Annette and Fein, Andreas (2003). Transformationsprozesse in Oasensiedlungen Omans. *Trialog*, 76, pp. 15–21.

Doherty, Gareth (2017). *Paradoxes of Green: Landscapes of a City-State*. Berkeley: University of California Press.

Douglas, Mary (1970). *Natural Symbols: Explorations in Cosmology*. London: Cresset Press.

Douglas, Mary (2006). A History of Grid and Group Cultural Theory. *Semiotics Institute Online. Semioticon 2006.* Available at: www.semioticon.com/sio/files/douglas-et-al/douglas1.pdf?lbisphpreq=1&file=douglas-et-al/douglas1.pdf [accessed 3 January 2018].

Dubai Internet City (2017). *Who We Are.* Available at: www.dic.ae/who-we-are/#get_intouch [accessed 3 December 2017].

Dubai Pearl (2017). *Project.* Available at: https://www.dubaipearl.com/about [accessed 3 December 2017].

Dubai Properties (2017). *Jumeirah Beach Residence.* Available at: http://www.dp.ae/about-dubai-properties [accessed 3 December 2017].

Dubai Statistics Centre (2014). *Population 2014.* Available at: https://www.dsc.gov.ae/Publication/Population%20Bulletin%20Emirate%20of%20Dubai%202014.pdf [accessed 3 December 2017].

Dubai Statistics Centre (2017). *Population Bulletin.* Available at: www.dsc.gov.ae/Publication/Population%20Bulletin%20Emirate%20of%20Dubai%202015.pdf [accessed 22 March 2017].

Dumont, Jean-Christophe, Spielvogel, Gilles and Widmaier, Sarah (2010). International Migrants in Developed, Emerging and Developing Countries: An Extended Profile. *OECD Social, Employment and Migration Working Papers No. 114.* Available at: www.oecd.org/migration/46535003.pdf [accessed 7 March 2018].

El-Katiri, Laura, Fattouh, Bassam and Segal, Paul (2011). *Anatomy of an Oil-based Welfare State: Rent Distribution in Kuwait.* Available at: www.eprints.soas.ac.uk/14265/1/Kuwait_2011.pdf [accessed 7 March 2018].

El-Samahy, Rami and Hutzell, Kelly (2014). In Search of Doha's Public Realm. *Urban Pamphleteer* 4, pp. 10–13.

Elsheshtawy, Yasser (2008). Cities of Sand and Fog: Abu Dhabi's Global Ambitions. In: Y. Elsheshtawy (ed.), *The Evolving Arab City.* London: Routledge, pp. 248–304.

Emaar (2017a). Dubai Marina Waterfront. Available at: https://www.emaar.com/en/what-we-do/communities/uae/dubai-marina/ [accessed 3 December 2017].

Emaar (2017b). *Emirates Hills.* Available at: http://www.emiratesliving.ae/en/about/communities/emirateshills.aspx [accessed 3 December 2017].

Engels, Friedrich (1968). *The Condition of the Working Class in England.* 1st ed. Stanford, CA: Stanford University Press.

Ernst & Young (2017). *Digging beneath the Surface. Is It Time to Rethink Diversification in the GCC.* Available at: www.ey.com/Publication/vwLUAssets/ey-is-it-time-to-rethink-diversification/$FILE/ey-is-it-time-to-rethink-diversification.pdf [accessed 3 December 2017].

Fainstein, Susan S. (2005). Cities and Diversity: Should We Want It? Should We Plan for It? *Urban Affairs Review*, 42(1), pp. 3–19.

Fattah, Hala (2016). Social Structures and Transformation in the Gulf and Arabia until 1971. In: J. E. Peterson (ed.), *The Emergence of the Gulf States.* London: Bloomsbury, 241–59.

Florida, Richard (2002). *The Rise of the Creative Class: And How It's Transforming Work, Leisure, Community and Everyday Life*. New York: Perseus Book Group.

Foster, Dawn (2016). Is Immigration Causing the UK Housing Crisis? *The Guardian*, 25 January 2016. Available at: www.theguardian.com/housing-network/2016/jan/25/is-immigration-causing-the-uk-housing-crisis [accessed 3 December 2017].

Fox, John, Mourtada-Sabbah, Nada and Al-Mutawa, Mohammed (2006). *Globalization and the Gulf*. New York: Routledge.

Freeman, Lance (1998). Interpreting the Dynamics of Public Housing: Cultural and Rational Choice Explanations. *Housing Policy Debate*, 9(2), pp. 323–53.

Friedmann, John (1986). The World City Hypothesis. *Development and Change*, 17(1), pp. 69–83.

Fromherz, Allen J. (2012). *Qatar: A Modern History*. New York: I. B. Tauris.

Fuccaro, Nelida (2007). Understanding the Urban History of Bahrain. *Critique: Critical Middle Eastern Studies*, 9(17), pp. 49–81.

Furlan, Raffaello and Faggion, Laura (2015). The Souq Waqif Heritage Site in Doha: Spatial Form and Livability. *American Journal of Environmental Engineering*, 5(5), pp. 146–60.

Gafoor, Abdul A. (1995). *Islamic Banking and Finance*. Available at: www.users.bart.nl/~abdul/chap4.html [accessed 19 October 2008].

Garba, Shaibu (2004). Managing Urban Growth and Development in the Riyadh Metropolitan Area, Saudi Arabia, *Habitat International*, 28, pp. 593–608.

Gardner, Andrew (2011). Gulf Migration and the Family. *Journal of Arabian Studies*, 1(1), pp. 3–25.

Gardner, Andrew, Pessoa, Silvia and Harkness, Laura (2014). *Labour Migrants and Access to Justice in Contemporary Qatar*. Available at: http://www.lse.ac.uk/middleEastCentre/publications/Reports/LabourMigrantsQatarEnglish.pdf [accessed 3 January 2018].

Gardner, Andrew, Pessoa, Silvia, Diop, Abdoulaye, Al-Ghanim, Kaltham, Trung, Kien Le and Harkness, Laura (2013). A Portrait of Low Income Migrants in Contemporary Qatar. *Journal of Arabian Studies*, 3(1), pp. 1–17.

Garreau, Joel (1991). *Edge City: Life on the New Frontier*. New York: Doubleday.

Gehl, Jan (1987). *Life between Buildings: Using Public Space*. London: Island Press.

General Secretariat of Development Planning (2008). *Qatar National Vision 2030*. Doha: Gulf Publishing and Printing Company.

General Secretariat of Development Planning (2009). *Advancing Sustainable Development, Qatar's Second Human Development Report*. Doha: Gulf Publishing and Printing Company.

General Secretariat of Development Planning (2011). *National Development Strategy 2011 – 2016*. Doha: Gulf Publishing and Printing Company.

Gerrity, Michael (2015). Dubai Property Correction Overshadowed by 5-Year Supply Mismatch. *World Property Journal* (8 June). Available at: www.worldpropertyjournal.com/real-estate-news/dubai-uae/dubai-property-report-2015-phidar-

advisory-dubai-residential-research-report-condo-prices-in-dubai-jesse-downs-914
2.php [accessed 3 December 2017].

Golubchikov, Oleg and Badyina, Anna (2012). *Sustainable Housing for Sustainable Cities: A Policy Framework for Developing Countries*. Nairobi, Kenya: UN-HABITAT. Available at: www.ssrn.com/abstract=2194204 [accessed 6 May 2017].

Gonzalez, Libertad and Ortega, Francesc (2009). *Immigration and Housing Boom: Evidence from Spain. Institute for the Study of Labor*. Available at: www.ftp.iza.org/dp4333.pdf [accessed 7 March 2018].

Gordon, Peter, Kumar, Ajay and Richardson, Harry W. (1989). The Influence of Metropolitan Spatial Structure on Commuting Time. *Journal of Urban Economics*, 26(2), pp. 138–51.

Government of Dubai (2005). *Dubai Strategic Plan 2015*. Available at: www.dubaiplan 2021.ae/dsp-2015-2/ [accessed 22 March 2017].

Government of Dubai (2007). *Urban Development Framework*. Dubai.

Government of Dubai (2016a). *Dubai Industrial Strategy 2030*. Available at: www. dubaiplan2021.ae/wp-content/uploads/2016/06/Dubai-Industrial-Strategy-2030.pdf [accessed 22 March 2017].

Government of Dubai (2016b). *Dubai Plan 2021*. Available at: www.dubaiplan2021.ae/dubai-plan-2021/ [accessed 22 March 2017].

Graham, Elspeth and Sabater, Albert (2015). Population Change and Housing across the Lifecourse: Demographic Perspectives, Methodological Challenges and Emerging Issues. *ESRC Centre for Population Change*, Working Paper Series 64.

Gröger, Maria, Schmid, Victoria and Bruckner, Thomas (2011). Lifestyles and Their Impact on Energy-Related Investment Decisions. *Low Carbon Economy*, 2, pp. 107–14.

Gulf Holding Company (2017). *Projects*. Available at: www.gfholding.com/Projects [accessed 3 December 2017].

Gulf Migration (2015). UAE: A Comparison of Average Monthly Salaries Received by Nationality Group of Workers. Available at: www.gulfmigration.eu/uae-a-comparis on-of-average-monthly-salaries-received-by-nationality-group-of-workers-in-us-selected-professions-2015/?print=pdf [accessed 3 January 2018].

Gurran, Nicole, Milligan, Vivienne, Baker, Doug and Bugg, Laura B. (2007). International Practice in Planning for Affordable Housing: Lessons for Australia. *Australian Housing and Urban Research Institute*. AHURI Postitioning Paper No. 99. Available at: https://www.ahuri.edu.au/__data/assets/pdf_file/0017/2834/AHURI_ Positioning_Paper_No99_International_practice_in_planning_for_affordable_ housing_lessons_for_Australia.pdf [accessed 3 January 2018].

Hakim, Besim S. (2007). Revitalizing Traditional Towns and Heritage Districts. *Archnet-IJAR: International Journal of Architectural Research*, 1(3), pp. 153–66.

Hall, Peter (1988). *Cities of Tomorrow*. 1st ed. Oxford: Blackwell.

Hall, Peter (1987). The Urbanization of Capital and Consciousness and the Urban Experience: Studies in the History and Theory of Capitalist Urbanization. *Economic Geography*, 63(4), p. 354.

Hanhörster, Heike (2001). Whose Neighbourhood Is It? Ethnic Diversity in Urban Spaces in Germany. *GeoJournal*, 51, pp. 329–38.

Hanif, Nadeem, Khaishgi, Amna E. and Fahy, Michael (2017). Affordable Homes Plan a Good Fit for Dubai. *The National*. Available at: www.thenational.ae/uae/governm ent/20170313/affordable-homes-plan-a-good-fit-for-dubai [accessed 6 May 2017].

Harrison, Fraker (2007). Where Is the Urban Design Discourse? *Places: Forum of Design for the Public Realm*, 19(3), pp. 61–3.

Harvey, David (1973). *Social Justice and the City*. 1st ed. Athens: Edward Arnold.

Harvey, David (1985). *Consciousness and the Urban Experience: Studies in the History and Theory of Capitalist Urbanization*. 1st ed. Baltimore, MD: The Johns Hopkins University Press.

Harvey, David (1989). *The Condition of Postmodernity*. Oxford: Blackwell.

Harvey, David (1997). Contested Cities: Spatial Process and Spatial Form. In: N. Jewson and S. MacGregor (eds), *Transforming Cities*. London: Routledge, pp. 19–28.

Hasanin, Abeer A. (2007). Urban Legibility and Shaping the Image of Doha. *Archnet-IJAR: International Journal of Architectural Research*, 1(3), pp. 37–54.

Hawker, Ronald (2008). *Traditional Architecture of the Arabian Gulf: Building on Desert Tides*. Southampton: WIT Press.

Heeg, Susanne (2008). *Von Stadtplanung und Immobilienwirtschaft*. Bielefeld: transcript Verlag.

Hertog, Steffen (2014). Arab Gulf States: An Assessment of Nationalisation Policies. In: *Gulf Labour Markets and Migration*. Available at: www.cadmus.eui.eu/bitstream/ handle/1814/32156/GLMM%20ResearchPaper_01-2014.pdf?sequence=1 [accessed 22 March 2017].

Hojrup, Thomas (2003). *State, Culture, and Life Modes: The Foundations of Life Mode Analysis*. London: Ashgate.

Hopper, Matthew S. (2014). The African Presence in Eastern Arabia. In: L. G. Potter (ed.), *The Persian Gulf in Modern Times*. New York: Palgrace Macmillan, pp. 327–50.

Hui, Eddie C. M., Li, Si M., Wong, Francis K. W., Yi, Zheng and Yu, Ka H. (2012). Ethnicity, Cultural Disparity and Residential Mobility: Empirical Analysis of Hong Kong. *Habitat International*, 36(1), pp. 1–10.

Human Rights Watch (2012). *Building a Better World Cup. Protecting Migrant Workers in Qatar Ahead of FIFA 2022*. Available at: www.hrw.org/sites/default/files/reports/ qatar0612webwcover_0.pdf [accessed 3 January 2018].

International Monetary Fund (2009). *International Transactions in Remittances: Guide for Compilers and Users*. Washington, DC: IMF.

Jacobs, Jane (1961). *The Death and Life of Great American Cities*. New York: Vintage Press.

Jacobs, Jane (1969). *The Economy of Cities*. 1st ed. New York: Random House.

Jaidah, Ibrahim and Bourennane, Malika (2009). *The History of Qatari Architecture 1800-1950*. Milan: Skira.

Jarvis, Adrian and Lee, Robert (2008). *Trade, Migration and Urban Networks in Port Cities, 1640-1940*. Liverpool: Liverpool University Press.

Jayet, Hubert, Rayp, Glenn, Ruyssen, Ilse and Ukrayinchuk, Nadiya (2014). *Immigrants' Location Choice in Belgium*. Institut de Recherches Economiques et Sociales de l'Universite catholique de Louvain. Available at: www.sites.uclouvain.be/econ/DP/IRES/2014004.pdf [accessed 7 March 2018].

Jones, Peter, Roberts, Marion and Morris, Linda (2007). *Rediscovering Mixed-use Streets: The Contribution of Local High Streets to Sustainable Communities*. Bristol: Policy Press in association with the Joseph Rowntree Foundation.

Kamrava, Mehran (2016). *Gateways to the World: Port Cities in the Persian Gulf*. London: Hurst Publishers.

Kanna, Ahmed (2011). *Dubai: The City as Corporation*. Minnesota: University of Minnesota.

Kavaratzis, Mihalis and Ashworth, G. J. (2005). City Branding: An Effective Assertion of Identity or a Transitory Market Trick? *Journal of Economic and Social Geography*, 96(5), pp. 206–514.

Keating, Michael (2001). Governing Cities and Regions: Territorial Restructuring in a Global Age. In: A. Scott (ed.), *Global City Regions*. Oxford: Oxford University Press, pp. 371–91.

Kelbaugh, Douglas (2000). Three Paradigms: New Urbanism, Everyday Urbanism, Post Urbanism—An Excerpt From the Essential Common Place. *Bulletin of Science, Technology & Society*, 20, pp. 285–9.

Khalaf, Sulayman N. (2006). The Evolution of the Gulf City Type: Oil and Globalization. In: J. W. Fox, N. Mourtada-Sabbah and M. Al-Mutawa (eds), *Globalization and the Gulf*. New York: Routledge. pp. 245–63.

Kunstler, James H. (1993). *The Geography of Nowhere*. New York: Touchstone.

Law, Rosanna (2014). The Paradox of Msheireb. *Urban Pamphleteer*, 4, pp. 8–9.

Law, Rosanna and Underwood, Kevin (2012). Msheireb Heart of Doha: An Alternative Approach to Urbanism in the Gulf Region. *International Journal of Islamic Architecture*, 1(1), pp. 131–47.

Lefebvre, Henri (1991). *The Production of Space*. Oxford: Blackwell.

Lefebvre, Henri (2003). *The Urban Revolution*. 1st ed. Minneapolis: University of Minnesota Press.

Lusail City (2017). *Lusail City*. Available at: http://www.lusail.com/ [accessed 19 December 2017].

Marans, Robert W. (2012). Quality of Urban Life Studies: An Overview and Implications for Environment-Behaviour Research. *Social and Behavioral Sciences*, 35, pp. 9–22.

Marcus, Clare C. (1997). *House as a Mirror of Self*. Berkeley, CA: Conari Press.

McIntosh, James, Trubka, Roman J., Kenworthy, Jeffrey R. and Newman, Peter W. (2014). The Role of Urban Form and Transit in City Car Dependence: Analysis of

26 Global Cities from 1960 to 2000. *Transportation Research Part D: Transport and Environment*, 33, pp. 95–110.

Meinel, Ute (2002). *Die Intifada im Ölscheichtum Bahrain*. Münster: LIT Verlag.

Merrifield, Andy (2002). *Dialectical Urbanism: Social Struggles in the Capitalist Society*. 1st ed. New York: Monthly Review Press.

Ministry of Development Planning and Statistics (2015). *Census 2015*. Available at: www.mdps.gov.qa/en/knowledge/Publications/Other/Census%202015.pdf [accessed 3 January 2018].

Ministry of Development Planning and Statistics (2016). *Population and Social Statistics*, 2016. Available at: www.mdps.gov.qa/en/statistics/Statistical%20Releases/Population/Population/2015/1_Population_2015.pdf [accessed 22 March 2017].

Ministry of Housing (1996). *General Report on Housing and Urban Development in Bahrain*. Istanbul: The United Nations Conference on Human Settlements – Habitat II, City Summit.

Mirincheva, Velina, Wiedmann, Florian and Salama, Ashraf M. (2013). The Spatial Development Potentials of Business Districts in Doha: The Case of the West Bay. *Open House International*, 38(4), pp. 16–26.

Mohamad, Robina and Sidaway, James D. (2012). Spectacular Urbanization Amidst Variegated Geographies of Globalization: Learning from Abu Dhabi's Trajectory through the Lives of South Asian Men. *International Journal of Urban and Regional Research*, 36(3), pp. 606–27.

Mohammed, Sara I., Graham, Daniel J. and Melo Patricia C. (2017). The Effect of the Dubai Metro on the Value of Residential and Commercial Properties. *Journal of Transport and Land Use*, 10(1), pp. 263–90.

Molotch, Harvey (1976). The City as a Growth Machine: Towards a Political Economy of Place. *American Journal of Sociology*, 82, pp. 309–32.

Msheireb Properties (2013). *About Msheireb Downtown Doha*. Available at: http://www.msheireb.com/msheireb-downtown-doha/about-msheireb-downtown-doha/ [accessed 3 January 2018].

Mumford, Lewis (1968). *The City in History: Its Origins, Its Transformations, Its Prospects*. Boston, MA: Mariner Books.

Nadjmabadi, Shahnaz R. (2009). The Arab Presence on the Iranian Coast of the Persian Gulf. In: L. G. Potter (ed.), *The Persian Gulf in History*. New York: Palgrave Macmillan, pp. 129–45.

Nagy, Sharon (1997). *Social and Spatial Process: An Ethnographic Study of Housing in Qatar*. Philadelphia: University of Pennsylvania.

Nagy, Sharon (2006). Making Room for Migrants, Making Sense of Difference: Spatial and Ideological Expression of Social Diversity in Urban Qatar. *Urban Studies*, 43, pp. 119–37.

Nakheel (2017a). *Palm Jumeirah*. Available at: http://www.nakheel.com/en/communities/palm-jumeirah [accessed 3 December 2017].

Nakheel (2017b). *Jumeirah Heights*. Available at: http://www.nakheel.com/en/comm unities/jumeirah-heights [accessed 3 December 2017].

Narwold, Andrew and Sandy, Jonathan (2010). Valuing Housing Stock Diversity. *International Journal of Housing Markets and Analysis*, 3(1), pp. 53–9.

The National (2017). *Dubai Real Estate Had a Sluggish Year of Fewer Trades and Turnover*. 14 January 2017. Available at: www.thenational.ae/business/property/dubai-real-estate-had-a-sluggish-year-of-fewer-trades-and-turnover [accessed 6 May 2017].

Newman, Peter and Kenworthy, Jeffrey (1999). *Sustainability and Cities: Overcoming Automobile Dependence*. 2nd ed. Washington, DC: Island Press.

Newmark, Norma L. and Thompson, Patricia J. (1977). *Self, Space and Shelter*. San Francisco, CA: Canfield Press.

Nicholas, Sarah (2010). Al Zaab Neighbourhood in Abu Dhabi. In: *The National*, 25 September 2010. Available at: www.thenational.ae/lifestyle/home/al-zaab-neighbourhood-in-abu-dhabi-1.593982 [accessed 3 January 2018].

Nietzsche, Friedrich W. (2008). *The Birth of Tragedy: Out of the Spirit of Music*. Oxford: Oxford University Press.

Oxford Business Group (2008). *The Report: Bahrain 2008*. Oxford: Oxford Business Group.

Oxford Business Group (2013). *The Report: Bahrain 2013*. Oxford: Oxford Business Group.

Oxford Business Group (2017). *The Report: Bahrain 2017: Construction & Real Estate. Sustainability in the Gulf: Challenges and Opportunities*. Available at: https://oxfordb usinessgroup.com/bahrain-2017/construction-real-estate [accessed 19 December 2017].

Pacione, Michael (2005). City Profile: Dubai. *Cities*, 22(3), pp. 255–65.

Pape, Heinz (1977). *Er Riad. Stadtgeografie und Stadtkartografie der Hauptstadt Saudi-Arabiens*. Paderborn: Schöningh Verlag.

Peck, Jamie and Tickel, Adam (1994). Search for a New Institutional Fix. In: A. Amin (ed.), *Post-Fordism: A Reader*. London: Blackwell, pp. 280–316.

Perry, John (2012). *Housing and Migration. A UK Guide to Issues and Solutions*. Available at: www.cih.org/resources/PDF/Policy%20free%20download%20pdfs/ho usingandMigration2012.pdf [accessed 7 March 2018].

Peterson, J. E. (2009). Britain and the Gulf: At the Periphery of the Empire. In: L. G. Potter (ed.) The *Persian Gulf in History*. New York: Palgrave Macmillan, pp. 277–93.

Potter, Lawrence G. (2009). *The Persian Gulf in History*. New York: Palgrave Macmillan.

Powell, Walter W. and Snellman, Kaisa (2004). The Knowledge Economy. *Annual Review Sociology*, 30, pp. 199–220.

Prime Minister's Office (2010). *UAE Vision 2021*. Available at: www.vision2021.ae/en/ news/emiratization-efforts-private-sector [accessed 3 January 2018].

Purcell, Mark (2002). Excavating Lefebvre: The Right to the City and Its Urban Politics of the Inhabitant. *GeoJournal*, 58, pp. 99–108.

Radoine, Hassan (2010). *Souk Waqif, Doha, Qatar*. Available at: www.archnet.org/
    system/publications/contents/8722/original/DTP101221.pdf?1396271815 [accessed
    7 March 2018].

Rapoport, Amos (1990). *The Meaning of the Built Environment: A Non-verbal
    Communication Approach*. Tucson: University of Arizona Press.

Rapoport, Amos (2005). *Culture, Architecture, and Design*. Chicago, IL: Locke Science
    Publishing.

Ratha, Dilip (2017). Migration and Development: A Roadmap to a Global Compact.
    In: *Presentation to Meeting of the Regional Conference on Migration on the Global
    Compact on Migration*, 29 March, Washington, DC.

Ratha, Dilip and Plaza, Sonia (2014). Diaspora and Development: Critical Issues. In:
    S. I. Rajan (ed.), *India Migration Report 2014*. London: Routledge, pp. 1–21.

Ratha, Dilip and Shaw, William (2007). South–South Migration and Remittances.
    Working Paper 102, World Bank, Washington, DC.

Reef Island (2017). *Key Components*. Available at: http://www.reef-island.com/key-
    components [accessed 3 December 2017].

Reichert, Horst (1978). *Die Verstädterung der Eastern Provinz von Saudi-Arabien*, PhD
    thesis. Stuttgart: Universität Stuttgart.

Salama, Ashraf M. (2011). Trans-disciplinary knowledge for affordable housing. *Open
    House International*, 36 (3), pp. 7–15.

Salama, Ashraf M. (2014). Intervention Urbanism: The Delicacy of Aspirational Change
    in the Old Center of Doha. *Urban Pamphleteer*, 4, pp. 1–3.

Salama, Ashraf M. (2015). Urban Traditions in the Contemporary Lived Space of Cities
    on the Arabian Peninsula. *Traditional Dwellings and Settlements Review*, 27(1),
    pp. 21–39.

Salama, Ashraf M. and Gharib, Remah Y. (2012). A Perceptual Approach for
    Investigating Urban Space Diversity in the City of Doha. *Open House International*,
    37(2), pp. 24–32.

Salama, Ashraf M. and Wiedmann, Florian (2013a). The Production of Urban Qualities
    in the Emerging City of Doha: Urban Space Diversity as a Case for Investigating
    the 'Lived Space', *Archnet-IJAR: International Journal of Architectural Research*, 7(2),
    pp. 160–72.

Salama, Ashraf M. and Wiedmann, Florian (2013b). *Demystifying Doha: On
    Architecture and Urbanism in an Emerging City*. London: Routledge.

Salama, Ashraf M. and Wiedmann, Florian (2016). Perceiving Urban Livability in an
    Emerging Migrant City. *Proceedings of the Institution of Civil Engineers – Urban
    Design and Planning*, 169(6), pp. 268–78.

Salama, Ashraf M., Al-Maimani, Ahood and Khalfani, Fatma (2013). Understanding
    Inhabitants' Spatial Experience of the City of Doha through Cognitive Mapping.
    Open House International, 38(4), pp. 37–46.

Salama, Ashraf M., Wiedmann, Florian and Thierstein, Alain (2012). People and the
    City: Unveiling the Lived Urban Environment of Doha. *Qatar Foundation Annual
    Research Forum*, AHP36. Doha: Bloomsbury Qatar Foundation Journals.

Salama, Ashraf M., Wiedmann, Florian, Thierstein, Alain and Al Ghatam, Wafa (2016). Knowledge Economy as an Initiator of Sustainable Urbanism in Emerging Metropolises: The Case of Doha, Qatar. *International Journal of Architectural Research: ArchNet-IJAR*, 10(1), pp. 274–324.

Sanderock, Leonie (1998). *Towards Cosmopolis: Planning for Multicultural Cities*. Chichester: John Wiley & Sons.

Sanoff, Henry (1974). Measuring Attributes of the Visual Environment. In: J. T. Lang, C. Burnette, W. Moleski, D. Vachon (eds), *Designing for Human Behavior: Architecture and the Behavioral Sciences*. Stroudsburg: Dowden, Hutchinson and Ross, pp. 244–60.

Sanoff, Henry (2000). *Community Participation Methods in Design and Planning*. Chinchester: John Wiley and Sons.

Sassen, Saskia (1991). *The Global City: New York, London, Tokyo*. 1st ed. Princeton, NJ: Princeton University Press.

Sassen, Saskia (2002). Locating Cities on Global Circuits. *Environment and Urbanization*, 14(1), pp. 13–30.

Sassen, Saskia (2009). Cities Today: A New Frontier for Major Developments. *The Annals of the American Academy of Political and Social Science*, 626(1), pp. 53–71.

Savitch, Hank V. and Kantor, Paul (2002). *Cities in the International Marketplace*. Princeton, NJ: Princeton University Press.

Schlaffer, Edit and Kropiunigg, Ulrich (2011). Saudi Youth: Unveiling the Force for Change. *Gulf Analysis Paper*, Center for Strategic and International Studies. Available at: www.csis-prod.s3.amazonaws.com/s3fs-public/legacy_files/files/pub lication/111104_Gulf_Analysis_Saudi_Youth.pdf [accessed 3 January 2018].

Schmid, Christian (2005). *Stadt, Raum und Gesellschaft*. 1st ed. Stuttgart: Steiner.

Schmid, Heiko (2009a). Dubai: Der schnelle Aufstieg zur Wirtschaftsmetropole. In: E. Blum and P. Neitzke (eds), *Dubai – Stadt aus dem Nichts*. Berlin: Birkhäuser, pp. 56–73.

Schmid, Heiko (2009b). *Economy of Fascination. Dubai and Las Vegas as Themed Urban Landscapes*. Stuttgart: Gebrüder Borntraeger Verlagsbuchhandlung.

Scholz, Fred (1999). *Die kleinen Golfstaaten*. 2nd ed. Gotha: Justus Perthes Verlag Gotha GmbH.

Sieverts, Thomas (2000). *Zwischenstadt: Zwischen Ort und Welt, Raum und Zeit, Stadt und Land*. Bauwelt Fundamente, Band 118. Berlin: Birkhäuser Verlag.

Simpson, Colin (2012). *Dubai World Trade Centre Building: An Example for the Future*. Available at: https://www.thenational.ae/uae/dubai-world-trade-centre-building-an-example-for-the-future-1.362159 [accessed 7 March 2018].

Sinus Institute (2016). *Profile*. Available from Internet: www.sinus-institut.de/en/about -us/profile/ [accessed 3 January 2018].

Sit, Victor F. and Yang, Chun (1997). Foreign-investment-induced Exo-urbanisation in the Pearl River Delta, China. *Urban Studies*, 34(4), pp. 647–77.

Snoj, J. (2014). *Population of Qatar by Nationality*. Available at: www.bq-magazine.com/economy/2013/12/population-qatar-nationality [accessed 10 February 2017].

Soja, Edward (1989). *Postmodern Geographies: The Reassertion of Space in Critical Social Theory*. 1st ed. London: Verso.

Talen, Emily (2008). *Design for Diversity: Exploring Socially Mixed Neighbourhoods*. Oxford: The Architectural Press.

Taylor, Peter J. (2003). *World City Network: A Global Urban Analysis*. London: Routeledge.

UN Habitat (2017). *Governance*. Available: www.unhabitat.org/governance/ [accessed 6 May 2017].

United Nations (1987). *Report of the World Commission on Environment and Development: Our Common Future*. Available at: http://www.un-documents.net/our-common-future.pdf [accessed 10 February 2017].

United Nations (1998). *Recommendations on Statistics of International Migration*. Revision 1. Available at: www.unstats.un.org/unsd/publication/SeriesM/SeriesM_58rev1e.pdf [accessed 7 March 2018].

United Nations (2002). *Monterrey Consensus on Financing for Development*. Available at: www.un.org/esa/ffd/monterrey/MonterreyConsensus.pdf [accessed 7 March 2018].

United Nations (2005). *Fourth Coordination Meeting on International Migration. Department of Economic and Social Affairs*. Available at: www.un.org/esa/population/meetings/fourthcoord2005/P09_GCIM.pdf [accessed 7 March 2018].

United Nations (2017). *International Migration Report 2017. Highlights*. Available at: www.un.org/en/development/desa/population/migration/publications/migrationreport/docs/MigrationReport2017_Highlights.pdf [accessed 7 March 2018].

Veblen, Thorstein (2009). *The Theory of the Leisure Class*. Oxford World's Classics. Oxford: Oxford University Press.

Ventures Onsite (2015). 3800 Houses Being Built in New Northern Town of Bahrain to Address Shortage in Northern Governorate. *Ventures Middle East*. Available at: https://www.venturesonsite.com/news/3800-houses-being-built-in-new-northern-town-of-bahrain-to-address-shortage-in-northern-governorate/ [accessed 6 May 2017].

Walters, Glenn D. (2006). *Lifestyle Theory: Past, Present and Future*. New York: Nova Science Publishers.

Webber, Melvin M. (1963). Order in Diversity: Community without Propinquity. In: L. Wingo, Jr. (ed.), *Cities and Space: The Future Use of Urban Land, Essays from the Fourth RFF Forum*. Resources for the Future, Baltimore: Johns Hopkins Press, pp. 23–54.

Whyte, William H. (1980). *The Social Life of Small Urban Spaces*. Washington DC: Project for Public Spaces.

Wiedmann, Florian (2012). *Post-oil Urbanism in the Gulf: New Evolutions in Governance and the Impact on Urban Morphologies*. Stuttgart: SHV Verlag.

Wiedmann, Florian (2013). The Verticalization of Manama's Urban Periphery. *Open House International*, 38(3), pp. 90–100.

Wiedmann, Florian (2016). Real Estate Liberalization as Catalyst of Urban Transformation in the Persian Gulf. In: M. Kamrava (ed.), *Gateways to the World: Port Cities*. London: pp. 157–82.

Wiedmann, Florian, Salama, Ashraf M. and Ibrahim, Hatem G. (2016). The Role of Mega Projects in Redefining Housing Development in Gulf Cities. *Open House International*, 41(2), pp. 56–63.

Wiedmann, Florian, Salama, Ashraf M. and Mirincheva, Velina (2013). Urban Reconfiguration and Revitalization: Public Mega Projects in Doha's Historic Center. *Open House International*, 38(4), pp. 27–36.

Wiedmann, Florian, Salama, Ashraf M. and Mirincheva, Velina (2014). Sustainable Urban Qualities in the Emerging City of Doha. *Journal of Urbanism*, 7(1), pp. 62–84.

Wiedmann, Florian, Salama, Ashraf M. and Thierstein, Alain (2012). Urban Evolution of the City of Doha: An Investigation into the Impact of Economic Transformations on Urban Structures. *METU Journal of the Faculty of Architecture*, 29(2), pp. 35–61.

Wirth, Louis (1938). Urbanism as a Way of Life. *American Journal of Sociology*, 44, pp. 1–24.

Wirth, Eugen (1988). *Dubai: Ein modernes städtisches Handels- und Dienstleistungszentrum am Arabisch-Persischen Golf*. Erlangen: Selbstverlag der Fränkischen Geographischen Gesellschaft.

World Bank Group (1999). *World Development Report, 1999/2000: Entering the 21st Century*. New York: Oxford University Press.

World Bank Group (2016). *Migration and Remittance Factbook 2016*. 3rd ed. Available at: www.siteresources.worldbank.org/INTPROSPECTS/Resources/334934-11998079 08806/4549025-1450455807487/Factbookpart1.pdf [accessed 7 March 2018].

World Bank Group (2017). *Migration and Remittances. Recent Developments and Outlook. Special Topic: Global Compact on Migration*. Available at: www.pubdocs. worldbank.org/en/992371492706371662/MigrationandDevelopmentBrief27.pdf [accessed 7 March 2018].

The World Bank (2017). *Population Data*. Available at: https://data.worldbank.org/ country [accessed 3 December 2017].

Worldometers (2017a). *Bahrain Population*. Available at: www.worldometers.info/world-population/bahrain-population/ [accessed 22 March 2017].

Worldometers (2017b). *Kuwait Population*. Available at: www.worldometers.info/world-population/kuwait-population/ [accessed 22 March 2017].

Worldometers (2017c). *Qatar Population*. Available at: www.worldometers.info/world-population/qatar-population/ [accessed 22 March 2017].

Worldometers (2017d). *United Arab Emirates Population*. Available at: www.worldometers. info/world-population/united-arab-emirates-population/ [accessed 22 March 2017].

Wu, Weiping (2009). Temporary Migrants in Shanghai, China: Housing Choices and Patterns. In: S. Sassen (ed.), *Human Settlement Development*, 3, Oxford: Eolss Publishers, pp. 22–38.

Zahlan, Rosemarie S. (1979). *The Creation of Qatar*. London: Croom Helm.

Zahra, Maysa (2015a). The Legal Framework of the Sponsorship Systems of the Gulf Cooperation Council Countries: A Comparative Examination. In: *Gulf Labour Markets and Migration*. Available at: www.cadmus.eui.eu/bitstream/handle/1814/32250/GLMM_ExpNote_07-2014.pdf?sequence=1 [accessed 22 March 2017].

Zahra, Maysa (2015b). Bahrain's Legal Framework of Migration. In: *Gulf Labour Markets and Migration*. Available at: www.cadmus.eui.eu/bitstream/handle/1814/34579/GLMM_ExpNote_01_2015.pdf?sequence=1 [accessed 22 March 2017].

Zahra, Maysa (2016). Qatar's Legal Framework of Migration. In: *Gulf Labour Markets and Migration*. Available at: www.cadmus.eui.eu/bitstream/handle/1814/32154/GLMM%20ExpNote_02-2013.pdf?sequence=1 [accessed 22 March 2017].

Index